Marriages and Deaths
from
Steuben County, New York
Newspapers
1797–1868

Abstracted by
Yvonne E. Martin

Heritage Books
2012

HERITAGE BOOKS
AN IMPRINT OF HERITAGE BOOKS, INC.

Books, CDs, and more—Worldwide

For our listing of thousands of titles see our website at
www.HeritageBooks.com

Published 2012 by
HERITAGE BOOKS, INC.
Publishing Division
100 Railroad Ave. #104
Westminster, Maryland 21157

Copyright © 1988 Yvonne E. Martin

All rights reserved. No part of this book may be reproduced or transmitted in any form or by any means, electronic or mechanical, including photocopying, recording or by any information storage and retrieval system without written permission from the author, except for the inclusion of brief quotations in a review.

International Standard Book Numbers
Paperbound: 978-1-55613-130-1
Clothbound: 978-0-7884-9463-5

TABLE OF CONTENTS

Preface	v
The Bath Gazette and Genesee Advertiser June 1, 1797-April 12, 1798 (scattered issues)	1
The Constitutionalist August 23, 1837-February 16, 1842	3
The Steuben Democrat November 15, 1843-May 22, 1844	31
Steuben Farmer's Advocate December 16, 1846-December 8, 1847 (Dec. 15, 1847-Dec. 6, 1848 missing)	35
The Steuben Democrat June 14, 1848-June 13, 1849	45
Steuben Farmer's Advocate December 13, 1848-December 2, 1852	53
The Voice of the Nation January 10, 1855-December 19, 1855	89
Steuben American January 2, 1856-May 6, 1857	99
The Addison Advertiser March 10, 1858-March 18, 1868	107
Index	139

PREFACE

This compilation, of marriages and deaths, has been extracted from seven Steuben County, New York, newspapers as located on microfilm at New York State Library, Albany, NY. The extractions cover the period from 1797 to 1868 depending on the availability of the selected newspapers. The majority of the notices relate to Steuben County residents although a few relate to well known people of that time and a few relate to people outside of Steuben County.

These extractions cover a period of time when civil vital records were practically nil in the county. This manuscript will be a great finding aid and time saver for anyone researching in Steuben County.

Abbreviations used are: ult. for ultimo meaning "the previous month", inst. for instant meaning "the current month", and sic which means "copied exactly".

There are approximately 5-6000 names mentioned in this manuscript.

Yvonne E. Martin

The Bath Gazette and Genesee Advertiser
Bath, New York
(1797-1798 sixteen scattered issues)

June 1, July 6, December 21, 1797; January 4, 18, February 1, 8, 15, 22; April 5, 12, 1798 no deaths or marriages.

Thursday October 12, 1797 - Married - Thursday last, by Doctr. James Faulkner Esq., Mr. James Woodruff to the agreeable Miss Hannah Huff, both of this place.

Thursday December 14, 1797 - Death - Lebeus Tubbs deceased 22 August 1797 at Newtown, Tioga County.

Thursday January 25, 1798 - Death - Died at Detroit, the 3d of October last, Capt. George Sytez, after a short illness. During the late struggle for independence, he bore a conspicuous character and as a citizen, that of an honest man.

Thursday March 1, 1798 - Married - By James Faulkner Esq., on Thursday last, Mr. John Wilson to Miss Betsey Dunn, daughter of Mr. Robert Dunn of York-Town, Pennsylvania.

Thursday March 15, 1798 - Married - On Tuesday last by Doctr. James Faulkner Esq., Patrick N. Kell merchant, to Miss Nancy Inslee, daughter of Mr. Joseph Inslee, all of this place.

The Constitutionalist
Bath, New York
August 23, 1837-August 15, 1838

Wednesday August 23, September 13, 27, 1837 no deaths or marriages. Wednesday October 4, 1837 - missing issue.

Wednesday August 30, 1837 - Died - In this town on 23d inst., Danford Warren, aged 31, son of Phineas Warren.

Wednesday September 6, 1837 - Married - At Hammondsport on 29th ult., by Rev. Delevan, John Faulkner of Urbana to Angeline Myrtle of Wheeler (sic).

Wednesday September 20, 1837 - Married - In this town on 13th inst., by Rev. Wheeler, John Kennard to Mary Whiting, dau. of Col. John Whiting.
Died - In this village on 12th inst., Ann Eloise, dau. of Hon. John Magee, aged 17 and a half months.
Died - On the 15th inst., Martha, adopted child of George Wilcox, aged two years.
Died - In this town on 12th inst., Nelson G., son of Peres Gilmore, aged 15 months.
Died - At Hammondsport Aug. 31st, of a pulmonary complaint, Emilie W. Delevan, wife of Rev. George D. Delevan; dau. of James Wiltse of Fishkill Landing, aged 24 years. She is mother of a little boy.

Wednesday October 11, 1837 - Married - In this town on 22d ult., by John D. Higgins Esq., James Stewart of Howard to Margaret Stewart, dau. of Henry Stewart of Bath.
Married - In Cameron Sunday last by J. D. Higgins Esq., Eber. L. Morton to Lucy Gustin, dau. of Gardner Gustin, all of Cameron.

Wednesday October 18, 1837 - Died - At Cohocton on 11th inst., Edwin Cook aged 22 years.

Wednesday November 22, 29, December 6, 1837 no deaths or marriages. December 13, 1837 issue missing.

Wednesday October 25, 1837 - Died - In Urbana on Monday Henry A. Townsend Esq., aged 68 years. A sermon will be preached at the Episcopal Church in Bath this afternoon.
Died - At Mud Creek on 18th inst., Eunice Moore, aged 25 years.
Died - From New Orleans Commercial Bulletin Sept. 15th, died in this city of prevailing fever on Wed. 12th inst., in his 27th year, William Wallace Whitney. He was born in Broome County, New York 1810 and was son of Gen. Joshua Whitney of Binghamton. He has left a bereaved wife and two children. The deceased came to this city three years ago to prosecute the claim of his wife, as legal heir of late Daniel Clark, to a very large estate; to recover which, suit is pending here in U. S. District Court.

Wednesday November 2(?), 1837 - Died - Mr. William Lyman, a most estimable man, who has sometime past been in the employ of Horace Hooker, was murdered in going from the Carthage railroad office to his home on North Clinton Street, Monday morning. (Rochester *Democrat*).
Died - In this village on 24th ult., Franklin Metcalfe, aged 26 years.

Wednesday November 8, 1837 - Married - In Prattsburgh on 15th ult., Joshua Ellsworth of Italy Hill, to Martha Francis of the former place.

Wednesday November 15, 1837 - Married - At Painted Post on 8th inst., Henry G. Cotton Esq., to Mary Bacon, dau. of Edward Bacon Esq.
Died - In this town on 12th inst., Mrs. S. E. Comstock, wife of Dr. A. L. Comstock, aged 28 years.

Wednesday December 20, 1837 - Died - In this village on 14th inst., Mrs. Ose Metcalfe, widow of the late John Metcalfe Esq., aged 44 years.

Wednesday January 17, 31, 1838 no deaths or marriages.

Wednesday December 27, 1837 - Married - In Cameron by Rev. Wisner, Jeremiah Murphy of Dixson's Ferry, Illinois to Clarissa A. Veile of the former place.
Married - At M'Clure's Grove, Kane County, Illinois on 16th Nov. last by Rev. John Blatchford, Capt. Louis T. Jamison of the U. S. Army to Mary E., dau. of Gen. George M'Clure.
Died - In Erwin, James Thompson (no date or age given).

Wednesday January 3, 1838 - Married - In Geneva on Wed. 13th ult. by Rev. Hay, Lemuel Hastings, merchant of Hammondsport to Mary Barnard of Geneva.
Married - At Painted Post on 24th ult. Philip Morse to Jane Grames, all of Bath.

Wednesday January 10, 1838 - Died - Samuel Contaranan of Howard, a very respectable citizen, hung himself in his chamber Monday last with a silk handkerchief.

Wednesday January 24, 1838 - Married - In this village on 17th inst., by John D. Higgins Esq., William R. Ketcham to Ruth E. Gifford.
Died - In this village on 20th inst., James, son of Mr. B. Wilkes, aged two years.

Wednesday February 7, 1838 - Married - In Addison on 28th ult., by Rev. William Sattle, formerly of Chenango to Maria Wells. (no groom named).
Married - In this village on 14th ult. Joseph Watkins to Eliza Bailey.
Married - In this town on 1st inst., by Rev. C. Wheeler, Townsend Allerton to Ann Chapin.
Died - In this village, a child of John W. Fowler, aged about six months.

Wednesday March 7, 14, 1838 - no deaths or marriages.

Wednesday February 14, 1838 - Married - In Wayne, on the inst. (sic) by Rev. S. White, Rev. Rowlett to Mary Ann Mitchell, dau. of John D. Mitchell Esq.

Wednesday February 21, 1838 - Married - In Howard on 14th inst. by Rev. Chandler Wheeler, Henry W. Chamberlain of this town to Angeline Bacon, dau. of Col. Simeon Bacon.
Married - In this village yesterday morning by Rev. Platt, Dr. Daniel M. Shipman to Sarah C. Townsend, all of this village.

Wednesday February 28, 1838 – Married – In this village on 21 inst. by Rev. Bostwick, Richard B. Stewart to Charlotte Metcalfe, dau. of Thomas Metcalfe Esq.

Married – In Howard by Rev. Elisha Brownson, Samuel Rider to Elizabeth Connor.

Wednesday March 21, 1838 – Married – In Boston on Saturday eve. last, by Rev. Peabody, Chaplain of the House of Representative, Rev. Edward N. Harris of Malden, member of the House to Sarah George age 16. He being a widower with three children. Mr. Harris resigned his seat in the House & has taken his young bride off to Methuen where has reoeived a call for a settlement over a Universalist Society at $800 per annum.

Wednesday March 28, 1838 – Married – At Wheeler on the 23d inst. by Rev. E. Everett, Sherman Rose to Mahala G. Stryker.

Married – At Hornby, on 15th ult. by Josiah Wheat, Esq., Abraham Whitney Jr. Esq. to Mercy Warner, only dau. of Alpheus Warner.

Married – In Jasper on 20th inst., Franklin Dennis to Martha E. Lamson.

Died – The Hon. John T. Irving, First Judge of the New York Court of Common Pleas, died on Thursday in the 60th year of his age. He was a brother of Washington Irving.

Wednesday April 4, 1838 – Married – In Tyronc on 31st ult. by Rev. Jonathan Ketchum of Barrington, Coonrad (sic) Fisher of Seneca, Ontario Co., to Arvilla Devoe, Tyrone.

Died – The body of Robert Barker, an elderly man of Colerain, Massachusetts was discovered in Sullivan on Saturday last dispelling all mystery in his murder. He left his home Sept. 1st, 1837 with intention of going to Onondaga County, New York to be married.

Wednesday April 11, 1838 – Married – In this village on 3d inst., by Rev. Platt, Lazarus Hammond Read Esq. of Hammondsport to Elizabeth L., dau. of the late William Woods.

Married – In this village on 7th inst. by William Hamilton Esq., Timothy Hastings of Wayne, a revolutionary pensioner to Mrs. Hannah Abel.

Died – In Cameron on 23d ult. Charles Wesley, son of Samuel Dickinson, in the 9th year of his age.

Wednesday April 18, 1838 - Married - In this village on 12th inst. by Wm. Hamilton Esq., Arnold Payne to Phebe C. Arnold, all of Cameron.

Died - In Hornellsville on 8th inst. Oliver Harding aged 83 years. Mr. Harding was one of the first settlers in this section, a revolutionary war veteran and has received a liberal pension for a number of years.

Wednesday April 25, 1838 - Married - In this town on 19th inst. by Wm. Hamilton Esq., George Goodsell to Sally Ann Fulsom.

Married - At Angelica, Almon Beeman Esq., of Addison to Elmira Bostwick of Hornellsville.

Wednesday May 2, 9, 1838 no marriages or deaths.

Wednesday May 16, 1838 - Married - In Campbell Wed. 9th inst. by Rev. Hotchkin, Lucius M. Brown of Dansville to Susan T. Besley, dau. of Samuel Besley Esq. of the former place.

Married - At Seneca Falls Tuesday 8th inst., George Washington Ellis of Tyrone to Amelia Alexandrina Potts of the former place.

Wednesday May 23, 1838 - Married - In Hammondsport on 16th inst. by Rev. C. Wheeler, Nathaniel P. Williams to Elizabeth Quick.

Died - At Hopewell, Ontario County on 18th inst. aged 59 years, Joel Pratt Esq., early settler & long a resident of Prattsburgh.

Wednesday May 30, 1838 - Married - In Stamford, Connecticut on 9th inst. by Rev. Todd, Francis S. Ellas, assistant teacher in Clinton Institute, Oneida Co., to Sarah E. Hoyt, formerly of Buffalo.

Died - In this town on 20th inst. Sarah Maria Walker, dau. of James Walker, aged 14 years.

Died - In Prattsburgh yesterday of consumption, Rev. Robert L. Porter, aged 27 years.

Wednesday June 6, 1838 - Married - In this village on Thursday last by Rev. Platt, Peter Halsey to Lucia Johnson.

Died - In Dansville at the home of Amos Preston on 7th May last, of consumption, a stranger named Caleb Cole aged 50 years, tin peddlar.

Died - At Randolph, Portage County, Ohio on 20th April last Thomas Mitchell, son of J. B. Mitchell Esq. of Wayne, cause inflammation of brain, interred at Wayne.

Died - In Pulteney on 10th May aged 54 years, Wealthy Sheldon, wife of Col. Daniel Sheldon, sermon by Rev. Elijah Wollage.

Wednesday June 13, 29, 1838 no deaths or marriages.

Wednesday June 27, 1838 - Married - At Greene, Chenango County on 12th inst. Joseph G. Masten Esq. of Buffalo to Christina Cameron of Greene.

Wednesday July 4, 1838 - Married - At Tyrone, by Rev. Jonathan Ketchum of Barrington to Betsey House of the former place. (no groom stated).

Wednesday July 11, 1838 - Married - In this town on 4th inst. by Rev. Wisner, Daniel Knight to Emily Warren.
Married - In Wayne on morning of 4th inst., by Rev. James Rollett, Cyrus Powers of Urbana to Nancy Richmond of the former place.

Wednesday July 18, 1838 - Married - In this village on 12th inst., by Rev. Wheeler, Thomas Pancost Hughes to Mary French.
Married - In Howard on 1st inst., by Rev. Baldwin, Samuel Allen to Ann Stephenson; by Rev. Buzzle (sic), Michael Nipher to Hannah Persons; by D. Stephenson Esq., Hubart Allen to Lydia Baldwin; on 4th inst., by Rev. Elder Root, Jeremiah Bennett to Ann Winne, all of Howard.

Wednesday July 25, 1838 - Married - At Owego on 10th inst., by Rev. Marcus Ford of Newark, Hon. Stephen Strong, first judge of Tioga County to Mrs. Abigail Camp of same place.

Wednesday August 1, 1838 - Married - In this village on 30th ult., by Rev. Wheeler, Minor Coss to Harriet DeWitt, all of this town.

Wednesday August 8, 1838 - Married - At Oxford, Chenango County on 16th ult., by Rev. Bassett, Charles N. Shumway of Addison to Margaret A. Gile, dau. of William Gile Esq. of the former place.

Wednesday August 15, 1838 - no deaths or marriages.

Wednesday August 22, 1838 - Died - At Hornellsville on 4th inst., Elizabeth Kelly aged 31, wife of Dr. Manning Kelly.

Wednesday August 29, 1838 - Married - At Avoca by Rev. E. Everett, Harry Miller of Barre, Michigan to Jane F. G. Stanley.
Died - At Hammondsport on 23d inst., Edward son of Wm. Hastings, 16 mos.

Wednesday September 5, 1838 - Married - In this village on 30th ult., by Rev. J. H. Hotchkin, Mark Miller of Towanda to Sarah Stewart, dau. of Richard B. Stewart.
Married - At Holley, Orleans Co., on 20th inst. by Rev. Perkins, Wm. Briggs of this village to Cecelia B. Towle, of the former place.
Married - At Hornellsville on 25th ult., by Rev. Russell, Ralph Otis of Almond to Mary Smith - after a courtship of 20 minutes.
Died - At Ann Arbor, Mich., John A. Stocking of this town, aged about 60 yrs.

Wednesday September 12, 1838 - no deaths or marriages.

Wednesday September 19, 1838 - Married - In this town Thurs. 13th inst., by Rev. Wisner, Edward Lindsley to Mary B. Johnson.

Wednesday September 26, 1838 - Married - In Campbell on 18th inst. by Rev. Hotchkin, Charles Bonham to Mary B. Goodwin.
Married - At Sheffield, Berkshire County, Massachusetts on 20th inst. by Rev. James Bradford, Wilber C. Hare of South Egremont to Elizabeth E., dau. of Lay Shears Esq. of the former place.
Died - In this town on 17th inst. Franklin Glass of consumption, aged about 36, Mr. John Fassett, aged 37.

Wednesday October 3, 1838 - Married - In Hornby on 27th ult. by Elder Correll, Dayton Easling to Emeline Masters, eldest dau. of Nehemiah Masters Esq., all of Hornby.

Married - In Jasper on 27th ult. by Rev. Russell, Samuel F. Dennis to Sarah S. Woodward.

Wednesday October 10, 1838 - Married - In Pulteney by Rev. Elijah Wollage, John Knox Esq. of Painted Post to Mrs. Fannie Gustine, widow of the late Major Gustine of New Hampshire.
Married - In Canisteo on 19th ult. by Moses Hallett Esq., Josiah Millerd to Elizabeth Cornell.

Wednesday October 17, 1838 - Married - In Cameron on 9th inst. by Rev. S. Ottman, Mr. Abraham I. Walrath of Jasper to Sally Rodela, eldest dau. of George I. House.
Married - In Hornby on 11th inst., Mr. Levi Coy to Hannah A. Goodsell.
Died - In Painted Post Thursday last, 12 year old son of Mr. Marshall.

Wednesday October 24, 1838 - Married - At Hornby on 18th inst. by Rev. D. B. Butts of Addison, Alford Randall Esq. of Orange to Sally Ann Sayer of Hornby.
Married - In Hornellsville, Henry P. Clason to Harriet Lilly.
Died - At Penn Yan on Sunday morning, William Babcock Esq., formerly a member of Congress.

Wednesday October 31, 1838 - Married - At Chilicothe, Ohio on 8th inst., Rev. George H. Hastings of this village to Sarah E. Bartlett, dau. of Montgomery R. Bartlett of Utica, New York.
Died - On board a steamboat on Mississippi River, Charles May, Aged 28, formerly of this village. He was a pilot on the boat and was buried at Paducah, M'Cracken County, Kentucky near mouth of Tennessee River.
Died - At his residence in Penn Yan on Sabbath morning last, the Hon. Wm. Babcock, aged 53 years. Mr. Babcock was born & raised in Westmoreland, Cheshire County, New Hampshire. He came to Penn Yan about 1813. At formation of Yates County he was appointed County Treasurer and in 1830 elected oneof members of Congress for district composed of Ontario, Seneca, Wayne & Yates. He leaves a widow & 3 children. Funeral services were held in Presbyterian Meetinghouse by Rev. Miner. Interment in "City Hill" near Seneca Lake in Milo beside the ashes of his mother and two sisters.

Died - In Rushville at residence of her father, Dr. Bryant, on 15th inst., Caroline E. Babcock, wife of John C. Baboock of Penn Yan, aged 25 yrs.

Wednesday November 7, 1838 - Died - In this town on the 31st ult., Mr. Allen Blood, aged 38.
Died - At his residence in Williamsburg yesterday, Joseph Lancaster, founder of the Lancasterian system of education in this country. The sudden death of this gentleman was caused by being run over Monday in Elizabeth Street.

Wednesday November 14, 1838 - Married - In Jasper on Thursday 1st inst., by Elder Sherwood, Jarvis Talbot to Fidelia Jane Dennis.
Died - In this town on 10th inst., Jeremiah Dudley Esq., aged 85.

Wednesday November 21, 1838 - no deaths or marriages.

Wednesday November 28, 1838 - Married - In Wheeler on the 22nd inst. by Rev. Bostwick, Martin H. Rose, merchant, at Hammondsport to Eliza Ann Marshall dau. of Gen. Otto F. Marshall.
Died - In this village on 13th ult., William aged 15 months & on 23rd inst., Robert aged 16 months, twin sons of William Howell Esq.

Wednesday December 5, 1838 - Married - At Hornby on 17th ult., by Josiah Wheat Esq., Alanson Bixby to to Cornelia Rowe.
Married - Also on 28th ult,, by Rev. D. B. Cornell, Joseph Beckwith Esq. of Hornby to Hannah Gorton of Painted Post.
Married - In Wheeler on 31st ult., bv Rev. I. J. B. McKenney, Benjamin F. Stryker to Jane Lewis.
Married - On 1st inst. by same, David Strattan to Eliza Hawkenbury.

Wednesday December 5, 1838 - Married - On 3d inst. by same, Archillus Maker to Mary Ann Williamson.
Died - Deacon Abraham Townsend of Tyrone, Thursday afternoon last. (Dec. 1st)

Wednesday December 12, 1838 - Died - At Tyrone on 3d inst., Mr. Joseph Hause, aged 51 years.

Wednesday December 19, 1838 - Died - In Wayne on 5th inst., Emily White, wife of Issachar (sic) White of this village, aged 27.
Died - In Jasper on 27th ult., Eleanor Hunter, wife of Dr. Wm. Hunter, aged 30.

Wednesday December 26, 1838 - No deaths or marriages.

Wednesday January 2, 1839 - Married - In Bath on Thursday 27th Dec. by John W. Whiting Esq., William H. Tuttle to Mary J. Brooks.
Married - At Avoca on 25th ult., by Rev. S. Ottman, Adam Loucks to Jane M. Collier, all of Avoca.
Married - On 27th Nov. Major Abraham Van Buren (eldest son of President of United States) to Sarah Angelica Singleton, youngest dau. of Richard Singleton, at her father's house in Sumter District, South Carolina.
Died - In Howard on 22d ult., Ripley Calkins, aged 54 years.

Wednesday January 9, 1839 - Notice - As my wife Lucy has left my bed and board, I forbid all persons harboring or trusting her on my account after this date. Jasper. Jan. 1, 1839. James Quick.

Wednesday January 16, 1839 - Married - In Jasper on 1st inst. by Rev. S. Ottman, Daniel I. Deck to Eliza Merriam.
Died - At Buffalo, Jennette, dau. of T. J. Dudley, aged 2 years.
Died - In Bath on 14th inst., John, son of Cornelius Davis aged 2 years.
Died - We notice with regret the death of the talented and gentlemanly editor of the Albany *Daily Advertiser*, Col. J. B. Van Schaick.

Wednesday January 23, 1839 - Married - At Baton Rouge, Louisiana, Dr. Joseph Adams May, formerly of this village to Mary Stuart. (no date).

Wednesday January 30, 1839 - Married - At Hornellsville, by W. Burkick Esq., G. W. Clason of Hornellsville to N. Seward of Almond; by Rev. H. Cornell, W. Andruss to F. Russell.
Married - At Wayne on 28th inst., by Rev. Rollet, George Ferris of Tyrone to Ann Hudinot of the same place.
Died - In Prattsburgh of consumption on 21st Dec., Levinia Linsley, dau. of the late Dea. Abial Linsley, aged 40 yrs.

Wednesday February 6, 1839 - Married - On 23d ult., John Johnson of Guilford to Harriet Buckingham of Medina, formerly of this village.

Wednesday February 13, 1839 - Married - In Wheeler on Wednesday eve. 30th ult., by Rev. S. Ottman, John Sitaman to Maria Harris, both of Wheeler.
Married - In Jasper, Charles Bishop of Troupsburgh to Charity Brotzman; Mr. David Wass to Elizabeth Heckman; Robert H. Heckman to Betsey Deck.

Wednesday February 20, 1839 - no deaths or marriages.

Wednesday February 27, 1839 - Married - In this town on 20th inst., by Rev. Bostwick, Amos Stone of Urbana to Jane Mills of this place.

Wednesday March 6, 1839 - missing issue, 20, 27, April 10, 24, 1839 - no deaths or marriages.

Wednesday March 13, 1839 - Married - In this village on Wed. 6th inst. by Rev. Bostwick, Harvey Bull to Lucinda Towle.
Married - In Urbana on 27th ult., by Elder J. S. Chapman, James M. Wixson to Margaret W. Stout.
Died - In Jasper on 6th inst., Mrs. Catherine Kinney, aged about 24 years.

Wednesday April 3, 1839 - Married - In this town on 27th ult., by Rev. Platt, David Francis Woodward of Jasper to Phoebe Webster of this place.
Married - In this town on 28th ult., by Henry Pier Esq., Solomon Chase to Tripheny Hudson, all of this place.
Married - On 26th ult., by Rev. Bostwick, Mathew Shannon to Martha Fossett, all of this town.
Married - On 31st Ult., by H. Pier Esq., Frederick Costen to Nancy Latta, all of this town.

Wednesday April 17, 1839 - Married - On 7th inst., by Rev. Hurd, Gen. Samuel S. Haight of Angelica to Maria Cheeseman at the residence of her father in Allegany County.
Died - In this village on 13th inst., of consumption, Mary, dau. of A. R. Gould, aged 5 years 3 months.

Wednesday May 1, 1839 - Married - In Almond on 25th ult., by Rev. Bemis, John Rose to Eliza H. Mason, both of this village.
Died - In Wheeler on the 17th ult., Clarence S., only son of Nathan Barney, aged 1 year 3 mos.

Wednesday May 8, 1839 - Died - In Campbell at the house of W. D. Knox, 24th ult., John P. Ryerss of Lindsley, Steuben County, aged 67 years.
Died - In Jasper on 29th ult., Joseph Boyd in the 65th year of his age.

Wednesday May 15, 1839 - Died - In this village on Sunday last, Mr. X. West, aged about 55 years.

Wednesday May 22, June 26, July 3, 1839 - no deaths or marriages.

Wednesday May 29, 1839 - Married - In Howard on 21st inst., by J. S. Depue Esq., Rufus Fluent to Maria Jane Ross.
Married - In Canisteo on 22d by same, Mr. James Ross to Mehitabel Fluent.
Married - At Prattsburgh on 12th inst., by Rev. Gaylord, John Hinckley Esq. of Naples to Sophia Stewart. (Miss S. on Saturday afternoon before the wedding had the misfortune to lose the house in which she resided by fire her loss estimated at $500 was shortly made up to her in the manner mentioned).
Married - In Prattsburgh on 21 inst., by Rev. Gaylord, Erastus Hopkins of White Lake, Oakland Co., Michigan to Climena Clark.

Wednesday June 5, 1839 - Died - At Clinton, Michigan on 23d ult., Charles H. McClure, aged about 26, formerly merchant in this village and son of Finla (sic) McClure of this town.

Wednesday June 12, 1839 - Married - In this village on 30th ult., by Henry Pier Esq., John S. Eddy of Campbell to June Aldrich of Cameron.
Died - In this village on 5th inst., Mrs. Dyckman, wife of Oliver Dyckman, lately from Broome County.
Died - In Jasper on 28th May, Charlotte Phelps, wife of Milo Phelps, aged 41 years.

Wednesday June 19, 1839 - Married - In Jasper on 9th inst., by Elder Sherwood, Warren Talbot to Esther Ann Travace.

Wednesday July 10, 1839 - Married - In Trumansburgh, Tompkins Co., on 25th ult., by Rev. Locke, John Legro of Bath to Nancy M. Gleason of the former place.
Married - In Bath on 3d inst. by Rev. Platt, Julius C. Smead to Manda C. Selden.

Wednesday July 17, 1839 - Married - In Geneseo by Rev. Atkins, E. W. Patchin, M.D. of Sparta to Mary Ewerts of the former place.

Wednesday July 24, 1839 - no deaths or marriages.

Wednesday July 31, 1839 - Married - In this village on 24th inst., by H. Pier Esq., James Goodrich of Columbia, Bradford Co., Pennsylvania, to Polly Bell of this village.
Died - In Howard on 22d inst., Daniel Robinson, aged 67 years.

Wednesday August 7, 1839 - Married - In Dansville, Livingston Co., on 27th July by Rev. Ira Bronson, Wm. G. W. Warren formerly of Bath to Rachel Roberts of Geneseo.

Wednesday August 14, 1839 - Died - A little son of George Campbell was drowned in Crooked Lake, near this village on Saturday morning last. (Penn Yan *Whig*)

Wednesday August 21, 1839 - Married - In this town on 18th inst., by Rev. Rowe, Samuel Gillett to Anna Palmer.
Married - In this town by H. Pier Esq. on 14th inst., Joseph Keehler to Mrs. Lucetta Blood.
Died - In this village on 17th inst. of consumption, Eliza Forbes Lewis, aged 34 years, wife of Mr. James Lewis.
Died - In this town on 8th inst., Harriet Neally, wife of Samuel Neally, aged 34 years.
Died - At Ithaca on 11th inst., Jehiel Ludlow Esq., sheriff of Tompkins County, aged 41.

Wednesday August 28, 1839 - Married - In Urbana on 20th inst., by Rev. W. W. Bostwick, Zenos Cobb to Julia Baker, dau. of Samuel Baker.

Wednesday September 4, 1839 - Died -In this village on 29th ult., Dr. David Henry aged 50.
Died - In this town on 29th ult., a child of S. Reaser, aged 7 mos.

Died – In Dunstable, Massachusetts, Zebedee Kendall, father of the Postmaster General, died Wed. last at his residence, in his 84th year.

Wednesday September 11, 1839 – Married – In Painted Post on 3d inst., by Rev. Smith, A. L. Smith Jr. of Hornellsville to Sarah Young of Painted Post.

Married – In Jasper on 12th ult., by D. Simpson Esq., William Burton to Mary Heliker.

Married – In Woodhull on same day by Calvin Searls Esq., Nelson Pomeroy to Jemima Hutchison.

Died – At his residence in Erwin on Friday 6th inst., Francis Erwin, aged 59 years 6 months. Mr. Erwin was formerly a resident of Easton, Pennsylvania, coming to this county in its early settlement where he has since continued to reside.

Died – In Tyrone, Steuben Co., Sept. 1st, Daniel Fleet, son of Abram Fleet, aged 17 years.

Wednesday September 18, 1839 – Died – On 2d inst., at Prattsburgh of consumption, Mary Niles, dau. of Doct. Noah Niles in the 21st year of her age. At the early age of 17 years, Miss Niles became principal of the female department in the academy at Dansville.

Wednesday September 25, 1839 – Married – In West Fayette, Seneca Co., on 10th inst., by Rev. Scofield, Edmund Backman of Pultney to Mary Voorheis of the former place.

Married – In Pulteney on 11th inst., by Rev. Babbitt, Sebring Voorheis of Van Burke, Wayne County, Michigan to Sarah Backman of the former place.

Wednesday October 2, 1839 – Married – In this village Thursday last by Rev. Platt, Hon. Francis Moore Jr. late mayor of Houston and editor of the Texas *Telegraph* to Elizabeth M. Wood, dau. of Benjamin H. Wood Esq.

Married – At Addison on the 1st Sept. by Russell Root Esq., C. M. Griswold to Sophronia Mosier.

Married – On 5th ult., by H. H. Birdsall Esq., E. A. Buck to Catherine A. Jones.

Married – On 8th ult. by Rev. J. Powers, Elnathan G. Brown to Betsey Kane.

Married – In Howard on 4th ult., by Rev. Wm. Goodell, Erastus Spalding to Eliza Walker.

Married – Also on 10th ult., by the same, Stephen Allen to Caroline Meeks, all of Howard.

Died - In this village on Sunday evening last, Robert Campbell, son of Matthew Schermerhorn, aged 17 mos. (sic).

Wednesday October 9, 1839 - Died - In Urbana on 27th ult., James Brundage Esq., aged 74 years.
Died - In Illinois, Brigham Hanks Esq., formerly of this town.
Died - In Texas, Mary Jameison, wife of Capt. Jameison and dau. of Gen. George McClure, formerly of this place.

Wednesday October 16, November 27 missing, November 6, 13, 1839 no deaths or marriages.

Wednesday October 24, 1839 - Married - At Hornby on 18th inst., by Rev. D. B. Butts of Addison, Alford Randall Esq. of Orange to Sally Ann Sayer of Hornby.
Married - In Hornellsville, Henry P. Clason to Harriet Lilly.
Died - At Penn Yan on Sunday morning William Babcook Esq., formerly a member of Congress.

Wednesday October 30, 1839 - Married - In Wheeler on 19th inst., by M. Brown Esq., John Brownwell to Sally Ann Trencher.
Died - At Cameron on 24th inst., Maryann, wife of Maj. James Lawrence, aged 33 years. She left an affectionate husband & six children.
Died - In this town on 26th ult., Clarissa Taylor, wife of Dugald C. Taylor, & dau. of Caleb Farnam Esq., aged 30 years.

Wednesday November 20, 1839 - Married - On the 30th ult., by Rev. John Smith, Wm. J. Gilbert Esq., to Rachel A., dau. of the late Capt. Samuel Erwin, all of Painted Post.
Died - At Westfield, Chatauqua County, of Apoplexy on 25th ult,, Maria Seward, wife of B. J. Seward Esq., (brother of Gov. Wm. H. Seward).

Wednesday December 4, 1839; January 1, 1840 no deaths or marriages. Wednesday January 22, 1840 missing issue.

Wednesday December 11, 1839 - Married - In Howard on 4th inst., by A. M. Leigh Esq., Chauncey Rathbun to Jane McNaughton.
Notice - Whereas my wife Betsey Ann has left my bed & board without any cause or provocation, I forbid all persons

from harboring or trusting her on my account, as I shall pay no debts of her contracting. Starkey. Dec. 2, 1839. Daniel Eddy.

Wednesday December 18, 1839 - Married - On 15th inst., by Rev. Hoag, John D. Towle to Elizabeth Aser, both of Howard.
Died - In Dansville on 10th inst., Benjamin Burgher, aged about 50.

Wednesday December 25, 1839 - Married - On 15th inst., by J. R. Ketchum Esq., Sam'l D. Sillick to Julia Ann Lloyd, all of Cameron.

Wednesday January 8, 1840 - Married - In Addison on 29th ult., by Rev. Aldrich, James Swarthout to Julia Wells of Leicester, Livingston County.
Married - In Urbana 19 ult., by Rev. W. W. Bostwick, Henry Miller of Mount Morris, Livingston Co., to Sarah Townsend of the former place.
Died - In Addison 21st ult., Olive Shumway, wife of Daniel Shumway, aged 58.
Died - On 18th Nov. last at Lodi, Seneca Co., Caroline C. Brinkerhoff, aged 25 years, wife of Jacob Brinkerhoff Atty.-at-law of Mansfield, Richland County, Ohio, formerly of this town.

Wednesday January 15, 1840 - Married - In this town 1st inst., by Rev. Wing, Hiram Small to Clarissa Emerson.
Married - In Cohocton 2d inst., by Rev. A. Chase, Lewis G. Feris, M.D. of Mount Morris, Livingston Co., to Sophronia, dau. of Simeon Holms, of the former place.
Married - In Cameron 8th inst., by E. D. Swartwood Esq., Dellevan Hallett of Canisteo to Harriet Swift of the former place.
Married - In this town 9th inst., by Rev. Wing, Andrew Rutherford to Roxana Emerson.
Married - In this village on 12th inst., by Henry Pier Esq., Ira Vaness of Hammondsport to Angeline Robinson of this village.

Wednesday February 26, 1840 missing issue; March 4, no deaths or marriages.

Wednesday January 29, 1840 - Married - In this village on 21 inst., by Rev. Platt, William A. Dutcher of Geneva, to

Mary B. Woods of this place.
Died - In Howard on 17th inst., Mrs. Anne Star, wife of William Star.

Wednesday February 5, 1840 - Married - On 28th ult., by Rev. Platt, Capt. Asa Cross to Catherine Bowlsby, all of this town.

Wednesday February 12, 1840 - Died - In this town on 10th inst., James F. Burnside aged 25. Funeral at Universalist Church in Kennedyville today at 1:00 o'clock.
Died - At his father's residence in Avoca on 8th inst., Charles Andrew Roof, son of Mr. Adam L. Peck (sic), aged 23 years.
Died - In this village on 3d inst., Sarah Elizabeth, child of Sylvanus Stephens.
Died - In this village on 5th inst., Nancy Maria, dau. of Walter F. Swezey, aged 11 months.

Wednesday February 19, 1840 - Died - Stephen Burroughs, whose name is familiar to all Americans, died at Three Rivers, Lower Canada, on 23d January. He was a native of Massachusetts. He visited this state during the last summer and attracted the eye of curiosity on steamboats, at hotels, etc.

Wednesday March 11, 1840 - Died - Francis Bloodgood Esq., Thursday last. He was for many years, Clerk of the Supreme Court, several years Mayor of the city & at time of death, President of the State Bank.
Died - In this village, of consumption on 4th inst., Mr. James Lewis, aged 34 years.

Wednesday March 18, 1840 - Married - On Thursday 12th inst., by Rev. Platt, at the residence of W. W. McCay Esq., in this village, James Stuart McCay, late of Mossesibe(?) County Antrim, Ireland to Hester Hamlin, ward of W. W. McCay.
Died - At his residence in town of Prattsburgh on 8th inst., Isaac Ainsworth in his 54th year.
Died - In Prattsburgh on 10th inst., George Rudd, infant son of J. Van Valkenburgh Esq.
Died - In Wheeler, of consumption on 12th inst., Harlow P. Katner, aged 21. In Urbana of dropsey, Gideon D. Bush, recently of this village, aged 26 years.

Wednesday March 25, 1840 - Died - At Elmira, Col. John Hensley in the 83d year of his age.

Wednesday April 1, 1840 missing issue; April 22 - no deaths or marriages.

Wednesday April 8, 1840 - Married - In Wheeler on 26th ult., by Rev. Nelson Hoag, Wm. Thompson to Hester Ann Steteer.
Died - In this village on 3d inst., George P. Graham, aged 18 years.
Died - In town of Bath on 6th inst., Miss Nancy Richardson.
Died - At Painted Post in this county on 24th ult., Mrs. Minerva, wife of John Mallory of that place, aged 36. About four weeks before her death, she gave birth to a daughter. The husband and five little children survive.

Wednesday April 15, 1840 - Died - Hon. Thaddeus Betts, Senator in Congress from Conn. died at Washington on 7th inst.

Wednesday April 29, 1840 - Married - In Burdett, Tompkins Co., on 8th inst., Dr. John W. Thompson, formerly of this village to Cordelia, dau. of Gen. D. Jackson of the former place.

Wednesday May 6, 1840 - Married - At Kennedyville, on 29th April last, by Harlow Smith Esq., Mr. Ansel Parker to Elizabeth G. Niles, both of Bath.

Wednesday May 20, 1840 - no deaths or marriages, June 3,24, July 1,8,15, 22,29, August 5, 12, 1840 missing issues.

Wednesday May 13, 1840 - Married - In Howard on 6th inst., by J. W. Whiting Esq., Daniel Hamilton to Marilla Bennitt, dau. of Gen. D. N. Bennitt.
Died - In this town of consumption on 10th inst., Phidelia, dau. of Edward Smith, aged 21 years.
Died - In Howard suddenly on 11th inst., Mrs. Sophronia Cole, relict of the late Hezekiah M. Cole, deceased.

Wednesday May 27, 1840 - Died - At Ottawa, Illinois of inflammation of lungs April 24th, James G. Higgins Esq., formerly of this village, aged 49, leaving a widow and seven ohildren.
Died - In Cameron on 22d inst., John Fluent, aged 39 years.

Wednesday June 10, 1840 - Married - In Howard on 7th inst. by J. W. Whiting Esq., Daniel Snyder to Betsey Ann Southard.
Died - At Elmira on 23d ult., Mrs. Maria D. wife of Ransom Birdsall, editor of *Elmira Republican*, aged 27 years.
Died - Departed this life at his residence in Prattsburgh on 3d June inst., Doct. Noah Niles, aged 61 years. Dr. Niles was a native of Colchester, Conn. coming to Prattsburgh in 1804. He was extensively known & esteemed for his medical skill. He was an able & liberal writer for columns of the *Panoplist* and *Missionary Herald*. The Franklin Academy remains a monument to his devotion in favor of Literature, owing its existence in a great measure to his personal efforts; he was licensed by the Methodist Episcopal Society as an exhorter in 1833 and ordained a minister of the gospel in 1836.

Wednesday June 17, 1840 - Married - In Tyrone on 7th June by S. H. Arnold Esq., Henry Mingas of Wayne to Mariah Christler of the former place.
Married - In Fairfield, Conn. on 4th inst., by Rev. Atwater, Thomas McBurney of Painted Post, N.Y. to Jane A. Mills, dau. of the late Elisha T. Mills Esq.
Married - In Campbell on 7th inst., by Rev. Beebe, David Gregory of Campbell to Julia Miller of Bath.

Wednesday August 19, September 23, 1840 no deaths or marriages. September 2, 1840 missing issue.

Wednesday August 26, 1840 - Married - On the 22d inst., by Rev. John ---ay, Lyman C. Wheat Esq., to Mary B. ---arnee, all of Hornby.
Died - At Benton Centre, Yates County Thursday of last week, Mrs. Julia Young, formerly of this village, aged 33 years.
Died - In Cohocton on 18th inst., Mrs. Mary Crouch, mother of Richard and Caleb Crouch, aged 96 years.

Wednesday September 9, 1840 - Married - In Avoca on 2d inst., by Rev. N. Hoag, Dr. Brayton Babcock, of Scottsville, Cortland County to Eunice Smith of the former place.

Wednesday September 16, 1840 - Died - In this town on 11th inst., Miss Lucietta Bishop, dau. of Robert H. Bishop, aged 32 years.

Died – In August last at Elgin, Kane County, Illinois, Mr. Boanerges(sic) Fluent, formerly of Cameron, in this county, aged about 74 years. Mr. Fluent was originally from Maine and was an early settler of Cameron. In the early part of the year 1839, he sold and pushed for the famed far west.

Wednesday September 30, 1840 – Married – On the 23d inst., by Henry Pier Esq., Harry Delong of Wayne to Mary Ann Talbert of the same place.
Died – On the 24th inst., at Bath, in the 34th year of her age, Clarinda Shaut, wife of Joseph Shaut. She left a husband & 8 children.

Wednesday October 7, 1840 – Married – In Painted Post on 29th ult., by Rev. John Smith, A. B. Beckwith of Bath to Martha C. Thompson of the former place. Died at Kennedyville on 4th inst., Maria Hall aged about 17 years.

Wednesday October 14, 1840 – Married – In this town on 7th inst. by Geo. Wheeler Esq., Calvin Magee to Harriet Smith.

Wednesday October 21, November 4, 11, 25, December 2, 30, 1840 – no deaths or marriages. Wednesday December 23, 1840 missing issue.

Wednesday October 28, 1840 – Married – In this town on 22d inst., by Rev. Wing, William J. Baldwin to Catherine Dow.
Married – In Sennett, Cayuga Co., on 17th inst., by Rev. Selah Stocking, Wm. H. Ongley of Jefferson, Chemung Co., to Mary H. Hickmott of Lockport, Niagra County.

Wednesday November 18, 1840 – Married – In Wayne on 10th inst., by Rev. James Rowlett, Capt. Abram Lozier to Mary Conklin.
Died – In this town on 3d inst., Samuel Thompson, aged 73 years.

Wednesday December 9, 1840 – Married – In Cameron on 26th ult., by Elder Moses Rowley, Peter Chase to Sarah McCollum.
Died – In Pulteney on Sunday 1st November last, John Prentiss Esq., in the 80th year of his age. Mr. Prentiss was a native of Lancaster, Worcester County, Mass. In the early part of his life he went to Vermont as a surveyor, pur-

chased and cleared a farm in the town of Rutland. His health failing, he commenced the mercantile business, continuing it for 6-8 years; he then returned to his native place & continued in commercial pursuits until the beginning of the late war, at which time he took final leave of Lancaster, came to this county & purchased the farm in Pulteney on which he resided until his death. Interred in the public burying ground of the Presbyterian Society of Pulteney, Rev. James H. Hotchkin performed the service.

Wednesday December 16, 1840 - Died - In this village on 9th inst., Mrs. Hannah May, in the 71st year of her age.

Wednesday January 6, 1841 - Died - In this village on 3d inst., Henry A. Graham, aged 17 years, 7 months.

Wednesday January 13, 1841 - Married - Auburn, Cayuga Co., on 28th ult., by Rev. Hopkins, L. H. Dewey, printer of Sackett's Harbor, Jefferson County to Harriet Y. Merriam of Auburn.

Wednesday January 20, 1841 - Married - In Cameron on 30th ult., by Rev. Rowley, William D. Swarthout to Amanda Northrup.
Died - In Parkhurst, Scott County, Iowa on 13th ult., William Row, aged 55 years, formerly of this town.

Wednesday January 27, 1841 - Married - At Ogdensburg, St. Lawrence County, on 19th inst., by Rev. Savage, David Rumsey Jr. Esq., of this village to Jane E., dau. of Hon. A. C. Brown of the former place.
Married - In Jasper on 20th inst., by Rev. Cressy, Levi Stockbridge, of North Hadley, Mass. to Syrena Lamson of the former place. At Trinity Church, Elmira 10th inst., by Rev. G. Winslow, Mr. Alexander Hess to Martha T., dau. of late Samuel S. Seeley.

Wednesday February 3, 1841 - Missing issue.

Wednesday February 10, 1841 - Married - In Pulteney on 28th ult., by Elder Stebbins, Lewis Longwell of Urbana to Rachel Rattan of the former place.

Wednesday February 17, 1841 - Died - At Erwin on 13th inst., Mrs. Mary Hempsted, aged 75 years, formerly of Hartford, Conn.

Wednesday February 24, 1841 - Married - In Campbell on 16th inst., William Bonham Esq., to Eliza Cook.
Married - In Dansville on 16th inst., by Elder Clark, Charles Markham to Olive Rider of Howard.
Died - In Caton, this county, on 25th ult., of dropsey, Edward Robbins, in the 75th year of his age, formerly of Guilford, Chenango County. In Hammondsport on 18th inst. of consumption, Sophia Aulls, aged 23 years.

Wednesday March 3, 1841 - Died - In this village on 26th ult., of scarlet fever, Charles son of John Magee Esq., aged 7 years.
Died - In this village on 24th ult., James R. L., son of Samuel H. Hammond Esq., aged 8 years.
Died - On the 27th ult., Catharine A., dau. of Norman Daniels, late of Troy, aged three years.

Wednesday March 3, 1841 - Died - At Greene, Chenango County, Sunday 31st of January, Mrs. Jane Cameron, wife of Charles Cameron Esq., aged about 65 years.

Wednesday March 10, 1841 - Married - In Pulteney on 27th ult., by Rev. James H. Hotchkin, William H. Hotchkin to Ann Eliza Perkins, both of the former place.

Wednesday March 17, 1841 - Died - In Prattsburgh on Wed. 10th inst., Charles V. Stone in the 35th year of his age.
Died - In this village on Saturday 13th inst., John, son of John Magee, Esq. In this town on 8th inst., James Little, aged about 40 years. In Prattsburgh on 14th inst., Joel Pratt, son of Elisha Pratt Esq., in the 20th year of his age.

Wednesday March 24, 1841 - Died - In Lindsley on 11th inst., the wife of Rev. David Harrower, aged 71 years. Sermon by Rev. S. R. Jones.
Married - In Reading on 18th inst., by John Jameson Esq., Ira Roberts to Huldah Maria Edgar.

Wednesday March 31, 1841 - Married - In East Bloomfield on 24th inst., by Rev. R. W. Hill, Daniel D. Beebe to Almira M. Hobart.
Died - In Cameron on 28th inst., Angeline, only dau. of David Dickinson, about 4 years of age.

Wednesday April 14, 1841 - Married - In this town on 8th inst., by Rev. Oris Frazier, Moses F. Whittemore, one of the proprietors of this paper, to Sally Webster.
Married - In Cohocton on 11th inst., by Constant Cook, Esq., Waterman Jenks to Keziah Eggleston.
Died - President William Henry Harrison died at 5 p.m. Saturday last in Washington, D.C.

Wednesday May 5, 19, June 9, July 7, 1841 no deaths or marriages.

Wednesday April 14, 1841 - Died - In this town on 10th inst., Ruth Amy, dau. of Noah B. Bacon, aged 15 years.
Died - Departed this life suddenly at his residence in Prattsburgh, on 3d inst., Burrage Rice Esq., in 59th year of his age. The deceased was the fourth son of Deacon Samuel Rice, formerly of Wallingford, Conn., where he was born 14 Sept. 1782 & at age 14 removed with his parents to Marcellus, Onondaga County. In 1806 he married a dau. of Capt. Joel Pratt of Prattsburgh, where he removed his family in 1809.

Wednesday April 21, 1841 - Died - In Cameron on 12th inst., Eliza Halliday, consort of Harvey Halliday in the 41st year of her age. She was a member of the Baptist Church. Departed this life at his residence in Prattsburgh on 11th inst., Horatio Hopkins aged 52 years.
Died - At Prattsburgh on 4th inst., Jonathan Sweet, aged 93 years. The deceased was actively engaged in the war of the revolution.

Wednesday April 28, 1841 - Married - In this village on Thursday eve 22d inst., by Rev. Oris Frazier, Mr. Joseph Shaut to Jane Ann Hendryx.
Died - In this village on 19th inst., John, son of John W. Fowler Esq., aged 2 years.
Died - On Thursday 22d inst., Charles, son of Hon. Z. A. Leland, in the 3d year of his age.

Wednesday May 12, 1841 - Married - In Howard on 2d inst., by Rev. Justus Bartholomew, Melancton Barber and Lucinda Rathbun.

Wednesday May 26, 1841 - Married - In Jasper on 19th inst., by Rev. Cressy, Edwin J. Batchelder to Sally Sharp.

Wednesday June 2, 1841 - Died - May 4th at Portland, Whiteside County, Illinois, Mrs. Rachel Rowe, consort of John S. Rowe, aged 40 years, formerly of this town.

Wednesday June 16, 1841 - Married - In Prattsburgh, 9th inst., by Rev. Wm. Goodall of Howard, Orson Simmons of Fredonia, Chatauqua Co., to Maria E. Gould of Prattsburgh.
Died - In this village on Sunday 13th inst., Elizabeth, consort of Adam Haverling, Esq., aged 62 years.

Wednesday June 23, 1841 - Married - In Rushville on 16th inst., by Rev. Gelston, Major George S. Ellas of this village to Amanda D., dau. of Hon. Chester Loomis of Rushville.
Married - In Prattsburgh on 17th inst., by Rev. Gaylord, Wm. Wheeler of Wheeler and Henrietta Johnson, dau. of S. A. Johnson Esq., of the former place.
Died - In Hornellsville on 16th inst., of Dropsey, George Isaac, eldest son of Isaac Borden, aged 11 years.
Died - On 14th inst., at his residence in Orleans, Ontario Co., Punderson B. Underhill, aged 56 years.

Wednesday June 30, 1841 - Married - In Hadley, Mass. on 26th ult., by Rev. Danforth, Charles E. Lamson, formerly of Jasper to Elizabeth Cook of the former place. In this village on the 27th inst., by Rev. Oris Frazier, Jerome Greenfield to Mary Gifford; by the same, at the same time & place, Mr. Orrin Rice to Sarah Morse, all of Bath.
Died - In Prattsburgh on 21st inst., Willard Ainsworth, aged 24 years.

Wednesday July 14, 1841 - Married - At the village of Painted Post July 7th, by Rev. S. S. Howe, Luke Coriell of Hornby to Martha Cushing of New Bedford, Mass.

Wednesday July 21, 1841 - Married - In this town on 11th inst., by J. S. Depue Esq., Jacob Covel to Mary Ann Emerson; also Daniel Shadduck to Harriet Emerson.

Wednesday July 28, August 4, 11, 18, 25, 1841 - no deaths or marriages.

Wednesday September 1, 1841 - Married - In this town on 29th inst., by Rev. O. Frazier, John Pike to Helen Lake.
Died - On the 23d inst., William, son of Sam'l. Nealy, aged 6 years of scarlet fever.

Wednesday September 8, 1841 - Married - At Campbell on 1st inst., by Rev. Davis, George Cook to Sarah Bonham, all of Campbell.
Married - On 6th inst., in Pulteney by Elder H. Stebbins, William H. Johnson of Trenton, Oneida Co., to Jane Williams of the former place. In this village on 1st inst., by Rt. Rev. Christopher Rush of New York, Richard Bogardus of Geneva to Mary Jane Lyon of Bath.
Died - In this village on 31st August Sarah, youngest dau. of James M'Beath, aged 16 months.
Died - At his residence in Cohocton 22d ult., after a protracted illness, Dr. Simeon Rosenkrans, formerly of Sussex Co., N.J. aged 67 years.

Wednesday September 15, 1841 - Married - In this town on 9th inst., by Rev. O. Frazier, James Fraser of York, Livingston Co., to Agnes Jane McPherson of this town. At the Presbyterian Church in Bath on 9th inst., by Rev. Isaac W. Platt, George White, merchant in Albany to Helen A. Taylor of Bath. In Homer, Cortland Co., on 6th inst., by Rev. L. A. Barrows, N. Pellet, editor of the Chenango Telegraph to Malvina, dau. of Ira Bowen of Homer.
Married - In Angelica on the 8th inst., by Rev. L. Thibou, Martin Adsit of Hornellsville to Esther Jane Charles of Angelica. In Prattsburgh on 12th inst., by Wm. M. Van Valkenburgh Esq., Wm. Moore to Elizabeth Fisher of the former place.
Died - In this village at the residence of L. Biles, Alexander M. Conner, aged 22 years.
Died - In Urbana on 8th inst., of consumption, Zopher Williams, aged 25 years. In Prattsburgh on 28th ult., of bilious fever, Simeon Hayes, aged 72 years 6 mos.

Wednesday September 22, 1841 - Died - In this town on 28th ult., John Gregg, aged 63 years.
Died - At his residence in Elmira on 12th inst., John Shockey, aged 72 years. Grenville Millen whose poetry has long been admired by the American public died at his residence in N.Y. city a few days since. He had been in feeble health sometime and spent last winter in Cuba.

Wednesday September 29, October 13, 1841 - missing issues.

Wednesday October 6, 1841 - Died - On 11th Sept. at Newton, Conn. while on a visit to her friends, Jane M. Curtis of Campbell, aged 16 years 7 mos.

Wednesday October 21, 1841 - Married - In this town on 16th ult., by Rev. Platt, Simeon P. Niles of Prattsburgh to Hannah Smith of Bath.
Died - Sunday 10th inst., on board the Steamboat on Lake Erie, Ellen Loomis, wife of Theron Loomis of Prattsburgh and dau. of the late Brigham Hanks. She was returning from Illinois religious revival. In this village on 15th inst., Wm. Tolliver, aged about 70 years.

Wednesday October 27, 1841 - Died - In Wheeler on 25th inst., suddenly of inflammatory rheumatism, Gifford Potter, aged about 40 years.

Wednesday November 3, 1841 - Married - In Wayne on the 28th ult., by Rev. James Rowlett, Alvin G. Hause of Tyrone to Miss Fidelia Noble of the former place. In Howard on 28th ult., by A. M. Leigh Esq., Mr. Lucius Peck to Mary Day.
Died - In Rochester on Friday 29th ult., Sarah C., wife of Dr. D. M. Shipman, formerly of this village.

Wednesday Nov. 10, 1841 - Died - At Prattsburgh of scarlet fever on 5th inst., Robert D. Porter, youngest son of Wm. L. & Olive L. Porter, aged 3 yrs. 11 mos.

Wednesday November 17, 1841 - Married - In Avoca on 9th inst., by Rev. O. Johnson, Joel H. Rice of Jackson, Mich., and Caroline L. Butler of Avoca, only dau. of Joseph Butler.
Died - In Wheeler of consumption on 12th inst., Christina, wife of G. W. Taylor, aged 48 years.
Died - On Fri. 5th inst., Samuel Westcot, aged 13 years was killed by the felling of a tree in Hornellsville by Mr. Clark. His parents are separated, his mother being in Michigan and the father is in Dansville of this county. The boy was interred in Hornellsville Cemetery, sermon by Rev. Brownal.

Wednesday November 24, 1841 - Married - In this village, 17th inst., by Rev. P. L. Whipple, Dr. George Norton of Shelby, Orleans County and Sarah E. Ellas of this village.
Married - In Rushville on 17th inst., by Rev. Gelson, Albert

M. Hobart of Prattsburgh & Mary Blodget of the former place.
Married - In Wheeler on 18th inst., by Rev. F. S. Gaylord of Prattsburgh, Ackerson Armstrong of Pulteney to Eliza Wheeler, dau. of Hon. G. H. Wheeler.

Wednesday December 1, 1841 - Married - In Wheeler on 28th ult., by Jacob Larrowe Esq., Capt. Silas Wheeler & Phidelia Frisbie, all of wheeler.

Wednesday December 8, 1841, January 5, 26, 1842 - no marriages or deaths.

Wednesday December 1, 1841 - Died - In Jasper Nov. 13, Demaris, wife of Joseph Batchelder, formerly from New Hampshire, in the 48th year of her age.

Wednesday December 15, 1841 - Married - In Kennedyville on 8th inst., by Wm. M. VanValkenburgh Esq., of Prattsburgh, Wm. H. Miller & Eleanor Gregory, both of Cameron.
Married - At West Troy on 2d inst., by Rev. Gregory, J. Eustace Whipple Esq., of Lansingburgh to Maria E. E. Viele of Albany.

Wednesday December 22, 1841 - Died - In this town on 15th inst., Dr. John Ellis, aged about 13 years (sic); on 17th George Ellis (same family) aged 23 years.
Died - At Rochester Dec. 9th of consumption, Mary Mathews, dau. of Gen. Vincent Mathews.

Wednesday December 29, 1841 - Married - In Prattsburgh on 23d inst., by Rev. A. Judson, Dr. Walter S. Cheney & Sarah L. Ainsworth, both of that place.
Died - Departed this life at her residence in Prattsburgh Tues. 21st inst., Mary, wife of Auren Daboll. Mrs. Daboll was a native of Litchfield, Conn. & removed to Prattsburgh in 1822.

Wednesday January 12, 1842 - Married - In Pike, Allegany County on Tues. 28th ult., by Rev. Wm. Conklin, Capt. William A. Cook of this village to Ellen C. Cook of Pike.

Wednesday January 19, 1842 - Married - In Pulteney on 9th inst., by Rev. Gould, Dyer S. Kip & Jane A. Parker, all of Pulteney.
Died - In Prattsburgh on 13th Dec. last of consumption,

Jemima, wife of William Vedder, aged 36. She leaves a husband & 6 children.

Wednesday February 2, 1842 - Died - In this town on 31 inst., Mrs. Cornelia Rowe, consort of Anson Rowe, aged 24 years.
Died - In this town on 18th inst., Rachel Amelia, infant dau. of the late Stewart K. Warren.

Wednesday February 9, 1842 - Died - In this village on Fri. 4th ult., Elisha Loder, aged 27 years.

Wednesday February 16, 1842 - Married - In Prattsburgh on 13th inst., by Wm. M. VanValkenburgh Esq., Caleb Baxter to Sophia Mann.
Married - At Elmira, Chemung Co., on 3d inst., by Rev. Spaulding, John S. Hoffman and Lydia Logan, formerly of this town.

The Steuben Democrat
Bath, New York
Nov. 15, 1843-May 22, 1844

Wednesday November 15, 1843 - Marriage - Thomas O. Page married Hannah Nettleton September 12, 1842 at Alben, Buffalo County, Tues. 17 inst., they arrived in Buffalo together to go west. On Saturday following, Page took all $300 of her money and left the city alone. He talked of going to Ft. Wayne.

Wednesday November 22, 1843 - Marriage - In this village on 18th inst., by Rev. P. Powers, John M. Mathewson of Benton, Yates County to Jane E. Nash, of this place.
Died - Isabel R. Keats, Louisville, Kentucky "accidentally" shot herself. She was a niece of John Keats, young English poet. (*Louisville Journal*).
Died - The Honorable Edward P. Livingston of Clermont, Columbia County, New York expired in the city of New York on Friday in the 64th year of his age. He was first chosen to the Senate nearly forty years ago. He was chosen Lieutenant-Governor in 1836 & once again to the Senate & voluntarily withdrew, owing to ill health in 1840.
Died - Three miles south of this village on Tuesday, three sons of Peter Colbert, Thomas, William & George aged 12, 10, & 8 years drowned at the millpond. (Burlington, Vt. *Free Press*).

November 29, Dec. 13, 20, 1843 - no deaths or marriages.

Wednesday December 6, 1843 - Marriage - In West Tyrone village on 29th ult., by Rev. James Roulette, Eli Northrop to Rachel Craft, all of Tyrone.
Marriage - Also in East Tyrone village at 12 o'clock between 4th & 5th inst., by Jesse W. Wells Esq., William Sargeant to Laura Dilliston.

Wednesday December 27, 1843 - Died - Negro Daniel executed Friday last. (Upper Marlboro, Md. *Gazette*).
Died - The body of Mrs. Miller aged 70, who had wandered from the home of her son near Cold Spring on the North River, was found at the foot of West Point mountain on Wednesday last.
Died - The Honorable Smith Thompson, an Associate Justice of the Supreme Court of the U. S. expired at his residence in Poughkeepsie, Monday last at advanced age of seventy-six years.

Wednesday January 3, 1844 - no deaths or marriages. Wednesday January 10, 24, February 7, 1844 - missing issues.

Wednesday January 17, 1844 - Died - On Thursday 11th inst., John M. Cook, son of Constant Cook Esq., of this village in the 16th year of his age.

EIGHT SOLDIERS OF THE REVOLUTION GONE

At Newark, N.J. on 26th ult., Heman Hatch a revolutionary patriot, formerly of Centreville, N.J.
AT Ashby, Mass. Abel Richardson, a revolutionary soldier aged 92 1/2 years. (N.D.)
At Brookfield, Ct. on the 16th ult., David Keeler in the 91st year of his age, a revolutionary soldier, & for more than 60 years a devout Christian.
Near Flemington, N.J. on 15th ult., Major John Howe, a distinguished soldier of the revolutionary war, in the 90th year of his age.
Near White House, Hunterdon County, Cornelius Messler, a soldier of the revolutionary war, in the 84th year of his age.
At Leominster, Mass., John Burdett, a soldier of the revolution in the 98th year of his age.
At Gardner, Maine, Jude Sawyer, a soldier of the revolution aged 93. He was in the battle of Bunker Hill.
At Litchfield, Ct., Amos Galpin, a soldier of the revolution aged 89.
Marriage - In Wheeler on 3d inst., by Seth Wheeler Esq., Jackson Early of Prattsburgh to Patricia Trenchard of Wheeler.
Marriage - In Bradford, Walter Mitchell Esq., merchant & Catherine Zimmerman, dau. of John Zimmerman.

Wednesday January 31, 1844 - Marriage - In this village on 24th inst., by Rev. S. Porter, Samuel Legro to Elmira Tiffany.
Died - In this town on 25th inst., John, son of James Smith, aged about 8 years.

Wednesday February 28, March 13, 27, April 3, 1844 - missing issues. March 20, 1844 - no deaths or marriages.

Wednesday February 14, 1844 - Marriage - In this village on 8th inst., by Rev. Porter, James S. Smith of Newfield, Tompkins County to Sally Ann Dudley of this village.
Marriage - In this village on 17th ult., by Rev. Whipple, James Webster to Caroline Beckwith.
Died - Another revolutionary soldier gone, Robert Harrison of Urbana, aged 90 years. (N.D.)

Wednesday February 21, 1844 - Married - In South Dansville on 19th inst., by Rev. Cobb, Caleb R. Disbrow of Bath, to Electa Griswold of the former place.

Wednesday March 6, 1844 - Married - In Bath February 29 by Rev. Jabez Chadwick, Anthony H. Rarrick of Tyrone to Sarah Campbell of Bath.
Died - Thomas Reynolds, Governor of Missouri, committed suicide on 9th ult., in a momentary aberration of mind produced by feeble health.
Died - Nicholas Biddle, Whig financier who was president of the United States Bank died at his residence in Bucks County, Pa. from dropsey, aged 54 years.

Wednesday April 10, 1844 - Died - On Sunday last Mason Edwards, son of the late George C. Edwards in his 19th year.
Run Away - Theodore French, minor son of J. P. French, Cameron, March 20, 1844.

Wednesday April 17, 1844 - Married - In South Pultney on 3d inst., by Rev. J. H. Hotchkin, Joseph B. Hotchkin of Prattsburgh to Desiah Dunning of the former place. In Prattsburgh on 11th inst., by Rev. B. C. Smith, Ezra C. Bramble to Lydia G. Lindsley, all of Prattsburgh.

Wednesday May 1, 1844 no deaths or marriages.

Wednesday April 17, 1844 - Died - Morgan Lewis expired at his residence in New York city at 12 o'clock Sunday. He served in the Colonial Government with honor during the Revolutionary War, in 1791 he succeeded Aaron Burr as Attorney General of the state; 1792 was appointed a judge of the Supreme Court, in 1801 Chief Justice; 1804 nominated & elected governor opposite Col. Burr and in 1810 returned to State Senate.

Wednesday April 24, 1844 - Married - On 17th inst. by Elder Jabez Chadwick, James Van Houton & Nancy K. Johnson, both of Bath.
Married - In this village on 22d inst. by Rev. I. W. Platt, James R. Dudley, merchant to Clarissa R. Edwards all of this place.

Wednesday May 8, 1844 - Died - The Hon. P. M. Bassier, M.C. from Louisiana, died at Washington on 24th ult. He was 47 years of age & belonged to one of Louisiana's oldest French families.
Died - In New York city on 29th ult., at the residence of his brother, George Newcomb of this town, aged 61 years.
Died - Elizabeth Trimble, aged 22 years, dau. of John Trimble of Mud Creek, disappeared February last. Her body was found floating in the Niagra River near the dam at Black Rock April 18, ult.

Wednesday May 15, 1844 - Death - In Hornellsville on Thurs. May 2d of consumption, Lydia Doty, aged 26 years, dau. of Christopher & Lucinda Doty.

Wednesday May 22, 1844 - Died - Mrs. Caroline Matilda Thayer, a writer of some eminence, & granddau. of Gen. Warren who fell at Bunker Hill, at Harrisonburg, La. some days ago.
Died - In this town on 20th inst., Mrs. Polly Barton, aged 28 years.
Married - On the 15th inst., by Elder Jabez Chadwick, Milo Palmer to Azilla Moore, both of Bath.
Married - Also on 20th of April by Elder C. D. Kinney, Norman Rowland to Hannah Towner, both of Avoca.
Married - In Pultney on 15th inst. by Rev. P. Powers, Leicester Lee of Bath to Salina Brundage of the former place.
Married - In this village on 19th inst., by Rev. P. Powers, Uriah Scutt of Dryden, Tompkins Co. to Sally Tyler.

Steuben Farmers Advocate
Bath, New York
Dec. 16, 1846 - Dec. 8, 1847

Wednesday December 16, 1846 - Married - In this town on 13th inst., by Elder Ira Brown, George Bellas to Jane Aber, all of this town.

Married - In Dansville, Livingston County by Rev. W. Corry on 7th inst., Joseph E. Palmer of Erwin to Elizabeth M. Vance of the former place.

Married - In Palmyra, Wayne Co., on 8th inst., by Rev. D. Harrington, John M. Francis, editor of the Troy Budget, to Harriet E. Tucker of the former place.

Wednesday December 23, 1846 - Died - In this town on 13th inst., John, infant son of Israel Morris of whooping cough.

Married - In Prattsburgh on 17th inst., by Rev. Smith, John V. Lewis to Helen Ann, eldest dau. of Abner P. Lyon Esq., all of Prattsburgh.

Wednesday December 30, 1846 - Married - At the Clinton House, in this village on the evening of 24th inst., by the Rev. L. W. Russ, Julius A. Reynolds to Mary Elizabeth Conklin, all of this place.

Died - William Hatch of Worthington, Mass. perished in the snow on the night of 25th ult., within ten rods of the house of his neighbor.

Died - On Friday 4th inst., a girl six years old, dau. of William Wadsworth, who has charge of the ferry at Lewiston was burned to death when her clothing caught fire. (Lockport *Democrat*).

Died - On Saturday last, a son of Jacob Kaylor Jr. of Royalton, aged between 2 & 3 years, whilst running backwards, fell into a pail of scalding water & survived only 22 hours. (Niagra *Courier*).

Died - The *Dundee Record* of 16th says that David Bain, of

this place, who was married to Eliza Walling on Wednesday evening last, died on Thursday (the next) night. He was about 40 years of age.

Wednesday January 6, 1847 - Married - In the town of Cohocton on 23 ult., by Rev. S. S. Brown, Myron Patchin Esq., to Rozilla Parmater, all of Cohocton.
Married - In Avoca, on 30th ult., by Rev. J. Strough, John Loucks to Nancy C. Zeilly, both of that town.
Married - In Howard on 1st inst., by W. B. Rice Esq., Franklin Cole to Hannah Mariah Clark.
Died - In this town on 29th ult., John Griffith in the 81st year of his age.
Died - In Avoca, on 1st inst., Mrs. Anna Maria Rice, aged 27 years, her birthday.

Wednesday January 13, 1847 - Married - In this village on 6th inst., by Rev. L. W. Russ, Nathan Stephens of Thurston to Ellen Schenck of Bath.
Married - In this town on 7th inst., by Rev. C. Wheeler, Mr. N. Sanger Wheeler to Barbara Lewis, all of this town.
Died - In this town on 8th ult., Katurah D., wife of Cameron Carruthers, and dau. of James Bowlby, aged 22 years.
Died - In Prattsburgh on 7th inst., James C. Johnson, son of Samuel C. Johnson Esq., aged 23 years.

Wednesday January 20, 1847 - Married - In Howard on 6th ult., by Elder E. Bronson, Peter Pickle (sic) to Clarissa Clark
Married - In this town on the 13th inst., by Rev. L. Merrill Miller, Daniel DeWitt of Bath, to Eliza Stephens of Chenango County. In Italy, Yates County on 6th inst., by Rev. Chatman, John C. Raymond to Sarah A. Cort, both of that place.
Died - Henry V. D. Williams of Lima, Ohio died at his residence on 18th ult., of hydrophobia. He was bitten in the arm by a dog on 21st October last, while on a visit to Marion, Ohio.

Wednesday January 27, 1847 - Died - Edward Monely was drowned on 15th inst., in the first lock at Syra-cuse, into which he fell while intoxicated. He left a wife and child.
Died - James Langford of Rome Twp., Susquehannah Co., Pa. shot his wife with a pistol on Monday 12th inst. Langford's wife was dau. of Mr. Briggs, a tavern Keeper at Athens, Pa. and his employer. Two young Germans named

John Morgeworth and Jacob Schmidt were drowned in crossing the river Monday night. (Troy Budget)

Wednesday February 3, 1847 - Married - In Napolian (sic), Michigan Alexander H. Corning, son of Rev. Alexander Corning and nephew of Erastus Corning of Albany, to Indiana Blood, dau. of Capt. Asa Blood of this village.

Died - Daniel Aiken died at Wexford, Upper Canada a short time since, age 120 years. He had during his life contracted seven marriages, had 570 children, grandchildren and great-grandchildren; 370 boys and 200 girls!

Wednesday February 10, 1847 - Died - In Prattsburgh on 29th ult., of typhus fever, Biny (sic) Megrady, aged 23 years.

Died - In Prattsburgh on 4th inst., of prevailing fever, Henry Cleveland, aged 21 years.

Died - On Sunday 10th ult., James C., son of S. A. Johnson, Postmaster of Prattsburgh; on 1st ult., his wife Elmira aged 47 years, dau. of Wm. Curtiss Esq., and the day following, his daughter, Helen aged 21 years.

Wednesday February 17, 1847 - Married - In Burns, Allegany County on 13th ult., by Rev. Twitchel, George Wentworth to Eunice Cruttenden, all of Burns.

Married - In Dansville, on 1st ult., by Charles Oliver Esq., Elnathan H. Wing of Cohocton, to Sally Oliver of the former place.

Married - In Howard on 31st ult., by Rev. L. Rose, Wm. R. VanCampen of Almond to Harriet A. Howard of the former place.

Married - At the same place by the same, on 7th inst., John Chubbuck to Frances B. Rathbun, all of Howard.

Married - In Kennedyville on 11th inst., by Rev. J. Case, Daniel Dervel of Bristol, Ontario County to Mrs. Lucia Ann Strickland of Bath, formerly of Connecticut.

Died - At Howard on 8th inst., Lester Hamilton, aged 16 years, son of the late John Hamilton, Esq.

Wednesday February 24, 1847 - Married - In South Dansville on 4th inst., by Rev. A. Berky, Christian Kaush to Maria E. Braunschweig, both of South Dansville. In Jasper on 18th inst., by Rev. Everest, George W. Punchis of Cameron to Martha Dennis of the former place.

Wednesday March 3, 1847 - Married - In this village on 27th ult., by Rev. L. Merrell Miller, Hezekiah S. Biles of Bath to Olive S. Griswould of Penn Yan. In Tyrone on 25th ult., by John Chambers Esq., Abel Houck of Bath, to Angeline Disbrow of Tyrone.

Wednesday March 10, 1847 - Married - On Thursday 4th inst., by Rev. L. Merrell Miller, Eli Bidwell Jr. to Louisa, dau. of Benjamin F. Dudley, all of Bath.

Married - In Bath on 2nd inst., by the same, Elisha Mack of South Dansville to Hannah Niles of Bath.

Married - In this town on 4th inst., by Rev. Sawyer, Capt. John L. Smith, to Lois M. Legro, all of this town.

Married - In Avoca on 2d inst., by Rev. J. Strough, Patrick Dyer to Mary Towner, both of this town.

Married - In Benton, Yates County on 4th inst., by Rev. H. Spencer, Andrew F. Chapman to Mary E. Hicks, both of Benton.

Married - In Addison on 2d inst., by C. Cole Esq., John Harvey to Harriet Crawford.

Wednesday March 17, 1847 - Married - In Mud Creek on 3d inst., James L. Brink to Harriet A. Pratt, both of Mud Creek.

Married - In Huron, Wayne County on 4th inst., by Rev. Wm. C. Clark, Abner P. Lyon of Prattsburgh to Laura Sheldon of the former place.

Married - In Thurston on 14th inst., by Rev. T. McElhana, Joseph Emerson to Harriet Jaquay, late of Hamilton, Madison County.

Wednesday March 24, 1847 - Married - In Elmira on 9th inst., by Rev. P. E. Brown, Asaph Carr to Cordelia Handy, both of Corning.

Married - In Elkland, Pa. on 11th inst., by Rev. Bronson, Heman (sic) W. Kingsbury of Dansville to Elizabeth Hammond of the former place.

Married - In Howard on the 15th inst., by Rev. L. Rose, James Yortan (sic) to Laura M. Smith, both of the above place.

Married - In Oakland County, Michigan on 13th ult., by Rev. John Smith, Wm. White, late of this place, to Angeline Hilton of the former place.

Died - At Prattsburgh on 17th inst., of typhus fever, Dewit (sic) C. Ainsworth, aged 21 years. A worthy member of the Lyceum of that town.

Died - In Napoleon, Michigan on 24th ult., Michael Lemon, formerly of Howard, Steuben County, N.Y. aged 70 years.

Died - In this village on 21 inst., John K. Calkins of inflammation of lungs, aged about 55 years.

Wednesday March 31, 1847 - Married - In this village on 28th inst., by A. D. Read Esq., Hiram Warner of Wheeler to Susan Osterhout, of Urbana.

Married - In Bath on 25th inst., by Rev. E. B. Fuller, David Longwell to Laura Campbell.

Died - In Rathboneville on 15th inst., at residence of his son-in-law Gen. R. Rathbone, John Fisher, in the 70th year of his age.

Died - In this village on Wednesday of scarlet fever, Fanny Delphene, dau. of James & Caroline Webster, aged 9 mos.

Died - In Corning Charles H. Powers, a worthy member Corning Division Sons of Temperance. (No date given).

Wednesday April 7, 1847 - Married - In Prattsburgh on 27th ult., by Rev. J. K. Tuttle, Horace Burk of Italy, to Sarah Ann Nobel of the former place.

Married - In Springwater on 25th ult., by Rev. W. F. Curry, Allen J. Parker of Dansville (late of Bath), to Harriet M. Ashley of Springwater.

Died - In Pulteney on 2d inst., Charles W., son of John Gload Esq., aged 6 years.

Wednesday April 21, 1847 - Died - In Kennedyville, on 30th ult., of consumption, Lydia Ann, only dau. of the late Franklin Glass, aged 17 years.

Wednesday April 14, May 5, 19, 1847 - no deaths or marriages.

Wednesday April 28, 1847 - Married - In Jasper on 20th inst., by Rev. G. T. Everest, James R. Sargent, to Permelia Whittemore.

Wednesday May 12, 1847 - Married - In this town on 10th inst., by Rev. H. Spencer, George C. Bellis to Jane Aber, all of Bath.

Died - In Elmira on 6th inst., James Nichoson (sic), aged 37 years.

Died - In New Berlin, Chenango County on 21st ult., M. Adaline Cook, aged 21 years 6 months. She was a teacher in the community.

Wednesday May 26, 1847 – Married – In Wheeler on 20th inst., by Hiram VanPelt Esq., James Jolley to Hannah Baker, all of that place.
Died – On 14th inst., in the town of Bath, Maria dau. of Samuel Benjamin, formerly of New Jersey, aged 23 years.

Wednesday June 2, 1847 – Married – In Prattsburgh on 15th ult., by Rev. Chapman, Hiram C. Clark to Mary C. Bardeen, both of Prattsburgh.
Married – In Italy, on 15th ult., by Rev. Chapman, John Knapp to Martha Edson, both of Italy, Yates County.
Married – In this village on 23rd ult., by Rev. E. B. Fuller, John D. Jacobus of Westchester County to Janett Alderman of Urbana.

Wednesday June 9, 1847 – Died – In Jasper of consumption on 29th inst., Amanda P., wife of Allen Drake, aged 36 years.

Wednesday June 16, 1847 – Died – In this village on 25th ult., Mariana Whiting, aged 2 years, 15 days, child of Mr. L. C. Whiting.
Died – In this village on 12th inst., Mary W., wife of W. O. Noble, aged 36 years.

Wednesday June 23, 1847 – Married – On 20th inst., by Rev. S. White of Pulteney, Henry G. Skinner of Prattsburgh to Mary Jane Waddell of the former place.
Died – In Thurston on 16th inst., Turzah E. Rutherford, aged 12 years, dau. of Edward Rutherford of said town.
Died – At the dwelling of his only brother in Urbana on 28th May, Benjamin Eaton aged 84 years 10 mos. He was a native of Massachusetts, in early life a soldier of the revolution, at age 25 emigrated to Painted Post, last eight years a member of Presbyterian Church in Hammsondsport.

Wednesday June 30, 1847 – Married – In Corning on 13th inst., by Rev. E. Hotchkiss, John B. Southwell of Monterey, to Jane E. Goodon of the former place.
Married – In Pulteney on 24th inst., by Rev. S. White, Samuel B. White of Starkey to Amanda Tomes of the former place.

Wednesday July 7, 1847 – Married – In the Baptist Church in this village on 4th inst., by Rev. H. Spencer, John H. Mills to Amelia I. Blood, both of Liberty.
Married – In this village on 5th inst., by same, Leonard G.

Coats to Nancy W. Grant all of Bath.
Married - In North Dansville on 19th February last, by Rev. E. H. Walker, John Case Jr. of Bath to Adaline Rector of Rome, N.Y.

Wednesday July 14, 1847 - Married - In this village on 24th ult., by Rev. E. B. Fuller, Peter Bundy of Otsego to Charlotte J. French of the former place.
Married - By the same on 1st inst., Hiram Snyder to Mrs. Elsa A. Smith, all of Bath.
Married - In South Dansville on 1st inst., by Rev. J. Selsmer, Willis Covil to Mary Custo, all of that place.

Wednesday July 21, 1847 - Married - In Jasper on 4th inst., by Elder Wm. G. Raymond, Joseph Wilcox of Troupsburgh to Jane Webster of the former place.
Died - At his residence in Wayne on 2d inst., Alexander Pattent, aged 64 years.
Died - At the residence of his father in this town, on 16th inst., R. Robie Frink, aged about 19 years.

Wednesday July 28, 1847 - Married - On the 20th inst., by James Shannon Esq., Oliver Monell to Mary Ann Skinner, all of Bath.

Wednesday August 11, September 1, 29, 1847 - no deaths or marriages.

Wednesday August 4, 1847 - Died - In this village on 29th ult., Pamelia, wife of Levi C. Whiting, Esq., & dau. of the late Hon. William Woods, aged 24 years.
Died - In this village on 30th ult., Martin Collins, aged about 55 years.
Died - In this town on 30th ult., Daniel Cooper, aged about 80 years.
Died - Departed this life at Lawrenceville, Pa. on 26th ult., Mrs. Maria Ford, dau. of the late Judge Lindsley & consort of the Hon. James Ford, member Presbyterian Church.

Wednesday August 18, 1847 - Died - In this town on 12th inst., Mrs. Catherine Roberts, relict of Joseph Roberts, aged about 70 years.
Died - In this town on 1st inst., Catherine, dau. of Wm. Little, aged 17 mos.

Wednesday August 25, 1847 - Married - In this village on 18th inst., by Rev. Corson, Henry W. Perine to Elizabeth S., youngest dau. of Capt. James Read all of Bath.
Died - At Canisteo on 17th inst., Mary Eason, infant dau. of Mr. Hart Eason, aged 16 months.

Wednesday September 15, 1847 - Married - In the town of Orange by Rev. Bryant R. Hurd, on 1st inst., Niles Payne to Patty Lewis all of Orange.
Died - In this town on 7th inst., Mrs. Mary Eaton, aged about 45 years, consort of Benjamin Eaton.
Died - In this village on 11th inst., Louesa M., wife of Doct. Jas. D. Doer, of dropsey and disease of the heart, aged 23 years.
Died - In Addison on 27th ult., Fanny E., dau. of Joseph & Fanny Fluent, aged 22 years.
Died - In Avoca on 12th inst., Elijah Straight, aged 71 years, member of Baptist Church.

Wednesday September 22, 1847 - Died - In Avoca on 14th inst., of quick consumption, Joseph Woodard, aged 79 years.
Died - In Corning on 7th inst., Samuel Hoyt, of appoplexy, aged 31 years.

Wednesday October 6, 1847 - Married - In Wayne on 23d inst., by Rev. B. Russell, Daniel Russell of Castleton, to Mariah Hunter of Wayne.
Married - In Wayne on 29th ult., by Rev. S. C. Mallory, George W. Curtis to Isabelle Swarthout, all of Wayne.
Married - In Pulteney on 30th ult., by Rev. P. Olney, Russell Sandford of Wayne to Laura Chapman of Pulteney.

Wednesday October 13, 1847 - Married - In Urbana on 12th inst., by Rev. L. W. Russ, Franklin Baker of Republic, Ohio to Mary Brundage, dau. of Wm. Brundage of Urbana.
Died - In Corinth, Vermont on 31st inst., Jonathan Robie, aged 76 years.

Wednesday October 20, 1847 - Married - In this village on 13th inst., by Rev. L. Merrill Miller, Geo. W. Hallock to Mary H., eldest dau. of Hon. W. S. Hubbell, all of this place.
Died - At Avoca on 17th inst., after a short illness, Henry Pawling, aged 59 years.
Died - In Howard on 18th inst., James Stewart, aged 32 yrs.

Wednesday October 27, 1847 - Married - In Bath on 21st inst., by Rev. S. W. Alden, Hon. Carlos Emmons of Springville, Erie County, to Mrs. Caroline Powers, widow of late Rev. Philander Powers of the Genesee Conference.

Married - At Italy Hill on 7th inst., by Rev. W. H. Husted, David Lare to Maria Smith, all of Italy.

Married - On the 23d inst., by Rev. Merrill Miller, James Babcock to Catherine VanGelder, all of this town.

Married - At St. Thomas Church in this village on 20th inst., by Rev. M. Corson, A. P. Ferris Esq., to Catherine, dau. of Capt. Reed, all of this village.

Wednesday October 27, 1847 - Died - At his residence at Young Hickory, Will County, Illinois on 27th ult., Chauncey Hoffman M.D., late of Chenango County, N.Y. aged 52 years. (Joliet *Signal*, Ill.).

Died - At Prattsburgh on 16th inst., of typhus fever, Mandeville Tuthill, in the 30th year of his age. He was a Baptist minister and a member of the Lyceum.

Died - In this village on 22d inst., Ralph F., son of Azel R. Gould, aged 14 months.

Died - In this village on 22d inst., Adelaide R., dau. of John Page, aged 3 years.

Wednesday November 10, December 1, 8, 1847 - no deaths or marriages. Wednesday December 15, 1847 through Wednesday December 6, 1848 missing.

Wednesday November 3, 1847 - Married - In this village on 24th inst., by Rev. S. W. Alden, Renald Dickinson to Lucy V. Noble, all of Urbana.

Married - In this village on 31st ult., by Rev. S. W. Alden, Joseph Thorp to Mary Towle, all of Bath.

Died - In Canisteo on Thursday last, Finla McGlure, aged about 47 years, eldest son of Gen. George McGlure, formerly of this town.

Died - In Fairport on 25th ult., Henry Brooks, son of Birdsey Brooks, Oakland County, Michigan aged 26 years.

Wednesday November 17, 1847 - Died - In this village on 15th inst., after a short & painful attack of paralysis, Charlotte, wife of James McBeth, formerly of New York city.

Wednesday November 24, 1847 - Died - In this town on 17th inst., Miss Hannah Hunter, aged 56 years.

The Steuben Democrat
Bath, New York
June 14, 1848-June 13, 1849

Wednesday June 21, 28, July 3, August 2, 1848 - no deaths or marriages.

Wednesday June 14, 1848 - Died - In this village on Wednesday 7th inst., James Shannon Esq., aged 38 years. He leaves a widow, an aged father, brothers & sisters. He was a lawyer.

Wednesday July 12, 1848 - Married - In Wheeler on Thursday 29th ult., by Elder C. D. Kinney, Jeremiah Olmsted, Esq., of Avoca to Charlotte Dygert, of the former place.
Died - In Wheeler on Friday 20th ult., Sylvenus Dygert, a revolutionary soldier aged 88 years.

Wednesday July 19, 1848 - Married - In Bath by A. D. Read Esq., on 5th inst., Rufus Smith to Polly Chase, all of Bath.
Married - In Bath by A. D. Read, Esq., on 10th inst., John Kelly to Margaret Collins, all of Bath.
Died - In Bath on the 31st ult., Harry Wyllys, aged 45 years.
Died - In Urbana on 8th February Martha Matilda Abbott, eldest dau. of Moses & Caroline Abbott, aged 16 years, 2 months & 6 days.
Died - In Urbana on 29 April, Hannah R. Randle, wife of Wm. Randle, aged 29 years, 1 month & 20 days.

Wednesday July 26, 1848 - Died - At the residence of her brother-in-law in Corning on 20th inst., Rosanna Mary Theresa, wife of George Messenger, one of the proprietors of this paper, aged 20 years.
Longevity - Mrs. Mary Bacon, aged one hundred & eight years, died in this city on Monday afternoon last. The accuracy of her age seems to be placed beyond controversy

by the following record in the office of the city clerk – "Mary Mathewson, dau. of John Mathewson & Phoebe, his wife, was born at Providence the 10th of June 1740". (Providence, R. I. *Journal* July 9th).

Wednesday August 9, 1848 – Married – In Bath on 3d inst., by Rev. S. W. Alden, Watermore Jenks to Eliza Ann Richardson, both of this village.

Wednesday August 16, 1848 – Married – In Bath on 9th inst., by Rev. L. M. Miller, Francis Ripley Esq., of Milwaukie (sic) to Christina G., dau. of John W. Fowler of this place.
Died – In this village on Wednesday August 9th, Lydia, dau. of Reuben Robie, Esq., aged 20 years.
Died – In this village on Monday last, Joseph, son of Hiram Small, aged about 5 years.
Died – In Urbana on Friday 11th inst., Catherine Faulkner, mother of John and Richard Faulkner, aged 88 years.

Wednesday August 23, 30, 1848 – no deaths or marriages.

Wednesday September 6, 1848 – Married – In Havana, Chemung Co., N.Y. on 31st ult., Mr. J. B. Look, printer formerly of Bath and Sarah M., only dau. of A. Fay Esq., of the former place.

Wednesday September 13, 1848 – Married – In this village on Tuesday 12th inst., by Rev. Corsen, at the residence of C. Cook Esq., Mr. Seymour of Massachusetts to Miss Eugene (sic) Brigham.
Died – In Wheeler on 25th ult., after an illness of 12 hours, Mr. T. W. Daniels, aged 52 years.
Died – In this town on 29th ult., Isaac Bean Esq., aged about 74 years. In this village on Saturday 2d inst., Charles B. Blood, aged 18 months, son of Charles Blood Esq.
Died – In this village on 12th inst., at 2 o'clock, Charles Blood Esq., merchant, aged 28 years.
Died – In this village on Sunday 3d inst., Arabella, dau. of John Magee Esq., aged about 7 years.
Died – In this village on Saturday 2d inst., Charles Purdy Esq., lost a son, age not communicated.

Wednesday September 20, 1848 – Married – In Bath on 14th inst., by Rev. L. M. Miller, Jefferson French to Mary, eldest dau. of Col. Phineas Warren, all of this place.

Wednesday September 27, 1848 - Married - In Howard on 12th inst., by Rev. L. Rose, Seymour Fordyce of Scipio, Cayuga Co., to Susan M. Alexander of the former place.
Married - In Wheeler on 19th inst., by Rev. Judd, P. R. House of Bath to Mary Guiwits (sic), of the former place.
Died - On Monday evening last, David, infant son of Hon. David Rumsey, Jr., of this village.
Died - In Wheeler on 29th ult., Joseph Harkinson, aged 45 years.
Died - In Thurston on Friday 28th inst., Philander Brown, son of Wm. Brown aged 19 years. Died in a farming accident.

Wednesday October 4, 1848 - Married - In this village on Wednesday 27th ult., by Rev. L. H. Corson, Mary McCay and Henry H. Cook of this village.
Married - Also at the same time & by the same, Frances McCay & N. W. Howell Jr. of Canandaigua; both ladies, daus. of W. W. McCay Esq., of this village.
Married - In this village August 8th by Rev. L. Merrill Miller, Elisa Clisdell and Mr. P. White.
Died - In the town of Caton, on 29th ult., Joseph Gillett, aged 80 years. Mr. G. was a veteran democrat and a lieutenant in the war of 1812.

Wednesday October 13, 1848 - Died - The *Christian Register* chronicles the death at Boxboro (sic) Maine on 19th & 20th Sept. of Albert & Alfred, twin sons of John W. & Sarah Jane Mulliken. But a few days before, they were baptised over the coffin of their mother.
Died - Mrs. Frances, wife of J. N. Moffit, died in Brooklyn on Friday evening 29th ult., aged 18 years 7 months. The funeral was held at the residence of her step-father, Judge Pierce in Brooklyn. Her remains were conveyed to Greenwood Cemetery. (True Son).

Wednesday October 18, 1848 - Married - In this village on Tuesday 17th inst., by Rev. L. Merrill Miller, Mrs. Amelia Southerland and Col. William Gamble, all of this place.
Married - In this village on Wednesday 11th inst., by Rev. L. Merrill Miller, John P. Losier to Louisa H. Gould of this place.
Died - In this village on Friday 13th inst., Mr. Isacher (sic) White, aged 43 years; on Sunday 15th inst., David, infant son of Isacher White, aged 2 years.

Wednesday October 25, 1848 - Died - In this village on 18th inst., Charlotte Hopkins, wife of Norman Hopkins, sister of Messrs. Edward & William Howell. (age not Communicated).
Died - In Addison on 7th of July last, Daniel, son of Andrew Helmer Esq., aged 33 years.
Died - In the same place on 8th inst., Charlotte, wife of Andrew Helmer Esq., aged 60 years.
Died - In Canisteo on 19th inst., Miss Baker, dau. of Noah Baker Esq., aged 19 years.
Died - In Campbell on 22nd inst., Robert T. Bonham, aged 69 years.

Wednesday November 1, 1848 - Died - Arcanum I.O.O.F. Lodge No. 352 of Hornelsville regrets the passing of Philo Walbridge, one of its members on Oct. 24, 1848.

Wednesday November 8, 1848 - Died - Gov. McNutt, ex-governor of Mississippi at Memphis, Tennesee, on 23rd ult.
Died - In Greenwood on 6th inst., Olive Stephens, aged 82 years, widow of the late Col. John Stephens.
Died - In Bath on 6th inst., Caroline L., wife of Joel H. Rice Esq., aged 29 years.

Wednesday November 15, 1848 - missing issue.

Wednesday November 22, 1848 - Married - In Thurston on 15th inst., by J. L. Depue Esq., Philander Calkins to Emily Colcord.
Married - In Thurston on 16th inst., by Rev. Swick, Mr. Wheeler of Bath to Emma Halliday of the former place.
Died - In this town 18th inst., Elizabeth, wife of Charles Peters, aged 26 years.

Wednesday November 29, 1848 - Married - In Cohocton on 20th inst., by C. J. McDowell Esq., Thomas F. Beemer of Cohocton to Maria E. Williams of Ithaca.
Married - In Geneva on 21st inst., by Esq. Mundy, Samuel T. D. Allen of Cohocton to Catherine E. Skutt of Naples, N.Y.
Married - In Howard on 26th ult., by A. S. Phillips Esq., James Head to Mrs. Ann Bennett.
Died - Rev. John C. Rudd D.D. at Utica, N.Y. on Wednesday last. He was distinguished minister of the Protestant Episcopal Church and editor of *The Gospel Messenger*.

Died - In Bath (Oak Hill) on 2d inst., Elijah Evans, aged 63 years.
Died - In Howard on 4th inst., Charles Graves, aged 61 years.
Died - In Campbell on 5th inst., Mrs. Knox, wife of Jno. Knox, aged 73 years.
Died - In Howard on 20th inst., John Madale, aged 43 years.
Died - In Greenwood on 6th inst., Andrew VanSickle in the 56th year of his age.

Wednesday December 6, 1848 - Obituary - of Mrs. Olive Stephens. She was dau. of Roswell Franklin, who with family settled in valley of Wyoming in spring 1770. Mr. Franklin held rank of lieutenant in 1778 during battle of Yankees and Pennenites. On 8th April 1781 Mrs. Franklin, her dau. Olive then 14 years and 3 younger children were captured and the house fired. A full account of further suffering can be read in *Historical Sketches of Roswell Franklin And Family* by Rev. Robert Hubbard of Danville and published in 1839. Col. John and Olive were among earliest settlers of Canisteo. They resided on a farm with son Elias Stephens Esq., until 20 years ago when they moved to Bath the residence of their son, Hon. Alexander H. Stephens. Col. Stephens died March 19, 1837 aged 70 years. Mrs. Stephens expired Nov. 6th aged 81 years, member Presbyterian Church.
Died - In this village on Monday 26th ult., Julina F., wife of Henry Loomis, aged 28 years.
Died - At Mud Creek on 1st inst., Lucy Hart, wife of Peter VanNess, aged 21 years.

Wednesday December 13, 1848 - Married - In Kennedyville, on 29th ult., by Rev. L. Merrill Miller, Mr. D. T. Toliver to Elizabeth Nichols, all of Bath.
Died - In this village on 8th inst., Harriet, wife of Cornelius Barrett, aged about 28 years.
Died - In this village on 8th inst., Charles E. Anthony of Fall River, Mass., aged about 22 years.

Wednesday December 20, 1848 - Died - In this town on 13th inst., Marcia Ann, wife of George W. Breck, in the 29th year of her age. Since her marriage she has resided most of the time at Vienna, to which place the body was returned.

Wednesday December 27, 1848 - Married - At Bedford Westchester County, N.Y. on 12th inst., by Rev. English, Ferril C. Dininny Esq., counselor-at-law of Addison to Attia Harford of New York city.

Wednesday January 3, 31, February 14, 21, 1849 - no deaths or marriages.

Wednesday January 10, 1849 - Died - In this village on 4th inst., Rachel Elizabeth, wife of P. S. Perine & dau. of the late John Brown of this place, aged 21 years.

Wednesday January 17, 1849 - Died - On Tuesday afternoon last, James Conner of Howell's Depot died from injuries due to a sleigh accident. He was single and about 45 years of age. (Goshen *Republican*).
Died - Mrs. Mills, between 50 & 60 years of age, residing in the town of Horne committed suicide on Wednesday last.
Illness - The N.Y. *Morning Star* of Saturday says Mr. Edwin Forest, the celebrated tragedian, lies dangerously ill at his house, No. 284 Twenty-second Street.
Married - In Greenwood on 30th ult., by Alvin Mead Esq., Daniel McGraw to Caroline E. Brundage, all of that place.

Wednesday January 24, 1849 - (GOLD! O.K. means OFF TO KALIFORNIA!)
Died - At Avoca 15th inst., of pneumonia typhoides, Eliza, dau. of Col. D. G. Skinner of Bath, age 15 years.

Wednesday February 7, 1849 - Married - In this village on Tuesday January 30th by Rev. L. Merrill Miller, John C. Calkins of Avoca to Abigail Mack of Bath.
Married - In this village on Saturday 3d inst., by the same, Andrew Stewart of Howard to Susan Bracker/Beacher(?) of Bath.
Died - In this village on Friday January 26, Hannah R. Cooper, aged 24 years 11 months of consumption.
Died - In this village yesterday Jane, wife of William S. Mullhollen Esq., aged 65 years. She lived & died a Christian.

Wednesday February 28, 1849 - Died - In Cameron on 26th inst., Jacob S. Yost, aged 39 years.

Wednesday March 7, 1849 - Died - On the 3d inst., of consumption, at his father's residence in Howard, George H. Merrell, in the 18th year of his age.

Wednesday March 14, 1849 - Married - In this village on 7th inst., by Rev. L. H. Corson, Dr. John B. Fleming to Hannah C. Brown, all of Bath.

Wednesday March 21, 1849 - Married - In Avoca, on 31st inst., by Rev. H. Spencer, Edward A. Sweet of Urbana to Meribah Gregory of the same place.
Married - In Wheeler on 31st inst., by the same Jacob Vanderwarkin to Mrs. Temma Elliott, both of Wheeler.
Married - On 15th inst. by Rev. S.. W. Alden, James Longwell to Mrs. Elizabeth Longwell (sic), both of Urbana.
Married - In Bath, by the same on 15th inst., Hiram Harris to Sally Ann Ingersoll, both of Bath.
Died - In Troupsburgh on 14th inst., Alanson Perry, aged 67 years. He was an early settler of Troupsburgh.

Wednesday March 28, 1849 - Died - In Avoca on 24th inst., Melvifa (sic), dau. of John & Amanda Olmstead, aged 3 years.

Wednesday April 4, 1849 - Married - In Lodi on 27th inst., by Rev. Davis, Ambrose Nicholson of Howard to Sophia Ellis of the former place.
Died - In Wayne on 12th ult., of consumption, Mrs. Adah Zillah, wife of Hon. Levi Knox, aged 48 years.

Wednesday April 11, 1849 - Married - On 4th inst., by Rev. S. W. Allen, Alonzo Willour to Adeline Nicholds, both of Bath.
Died - In Prattsburgh 25th ult., of heart disease, Miss Sophia L. Johnson, dau. of Samuel A. Johnson Esq., aged 22 years.
Died - At the Eagle Tavern in this village, on 2d inst., Nathaniel S. Loomis of Durhamville, Oneida County. He was a member of DeKalb Lodge No. 255.

Wednesday April 18, 1849 - Died - James Gillet Esq., of Sodus, Wayne County, died at 52 years of age, last winter of a hog bite.

Wednesday April 25, May 16, 1849 - no deaths or marriages.

Wednesday May 2, 1849 - Married - In Prattsburgh on 15th March last, William Long, from one of the islands of Great Britain, to Nancy Wallace, of the former place.

Wednesday May 9, 1849 - Married - In Bath May 3d, by Rev. A. C. Mallory, Charles Peters to Lucinda Crosby.
Died - In Bath on 3d inst., Peter Henry, son of Ira Erway Esq., aged 2 years 9 months 6 days.
Died - In Orange on 25th ult., Joshua Chamberlain, aged 76 years.

Wednesday May 23, 1849 - Murder - At Fairfield, Herkimer County, Little Falls May 12 inst., Mrs. Daniel S. Neily, by R. E. Dicker of Camillus, Onondaga County.

Wednesday May 30, 1849 - (Nationwide cholera epidemic)
Died - At the Eagle Tavern in this village on 29th inst., William P. Groce, aged 28 years. Mr. Groce was foreman in Messrs. Darling & Proctor's Clothing Establishment, had resided in this village about six months, and is understood to have been a native of Boston at which place his mother now resides. (Eastern papers, please copy).

Wednesday June 6, 1849 - Died - At Catskill on Friday last, Aaron C. Hall of Cholera.
Died - In this village on 28th ult., Samuel Shannon Esq., aged 59 years. Deacon Shannon was an early resident of this village & was several years our postmaster. (Dansville *Chronicle*).
Married - In Thurston on 26th ult., at Mr. A. B. C. (sic) Dickinson's by Wm. N. Smith Esq., Andrew Helmer Esq., of Addison to Mrs. Thankful Smith of Thurston.
Married - In Addison on 29th ult., by Rev. Parmelee, Robert Patterson to Miss Anthony.
Married - At Erwin Centre on 29th ult., Dr. McCall of Rushford, Allegany County to Miss Smith, dau. of Hon. Ancel C. Smith of Erwin.

Wednesday June 13, 1849 - Married - In Prattsburgh on 4th inst., by John Smith Esq., Mr. Anson Rowe to Lucy Jane Smith, all of Bath.
Married - In Wayne on 26th ult., by Rev. A. C. Mallory, Mr. William Morgan to Miss Cordelia M. Smith, all of Bath.

Steuben Farmers Advocate
Bath, New York
December 13, 1848-December 1, 1852

Wednesday December 13, 1848; February 7, 1849 - see *The Steuben Democrat* same dates. Wednesday January 3, 17, February 21, 1849 - no deaths or marriages.

Wednesday December 20, 1848 - Died - In Prattsburgh November 27th, Josiah Allis in the 70th year of his age. Mr. Allis was one of the pioneers of Prattsburgh, a patron & trustee of Franklin Academy.

Wednesday December 27, 1848 - Married - In Prattsburgh on 12th inst., by Rev. Purington, Rev. Howell Smith of Penn Yan to Frances DeGolia of the former place.
Married - In Italy, on 16th inst., by Rev. B. C. Smith, William M. Beeman to Elizabeth Fisher.
Died - At Pulteney on 11th inst., James H. Perkins, son of Capt. John Perkins, aged 24 years. Belonged to Church of Christ.

Wednesday January 24, 1849 - Died - In Howard on 20th inst., Mrs. Graves, consort of the late Charles Graves of said town, aged about 65 years.

Wednesday January 31, 1849 - Married - In Avoca on the 23d inst., by Rev. H. Spencer, John C. Hopkins to Laura B. Butler.
Died - In this town on 23d inst., Miss Abigail Wilber, aged 32 years.

Wednesday February 14, 1849 - Died - In this town on 7th inst., Joseph Emerson, of consumption, aged 60 years.

Wednesday February 28, 1849 - Married - In Bath on 11th inst., by Rev. Wm. Rutherford, Holms Harvey (sic) of Tompkins County to Mrs. Sarah Williour, of Bath.

Wednesday March 7, 1849 - Died - At the residence of his father at Painted Post, on Tuesday 27th ult., Samuel H. Adams, aged 28 years 2 mos. His remains were committed to the grave under direction of members of Painted Post Lodge No. 105 I.O.O.F.

Wednesday March 14, 1849 - Died - At Howard on 1st inst., Christopher Dolly, aged 73 years.
 Died - At Alfred Academy on 2d inst., Eliza Ford, dau. of Eli Ford of Howard, aged 16 years.
 Died - In Bath on 7th inst., Ezekiel Hunt, aged 77 years. A member of the Masonic fraternity.

Wednesday March 21, May 9, 16, 23, 1849 - no deaths or marriages.

Wednesday March 28, 1849 - Died - In Howard on 14th inst., Lewis Alden, son of Benjamin Alden, aged 18 years.

Wednesday April 4, 1849 - Married - In Elmira on 25th ult., by Rev. A. M. Ball, George W. Mason editor of the Elmira *Gazette*, to Elizabeth Collingwood.
 Died - In Patchenville on 23d ult., Wm. Henry Cotton, only son Edward & Phoebe Cotton, aged 3 years 5 months.
 Died - In Avoca on 29th ult., Phebe Clizbe, wife of Joseph Clizbe, in the 39th year of her age.

Wednesday April 11, 1849 - Died - In this town on 19th ult., Fanny, eldest dau. of James & Catherine Hunter, aged 5 years.
 Died - At Rochester April 3d, Harriet, wife of Capt. E. R. Bidwell, aged 59 years. She went to Rochester in the fall for treatment & her remains were brought to this place for interment.

Wednesday April 18, 1849 - Married - In this village Wednesday evening last, by Rev. L. M. Miller, George Stinsen of Mud Creek to Catharine Johnson of Dansville.
 Married - In Palmyra on 5th inst., by Rev. J. W. French, Leonard Walter Jerome of Rochester to Clarissa, youngest dau. of the late Ambrose Hall, of the former place.

Wednesday April 25, 1849 - Married - At the Methodist parsonage in Elmira Thursday 19th inst., by Rev. H. N. Seaver, Hiram Fife of Bath to Matilda Smith of Elmira.

Wednesday May 2, 1849 - Married - In Cameron April 23 by Rev. David Smith of Bath, George J. Bird of Canisteo to Nancy Daggart of the former place.

Wednesday May 30, 1849 - Died - In this village on 28th inst., Mrs. Franklin at an advanced age.

Wednesday June 6, 1849 - Died - At Canisteo on 30 March last, Elizabeth, wife of Uriah Stephens, aged 85 years.
Died - At Canisteo on 16th ult., Rachel Celestia, dau. of Franklin D. & Sophronia Stephens, aged ten years.

Wednesday June 13, 1849 - Married - In Tyrone on 6th inst., by Rev. B. Russell, Mr. H. T. Strawn of Ogden, Monroe County to Amanda E. Phillips, dau. of Samuel Phillips of the former place.

Wednesday June 20, 1849 - Married - On 17th inst., by Rev. S. W. Alden at the Methodist Episcopal Church in Bath, Wm. B. Brace of Ottawa, LaSalle Co., Ill. to Alvira Strait of the former place.

Wednesday June 27, 1849 - Married - At Buena Vista Hotel, Big Flats, on 5th inst., by Rev. Carr, John French of Cameron to Mary Overhiser of the former place.
Died - In Bath on 22d inst., Mrs. Levina Hunt, consort of the late Ezekiel Hunt, aged 74 years.

Wednesday July 4, 1849 - Married - On 19th ult., by Rev. C. C. Carr, James S. Woods Esq., of Elmira to Susan, dau. of Wm. VanDuser Esq., of Veteran, Chenango County.
Died - In this village on 27th ult., at the residence of his son, Charles W. Campbell Esq., Robert Campbell senior aged 85 years. Mr. Campbell was born in Scotland on 1st January 1765 in parish of Galston, Ayreshire, emigrated to this oountry in the spring of 1794 & landed at New York city where he resided until early summer 1796 when he came to this village. Member Presbyterian Church.
Died - In Greenwood on 18th June, Lucy Amidon, wife of Shepherd Amidon, aged 31 years 10 months.

Wednesday July 11, 1849 – Married – At the Episcopal Church in this village on Wednesday 4th inst., by Rev. Corson, Joshua W. Waterman Esq., of Detroit, Mich. to Eliza Cameron, dau. of Ira Davenport Esq., of this village.
Married – In Bath July 3d by Rev. B. B. Swick, Elias Parmer of Hammondsport to Hannah Aulls of the former place.
Married – In Bath July 9th by Rev. B. B. Swick, Simon Bixby of Hornby to Phebe T. Lake of the former place.

Wednesday July 18, 1849 – Married – In Milan, Ohio on 28th June by Rev. J. B. Taylor, Benjamin D. Patrick of Norwalk to Eliza P., dau. of Hon. Th. Maxwell of Elmira.
Died – Mrs. Madison, wife of ex-president Madison, at Washington Thursday last.

Wednesday July 25, 1849 – Died – On 6th inst., while on a visit at the residence of her son in Painted Post, Mrs. Sarah Patterson of this village aged 87 years.
Died – At his residence in Italy, Yates Co., on 12th inst., John Spore, aged about 89 years.
Died – In this town on 13th inst., John Knight aged 63 years. Terrible tragedy at Batele Crefk (sic), Mich., Ashbel Kellogg, former resident & well known as President of Bank of Salina, killed his son William Kellogg. (Syracuse *Reveille*).

Wednesday August 8, 22, 1849 – no deaths or marriages.

Wednesday August 1, 1849 – Married – At the Clinton House in this village on Sunday last, by A. D. Read Esq., Adolphus Welch to Hellen Marr Graham, both of Starkey, Yates Co.

Wednesday August 15, 1849 – Married – On Oak Hill Steuben Co., 22d ult., by Esq. Babcock, E. G. Richardson, prop. of the Dansville *Weekly Chronicle* to Mary Ann Stryker, both of Dansville.
Married – In Bath August 13th, by Rev. B. B. Swick, John Wilhelm to Emeline Nobles, all of Bath.
Died – At his residence in Woodhull, August 5, Wm. G. Porter, aged 33 years. He left a wife & 3 children to mourn his loss.
Died – In this town on 11th inst., Keziah Hamilton, aged 87 years. She was the widow of Daniel Hamilton, a soldier of the Revolutionary War.

Wednesday August 29, 1849 - Married - In this village on 23d inst., by Rev. L. M. Miller, Ithamar Webster to Harriet Nixon, all of this place.

Died - In Jefferson, Wisconsin at the residence of his son, Whittington Sayre Esq., of Elmira, aged 65 years.

Died - In Danville, Pa., 12th inst., of consumption, John McQuhae (sic), aged 34 years.

Wednesday September 5, 1849 - Married - At Howard on 15th inst., by Rev. D. M. Root, Dr. D. Starr of Wisconsin to Ann D. Abbott of Michigan.

Died - S. S. Seward, this venerable citizen (father of Hon. Wm. H. Seward) at his residence in Orange County on Saturday last.

Died - At his residence in Bath, on 1st inst., Capt. Asa Blood, aged 63 years, member & vestryman of Episcopal Church.

Died - In Corning on 24th ult., Mercy Bostwick, eldest sister of H. W. Bostwick Esq., aged 62 years.

Died - In Havana 25th ult., of cholera, Sidney S. Decker.

Died - In Bath on 29th ult., Elizabeth, infant dau. of Jesse & Annis Vanderhooven, aged 10 mos. 25 days.

Died - In this village Monday last, Eugene, infant son of Ella (sic) & Jane Ellis, aged 10 mos.

Wednesday September 12, 1849 - Married - The Rochester *Advertiser* of Monday publishes the marriage of Doct. J. K. Hardinbrook to Mrs. Lois Nott, widow of the late Thomas Nott at Sandusky City, Ohio.

Married - In Starkey, Yates Co., August 30th by Rev. J. Dodge, Thomas Clark senior, aged 99 to Mrs. Phebe Aspell aged 72, widow of the late Richard Aspell, all of Starkey.

Married - In this village on 9th inst., by Rev. L. M. Miller, William Smith, M.D., of Oswego, Ill. to Rebecca P., dau. of the late Capt. Blood of Bath.

Died - In Wayne August 24th of consumption, Warren Dodge, aged 33 years.

Died - In Cameron 5th inst., Harriet O., wife of Charles Chase & dau. of Nathaniel Bundy Esq.

Died - At South Cameron on 20th ult., John F. French Esq., aged 49 years.

Wednesday September 19, 1849 - Married - In this village on 18th inst., by Rev. Corson, Henry Loomis to Ann Eliza Swart, dau. of P. Swart, all of this place.

Married - In Avoca on 12th inst., by Rev. H. Spencer, John H. Shaver of Howard to Amanda Loucks of the former place.
Married - In Cohocton on 16th inst., by Rev. A. Adams, Silas Hulbert to Sophira (sic) Watkins, both of Cohocton.
Married - In Cohocton on 11th inst., by Rev. A. Adams, Devan Begole to Miss M. C. Wallace, dau. of Jas. Wallace Esq., all of Cohocton.
Married - By the same on 12th inst., Darius Field to Maria Knickerbocker.
Died - Doctor A. Brigham, Supt. & resident physician of the N.Y. state Lunatic Asylum, died Saturday at Utica, from an attack of chronic diarrhea. ("Atlas")

Wednesday September 26, 1849 - Married - In this village on 13th inst., by Rev. L. H. Corson, C. W. Hudson to Julia Ann Ellas, all of Bath.

Wednesday October 3, 1849 - Married - on 24th ult., by Rev. Chas. G. Somers, Alexander G., son of Philip Harman Esq. of New York to Martha O., only dau. of Francis Denham of Brooklyn.

Wednesday October 10, 1849 - Married - In this village on 26th ult., by Rev. L. M. Miller, Hezekiah Decker to Jane, dau. of Charles Smith, all of Bath.
Married - At Dansville on 2d inst., by Rev. Jesse Edwards, Alexander Edwards formerly of this village to Elizabeth McCurdy, dau. of James McCurdy, of the former place.
Died - The celebrated comedian Geo. H. Hill, commonly known as Yankee Hill, at Saratoga Springs, on 27th ult., at the Adelphi Hotel.

Wednesday October 17, 1849 - Married - In this village on 18th inst., by Elder Swick, John Eggleston to Harriet Emerson, all of this place.
Married - In Prattsburgh on 7th inst., by Rev. H. Spencer, Joseph H. Drake of Wheeler to Catharine Caster, of the former place.
Married - In Hornellsville on 16th ult., by H. Bennett Esq., Wm. Shinabarger to Phebe Coburn, both of the above place.
Married - In the same place on 1st inst., by H. Bennett Esq., George Shinabarger to Harriet Hill, both of Hornellsville.

Married - At Stockbridge, Ingham Co., Mich., on 4th August last, by Rev. S. Carey, J. F. Selden of Stockbridge to Eliza Davidson of Henrietta, Jackson Co., Mich.

Wednesday October 24, 1849 - Married - In the Presbyterian Church in Wayne, on 16th inst., by Rev. L. M. Russ of Hammondsport, Joseph N. Crane to Helena Ann Mitchell, dau. of John B. Mitchell, all of Wayne.
Married - In Urbana on 16th inst., by Rev. B. R. Swick, John Bush of Reading to Huldah A. Bennett, of the former place.

Wednesday October 31, 1849 - Died - In Bath on 22d inst., at the residence of his son, Sturges Bradley, in his 85th year.

Wednesday November 7, 1849 - Died - At Angelica, Allegany Co., Oct. 15th Major Moses VanCampen, one of the bravest officers of the Revolutionary Army. He was born 21st January 1757 in Hunterdon County, New Jersey, aged 92 years & 9 months.

Wednesday November 14, 1849 - no deaths or marriages.

Wednesday November 21, 1849 - Married - In Howard on 11th ult., by W. B. Rice Esq., Hiram Rathbun to Louisa Shearer, dau. of Robert Shearer, all of Howard.
Died - In this town on Friday last, Roswell R. Chapman, aged 72 years.

Wednesday November 28, 1849 - Died - In this village on 22d inst., Eli Bidwell senior aged 62 years. He was a native of East Hartford, Conn., where he was born September 20, 1788. At 17 years he came with an older brother and settled in Prattsburgh, where he has been a resident 36 years.
Died - In Prattsburgh Spence Gulick on 12th inst., by drowning while engaged in drawing logs from his mill pond.

Wednesday December 5, 1849 - Died - In Ithaca on 24th ult., at the residence of T. C. Thompson, Mrs. Indiana Blood, wife of the late Capt. Blood of this village, aged 57 years.
Died - In Bath November 10th, Mr. Joseph G. Rockwell, a teacher in the "Haverling Union School", aged 26 years.

Wednesday December 12, 19, 1849 - no deaths or marriages.

Wednesday December 26, 1849 - Died - In this village on Thursday last, Harriet Watkins, wife of Simon Watkins, aged 58 years. She was an exemplary member of the New School Presbyterian Church.

Wednesday January 2, 1850 - Died - At his residence in Tyrone, John C. Bodine, aged 64 years, an early settler of that town.

Wednesday January 9, 1850 - Married - In Ithaca on Wednesday 26th ult., by Rev. Henry, Hon. Edwin F. Church of Bath to Catharine Andrus of Ithaca.
Died - In Syracuse on 1st inst., by suffocating himself with the fumes of charcoal, Rensselaer Van Rensselaer, a native of Albany & son of Gen. Solomon Van Rensselaer of Albany. He became well known in the Canadian War.

Wednesday January 16, 1850 - Died - Suddenly in this town on Saturday last, Mrs. Nancy Rutherford, dau. of Henry McElwee.

Wednesday January 23, 1850 - Married - In Wheeler on 8th inst., by Rev. H. Spencer, Lyman Arnold of Avoca to Mary Jane McNeil of the former place.
Married - In Bath on 15th inst., by Rev. B. R. Swick, Darwin A. Parsons of Bath to Lucy Sane (sic) Walling, of Campbelltown.
Died - In Avoca on 8th inst., Miss Mary Ann Salmon, aged 25 years.
Died - In Howard on 8th inst., Elizabeth, wife of Sam'l. Stewart 3d, dau. of John & Elizabeth McElwain, aged 34 years.
Died - On 11th inst., at the residence of her son-in-law Dr. Robert W. Cook in Hollindell, Monmouth County, N.J., Mrs. Elizabeth Gansevoort, relict of the late Conradt Gansevoort of Albany and mother of John R. Gansevoort Esq., of this village, 82 years of age.

Wednesday January 30, 1850 - Married - In Janesville, Wisconsin on the 8th inst. John G. Wheeler formerly of this village, to Emily E. Wait of the former place.

Wednesday February 6, 1850 - Married - In Wayne January 27th, by Rev. A. C. Mallory, Joseph L. Cain of Wayne to Nancy Tyler of Mud Creek.

Wednesday February 13, 1850 - Married - On Sunday 30th December by Rev. Pope, Master William Simmons aged 15 years to Miss Sarah Simmons aged 14, all of Pendleton Co., Va.

Died - In Prattsburgh on 2d inst., Henry Van Housen formerly of Howard, in the 75th year of his age.

Died - In this village on 5th inst., Richard, son of Thomas & Lorinda Baily, aged 11 months.

Wednesday February 20, 1850 - Married - In Wheeler on 10th inst., by A. P. Lyon Esq., Peter Stoddard to Thankful Welch, both of Wheeler.

Died - In this town on 13th inst., Mrs. Lucy Chapin in the 86th year of her age.

Died - In Canisteo January 28th, Calvin Frace aged 22 years.

Died - In Canisteo February 8th, Rachel, wife of Capt. Nathan Stephens, aged 67 years.

Wednesday February 27, 1850 - Married - In Prattsburgh on 21st inst., by Rev. B. C. Smith, Rev. James R. Pinneo to Mrs. Melissa E. Linsley.

Married - In Bath on 17th inst., by Rev. B. R. Swick, Alpheus R. Ballard to Emeline Cooper, both of Wheeler.

Died - In Corning Friday last, Bradford A. Potter, aged about 56 years.

Wednesday March 6, 1850 - Married - In Bath March 2d by Rev. B. R. Swick, Ira McGonegal to Mary Owen, all of Bath.

Married - At Urbana on 26th February by Rev. Geo. Hood, George H. Ellas of Decatur, Adams Co., Ind. to Phebe Bronson of Urbana.

Married - In Prattsburgh on 27th ult., by Rev. B. C. Smith, John R. Selover to Mary Frances Lewis.

Died - In Urbana February 26, Charles Andrew, son of Tobias and Mary Salsbury, aged 6 years one month.

Wednesday March 13, 1850 - Died - At Jacksonville, Florida 20th January, whither he had gone in pursuit of his health, Levi B. Harrower, son of B. Harrower Esq., of Lindley.

Wednesday March 20, 1850 - Married - At the cottage of Judge Denniston, Prattsburgh on 12th inst., by Rev. B. C. Smith, Walter S. Cheevy, M. D. to Louisa Falls.

Married – In Bath on 11th inst., by Rev. J. R. Tuttle, Joseph Butler Warren to Elizabeth Brooks, all of Bath.

Died – In this village on 6th inst., Miss Nancy Metcalfe, aged 82 years.

Died – In Orange on 26th ult., of consumption, Nancy, dau. of Jacob Frost, in the 15th year of her age.

Wednesday March 27, 1850 – Married – In this town on 14th inst., by Rev. Wilbur, John Walker to Mary Bishop, all of this town.

Married – In Avoca on 14th inst., by Rev. H. Spencer, Lemmuel H. Ferris of Bath to Eliza Ann McDowell, of Howard.

Died – In Lebanon, Madison Co., N.Y. on 30th January, Jacob Hartshorn Esq., aged 72 years.

Died – In this village on Saturday last, Miss Nancy McCalla, aged 69 years.

Died – In Big Flats on Wednesday last, Mary Harrower, wife of the late Levi B. Harrower.

Wednesday April 3, 1850 – Died – In Wheeler on 28th ult., Phillip Myrtle, aged 75 years. He was a native of Penna. & one of the oldest residents of the county.

Died – Mrs. Rachel Willour, wife of Jacob Willour, departed this life the 25th ult., in the 53d year of her life.

Wednesday April 10, 1850 – Married – In Bath on 26th ult., by Rev. J. C. Mallory, Aaron Aber to Elizabeth Ann Cornwell, both of Bath.

Married – In Bath on 29th ult., by Mr. W. B. Price Esq., Horace Graves of Howard to Dorcas M. Willis of Bath, dau. of Orren Willis.

Married – In Prattsburgh April 2d by Rev. B. C. Smith, William S. Foster to Helen W. Fay.

Married – In Cohocton on 2d inst., by Rev. H. Spencer, James Page to Lucinda A. Loomis, both of Cohocton.

Died – In this village on 2d inst., Hily Ann Swick, wife of Rev. B. R. Swick, aged 44 years.

Died – In Thurston on 28th ult., Jonas Youmans, aged 92 years, 10 months, 11 days. He was one that fought for liberty through the Revolutionary War.

Died – In Poughkeepsie April 3d, Theodore F. Clarke, son of the late Jas. C. & Eliza A. Clarke of Newburgh, aged 19 years 10 days.

Wednesday April 17, 1850 - Married - In Prattsburgh on 9th inst., by Rev. B. C. Smith, Amos Parks to Mary Jane Lafurge.
Died - In Pulteney March 27th, Capt. John Perkins, aged 66 years.
Died - At Liberty on 8th inst., Mrs. Elizabeth Graves, relict of the late Randall Graves Esq., aged 51 years.
Died - In Bradford on 9th inst., Charles Franklin of consumption, aged about 35 years.
Died - In Monterey on 1st inst., of numb palsy, David Davidson, aged 71 yrs.
Died - In Monterey on 2d inst., Joel Johnson, aged 81 years.

Died - In Bradford on 6th inst., Stephen, son of John S. Sprague, aged 16 years.
Died - Near Jefferson on 10th inst., Walter Dickinson, aged 58 years.

Wednesday April 24, 1850 - Married - In Marcellus, N.Y. on 28th ult., Sylvester Smith to Lydia Duncan; Sereno Smith to Cathia Duncan; & Charles Duncan to Emma Smith, all of that place.
Married - In Prattsburgh on 16th inst., by Rev. B. C. Smith, Henry Ford to Mrs. Electa Wilson.

Wednesday May 1, 1850 - Married - In Prattsburgh on 24th ult., by Rev. B. C. Smith, Alanson E. Briggs to Betsey E. Hilton.
Married - In Oakley, Oakland Co., Mich. on 20th ult., by Rev. Hyde, Otis H. Waldo Esq., of Milwaukee to Gertrude C., dau. of J. VanValkenburgh.
Died - In California recently, Charles Roberts, late of Reading, Steuben County, aged 30 years.
Died - In Orange on 16th ult., Henry C., son of Albert & Mary C. Lynch aged 16 years.

Wednesday May 8, 1850 - Married - In this village on 1st inst., by Rev. L. Merrill Miller, T. J. Aber to Samantha B. Bramble, all of Bath.
Married - In this town on 29th ult., by Rev. A. Wright, Henry Norris to Lucy Wheeler.
Married - In Howard on 28th ult., by Wesson B. Rice Esq., Daniel H. Rose of Howard to Martha Ann Goff of the former place.

Wednesday May 15, 1850 - Married - In Hornellsville on 1st inst., by Rev. H. Pattengill, Hiram Bennett Esq., to Eliza Doty, all of Hornellsville.

Died - Ruhama Drake, wife of Deacon Drake, departed this life in Jasper on April 30, aged 59 years, 1 month & 14 days.

Wednesday May 22, 1850 - Married - Mr. Francis Parkman Jr., only son of the late Dr. Geo. Parkman of Boston was married on Monday last at Kings Chapel to a dau. of Dr. Jacob Bigelow, of the same city.

Married - At the Methodist Church in this village on 21st inst., by Rev. D. Nutten, T. W. Whiting to M. J. Lambert.

Married - In this village on 18th ult., by Rev. J. K. Tuttle, Amos Emerson to Helen Cornelia Eggleston, all of Bath.

Died - In Addison this county, Mrs. Walton died a few days ago, having been sick for several weeks.

Wednesday May 29, June 5, 1850 - no deaths or marriages.

Wednesday June 12, 1850 - Married - In Howard on 25th ult., by Rev. L. Rose, George Case to Harriet Graves, all of Howard.

Wednesday June 19, 1850 - Married - In Prattsburgh on 5th inst., by Rev. B. C. Smith, Abraham Q. Lewis to Catherine B. Downs.

Married - In Elmira on 6th inst., by Rev. P. H. Fowler, Henri (sic) Park of Addison to Mary E. McNulty of Big Flats.

Married - In Hornellsville on 16th ult., by Rev. H. Pattengill, William Ross of Reading to Sarah C. Reed of the former place.

Married - By the same on 4th inst., in Canisteo, Frederick B. Landers of Hornellsville to Sarah W. Mulhollon of Canisteo.

Married - In Albany on 12th inst., by Parker Sargent Esq., John C. Osterhout to Mary Kelly, both of Corning.

Died - In Tyrone June 8th, Harriet Melvina, only dau. of Mrs. Tuthill, aged three years 6 months.

Wednesday June 30 (sic), 1850 - Married - In Elmira on 18th inst., by Rev. A. Hull, Joseph H. Harris to Mary Walbridge Cooley, dau. of Major L. J. Cooley.

Died - In this town on 18th inst., of consumption, Nancy Adaline, wife of Alonzo Willour, aged 21 years.

Died - In this village on Sunday night last, Ithamer Webster, aged 26 yrs.

Wednesday July 3, 1850 - Married - In this village on 30th inst., by Rev. B. R. Swick, Henry L. Stark to Almira Stark (sic), all of this place.
Died - On 6th ult., at the age of 23, Sarah Starkweather, step-dau. of Deacon Julius Bartlett of Prattsburgh.
Married - In this village on 19th ult., by Rev. J. K. Tuttle, Job Loder to Jane Maxwell, all of this place.

Wednesday July 10, 1850 - Married - In Prattsburgh on 2d inst., by Rev. B. C. Smith, Jacob Hogeland to Mrs. Harriet Parsons.
Married - On 4th, by the same, Phillip K. Stoddard, M.D. to Sarah Jane Lewis.
Married - In Wheeler on 4th by the same, Edward S. Pangburn to Catherine Small.
Died - In this village on Friday 28th ult., of bilious fever, Elizabeth Breck, aged 68 years, wife of Joseph Breck of Bath. Mrs. Breck came to this place to visit her son, A. Y. Breck and was taken sick the day she intended to start for home, Warsaw, Wyoming County, N. Y. Member of First Presbyterian Church Constitutional of Bath. She leaves a husband, 8 children & 19 grandchildren.

Wednesday July 17, 1850 - Married - In Avoca July 15th, by Rev. N. Sawyer, Thomas H. Zeilley of Peterborough, C. W. (Canada West/Ontario) to Ann Tooker of Elmira.
Married - In Campbell June 26th, by Rev. R. M. Beach, Joseph Chapin to Elizabeth P(l/r?)att, both of Campbell.
Died - In this village on Friday 5th inst., Mrs. Elizabeth Taylor, wife of G. W. Taylor, aged 35 years 4 months.
Died - In this town on 5th inst., Elder Elisha Martin, aged about 65 yrs.
Died - In this village on Friday last, of consumption, Thomas Woodward aged 22 years.

Wednesday July 24, 1850 - Married - On the 17th inst., by Rev. D. Nutten of Bath, Trumbull L. Bennett, M. D. of Lima to Elizabeth S., dau. of Major E. L. Paine of Canisteo.
Married - In this village on 21st inst., by Elder Mallory, John Rugar to Jane Alden.

Wednesday July 31, 1850 - Died - In Cameron on 24th inst., Wickham R., son of Dr. Wickham R. and Jane R. Crocker, aged 11 months.
Died - In this village on Sunday last, Charles, son of Mrs. Ellen Blood, aged 1 year 6 mos.
Elopement (sic) - Rosina Puffer left Tisdale Puffer, her husband at Hartsville July 8, 1850.

Wednesday August 7, 1850 - Married - In Hartsville on 31st ult., by C. C. Purdy Esq., Shepherd Amidon Esq., formerly of Greenwood to Betsey Maria Razey, of Almond.
Died - In this village on 3d inst., Hannah Fowler, dau. of John W. Fowler Esq., aged 9 years 4 months 17 days.

Wednesday August 14, 1850 - no deaths or marriages.

Wednesday August 21, 1850 - Married - In Waterloo, Seneca Co., on 18th inst., Joel H. Rice of Bath to Mrs. C. A. Turner of Waterloo.
Married - At Athens, Pa. on 15th inst., by Rev. C. Thurston, Henry H. Hull, editor of the *Steuben Courier*, to Clara, dau. of Hon. Horace Williston of Athens.
Married - In South Dansville on 8th inst., by Rev. H. Spencer, William H. Guiwits (sic) of Wheeler to Mary J. Kelly of the former place.

Wednesday August 28, 1850 - Married - In Bath August 12th by Rev. B. R. Swick, Seneca Watson to Lydia Mills, all of Bath.
Died - In Cambridge, Washington Co., 22d inst., of typhoid fever, James M. Stevenson Esq., for many years editor & proprietor of the *Troy Daily Whig*. (Troy Budget).
Died - In this village on 22d inst., Simon Watkins, a colored man in his 65th year. He was born a slave in Virginia and came to this country with his master Capt. Helm, more than forty years ago. Simon was tall and well proportioned, with good features for one of his race and he was a vigorous, athletic, powerful man. He conducted business as a butcher and buying & selling produce.
Died - In Bath August 19th, Mary Jane Elizabeth Youmans, aged 14 years, 4 months 6 days.
Died - In Bath August 25th, Augustus D., son of Jared Smith, 21 months.

Wednesday September 4, 1850 - Died - At the residence of her sister, at White Deer Mills, Union County, Pa., on 15th

August of dysentery, Miss Sophia Noble, dau. of Harvey Noble of Urbana in this county.

Died - In Owego August 28th, Mrs. Elizabeth Smith in the 54th year of her age, mother of Frederick Ward of this village.

Died - In this town 25th ult., very suddenly Mrs. Sarah B. Warren, wife of Jonathan Warren & only dau. of J. T. & Lucretia Johnson of this village in the 39th year of her age.

Wednesday September 11, 1850 - Married - In Avoca on 5th inst., by Rev. Wm. Bradley, Kendrick Daniels to Sarah H., second dau. of Col. Phineas Warren, all of Bath.

Married - On 10th ult., by J. Ashworth, William Smith of Troupsburgh to Lucinda H. Persons of Woodhull.

Married - In Jasper on 30th June by Elder J. B. McKenny, Wm. Persons of Woodhull to Amy McPherrons of Cameron.

Married - Samuel Graham and Hannah Wilhelm, both of Woodhull on 20th August by Esq. Persons.

Died - In Canandaigua on 24th ult., of chronic diarrhea, Mary, wife of W. Francis Melony and youngest dau. of L. J. Woodruff, aged 20 years 6 months.

Died - At his residence in Warsaw, Tues. Sept. 10th, Samuel S. Blanchard Esq., editor of the Western (Warsaw) New Yorker. He held the office of Sergeant-at-Arms in the Assembly of this state a year ago. (Rochester *American*).

Wednesday September 18, 1850 - Married - In this village on 14th inst., by Rev. B. R. Swick, Ambrose Conklin to Lucy E. Fluent, both of Addison.

Married - In Cohocton on 10th inst., by Rev. L. W. Russ of Hammondsport, Geo. H. Chapman, merchant of North Urbana to Amanda M. Walling of the former place.

Married - In Howard on 11th inst., by Rev. N. Sawyer, Charles Higgins to Loana, dau. of Seth Rioe Esq., all of Howard.

Died - At Coloma, California on 15th July last, James H. Read M. D., son of Capt. James Read of this village, age 27 years.

Died - In this village on 7th inst., of congestion of the brain, Mary, youngest dau. of Martha and Alexander Hess, aged 4 months 12 days.

Died - In this village on 12th inst., of apoplexy, Rhoda Goodrich in the 74th year of her age.

Wednesday September 25, 1850 - Married - In this village on 18th inst., by Rev. L. M. Miller, Edward Howell Jr. to Mary L., dau. of John R. Gansevoort.

Wednesday October 2, 1850 - Married - In Bath on 17th ult., by Rev. B. R. Swick, Rev. A. B. Chase of Cameron to Elizabeth B. Towle of Howard.
Died - In this village on 28th ult., Gelina F., dau. of Henry Loomis.

Wednesday October 9, 1850 - Died - In Bradford on Wednesday last, Jonathan Tobias was killed instantly in an accident at Munson's Steam Mills.
Died - On 2d inst., at the residence of her daughter Mrs. Mills at Alden, Erie Co., N.Y., in her 84th year, Mrs. Sarah S. Rogers, relict of Samuel Rogers, formerly of Unadilla, Otsego Co., and mother of Dr. G. A. Rogers of this village.
Died - In this village on 5th inst., Mrs. Philance (sic) T. Barney, wife of Nelson Barney, aged 35 years 6 months 4 days.
Married - At Mud Creek on 29th ult., by Rev. J. C. Mallory, Daniel Tucker to Susannah C. Brink, both of the above place.
Married - At the same place & time, by the same, William E. Bidwell of Bath to Sarah M. Brown of Cleveland.

Wednesday October 16, 1850 - Married - In Bath 9th inst., by Rev. Almon Gregory, Rector of St. Thomas Church, Alva E. Brown to Sarah H. Hamilton, youngest dau. of Wm. Hamilton, all of Bath.
Married - In Hammondsport on 12th inst., by Rev. Wilson, John Durkee to Adeline Erwin, both of Bath.
Married - In this village on 13th inst., by Rev. Wright, Ephraim Aulls to Mary Bryant, all of this town.

Wednesday October 23, 1850 - Married - In Howard on 16th inst., by Rev. L. Rose, Joseph H. VanHousen of Prattsburgh to Catharine VanWie, of the former place.
Married - In the town of Wheeler on 17th inst., by Rev. Jno. Selmser, Wm. H. VanDusen to Nancy Bellinger.

Wednesday October 30, 1850 - The village and post office formerly known as Mud Creek in this county has been changed to the name of Savona.
Married - In Howard on 23d inst., by Rev. L. Rose, Luther Hull to Louisa E. Smith, both of Howard.

Died – In this village on 25th inst., after a long and severe illness, Gideon Walker, aged 80 years formerly of Hartford County, Conn.

Died – In Avoca on 22d inst., Riohard VanBuskirk, aged 62 years.

Wednesday November 6, 1850 – Died – The Honorable Samuel Young, at his residence in Ballston, yesterday morning, it is supposed by apoplexy, aged about 72 years. (New York *Post* Nov. 4).

Wednesday November 13, 1850 – Married – In this town on 31st ult., by Rev. B. R. Swick, Henry VanGelder to Polly Veley, all of this town.

Died – In Hornellsville Nov. 5th of bilious fever & diarrhea, Jemima Mason, wife of Elliott Mason, aged 41 years.

Wednesday November 20, 1850 – no deaths or marriages.

Wednesday November 27, 1850 – Married – In Bath on 24th inst., by Rev. B. R. Swick, A. M. Goodrich of Albany to Amanda C. Reed of Bath.

Married – In Gibson on 21st inst., by Esq. Peak, Thomas Eaton of this town to Mrs. Mercy Yost of Cameron.

Married – In Dansville on 19th inst., by Rev. J. Chapman, Wm. H. Van Allen of Scio, Allegany Co., to Nancy M. White, dau. of Lugher White Esq. of Dansville.

Married – In Corning on 14th inst. by Rev. A. L. Brooks, Chas. H. Berry Esq. to Frances Hubbell, all of the above place.

Died – In this village on 17th inst., Sarah Jane, dau. of A. H. Silsbe, aged 2 years 4 months.

Wednesday December 4, 1850 – Married – In Geneva on 30th ult., by Rev. Abel Haskell, Elisha Holton of Bath to Mary A. Wright of Grafton, Vt.

Married – In Bath on 17th ult., by Rev. N. Sawyer, Nehemiah Hallet of Wellsville, Allegany Co., to Harriet Smith, dau of T. J. Smith Esq.

Married – Also on 24th ult., by the same, Walter Dygert to Rhoda Willis, all of Bath.

Died – In Hornellsville on 25th November, Jane Magee, wife of Thomas J. Magee, aged 43 years.

Died – In this town on 29th ult., Calvin Simmons aged 60 years.

Wednesday December 11, 1850 - Married - In this village on 27th ult., by Rev. Miller, J. C. Jackson of Otis, Mass. to Miss H. M. Miller of Rochester.
Died - In this town on 28th ult., Mrs. Mary Wheeler, consort of Jeremiah Wheeler, deceased, in the 90th year of her age.

Wednesday December 18, 1850 - Married - In Bath on 8th inst., by Rev. B. R. Swick, John Dygert of Avoca to Aurissa V. Merrill of Howard.
Married - By the same and in the same place on 14th inst., John W. Gould to Jane A. Morgan, all of Bath.
Died - In this village on 12th inst., Nancy Whiting, wife of Leonard Coats and dau. of Col. Stephen Grant in her 28th year.

Wednesday December 25, 1850 - Married - On the 23d inst., by Rev. A. Lloyd, Harmon M. Hamilton one of the teachers of the "Haverling Union School" to Annis S., eldest dau. of Orrin Smith Esq., all of this village.
Married - In Campbelltown Dec. 11th by Rev. J. C. Mallory, Myron W. Brown of Thurston to Calcina E. Stewart of the former place.
Married - In Savonia (sic) Dec. 12th by the same, Wm. H. Abel to Sarah F. Van Amburg, all of Savonia (sic).
Married - By Rev. Mallory, John Garlinghouse of Michigan to Mary Jane Benedict of Urbana, N.Y. (No date given).

Wednesday January 15, February 5, 12, March 26, 1851 - no deaths or marriages.

Wednesday January 1, 1851 - Married - In Savona Dec. 25th, by Rev. J. C. Mallory, George F. Ellison and Mary E. Sanderson, both of Corning.
Married - At the same time & place, by the same, Alonzo Herrington and Nancy E. Bartholomew, all of Savona.
Died - In Avoca on 21st inst., Richard Collier in the 91st year of his age, formerly of Green Co., N.Y.
Died - At Horseheads on 22d Dec., Porcia Maria, wife of Charles Underhill, in the 44th year of her age.

Wednesday January 8, 1851 - Married - In Wayne Dec. 25th by Rev. A. C. Mallory, Alvin H. Curtis of Wayne and Sophrona Jacobus of Urbana.

Wednesday January 22, 1851 - Married - In Elmira on 15th inst., by Rev. Hood, Joseph Breck formerly of Bath, to Mrs. Cahill, both of Elmira.

Married - In Reading January 11th by Elder Donaldson, Peter Drake of Jasper to Susan Simmons of the former place.

Married - In this village at the residence of Sheriff Allen on 13th inst., by Rev. George, Asaph Allen Esq. of New Hudson, Allegany Co., to Mrs. Marietta Perine, of this place.

Died - In Pulteney on 7th inst., Eleanor Watrous, wife of John Watrous of Pulteney and dau. of the late Robert Downey of Yates Co., in her 46th year.

Died - At his residence in Mt. Morris, on 10th inst., Doct. Lewis G. Ferris, aged 36 years 9 months.

Died - In Danville, Pa. on 9th inst., Helen, wife of B. K. Rhodes Esq. & dau. of the late Hon. David Petrikin.

Died - At Aiken, South Carolina Nov. 30th, 1850 Dr. Trumbull L. Bennett of Lima, N.Y. aged 26 years.

Wednesday January 29, 1851 - Married - In Bath Jan. 27th by Rev. B. R. Swick, Gilbert N. Perry of Caneadea, Allegeny Co., to Martha Ellis of Bath.

Married - On 22d of Jan. by Elder O. P. Alderman, Isaac Skinkle of Thurston to Catharine V. Collier of Bath.

Married - On 8th Dec. by the same, Vestus D. Allen of Bath to Mrs. Rachael Polmateer of Avoca.

Died - In Lockport, N.Y. Jan. 25th, Alvah Hill, sheriff of Niagara Co., at half past 12 o'clook today.

Wednesday February 19, 1851 - Died - In Howard on Saturday last, Abram Whiting, son of John W. Whiting, aged about 18 years.

Wednesday February 26, 1851 - Married - In Corning on 12th inst., by Rev. Young, Mr. Brazilla Dana to Ann Eliza Weeks, both of Corning.

Married - In Pittsburg on 18th inst., Capt. John Hartman, a soldier of War of 1812 aged 70 years, to Miss Richardson, aged 20 years.

Wednesday March 5, 1851 - Bounty Land Warrant - The first one we have seen, was obtained by R. B. VanValkenburgh Esq. for John Nichoson Esq. of Cohocton (for 80 acres) who served in Capt. James Read's Company, 2d Regiment, in War of 1812.

Married - In this village Feb. 12th, by Rev. J. C. Mallory, Richard Collier and Mary Crosby, all of Bath.

Married - In this village on 26th ult., by Rev. L. Merrill Miller, William Clisdell of Bath to Hannah McChesney of Howard.

Died - At Cameron on 19th ult., of tubercular phthisic (sic), Jane R., wife of Dr. Wickham R. Crocker in the 27th year of her age.

Died - In Prattsburgh on Feb. 21st, Mr. Brayton Hays, aged 46 years.

Wednesday March 12, 1851 - Married - In Wayne March 5th by Rev. A. C. Mallory, Theodore B. Kinney of Wheeler to Elizabeth Van Ness of Urbana.

Married - In Urbana March 5th by the same, Nathaniel Crawford of Wayne to Emily Brundage of the former place.

Died - In this village on Saturday last, William Edwards, aged 71 years. Mr. Edwards was one of the earliest settlers of this village, having resided here fifty years, and was a member of the Masonic order.

Wednesday March 19, 1851 - Married - In Wayne on 13th inst., by Rev. Russell, Jacob R. Hovey of this village to Mary E. Olmstead, dau. of Aaron Olmstead of Wayne.

Wednesday April 2, 1851 - Died - Eunice A. Hoagland, eldest dau. of Abraham Hoagland of Howard, while pursuing her studies at Alfred Institute, at that place of typhoid fever March 19th, aged 25 years.

Died - In Savona on 7th inst., Amanda Whitaker, aged 14 years.

Wednesday April 9, 1851 - Died - In this village today, James Kane.

Died - In Avoca 6th inst. George W. Burnham Esq., aged 43 years, he was a native of this town & had resided in Avoca since its first organization.

Wednesday April 16, 1851 - Married - In Avoca on 27th ult., by Rev. Strough, John G. Eacker of Palatine, Montgomery County, N.Y. & Elizabeth Shaver, dau. of Henry Shaver.

Wednesday April 23, 1851 - Died - In this town on 28th ult., Lydia Thompson, widow of the late Samuel Thompson, aged 80 years.

Died - In this village on Monday last, James W., son of the Hon. Reuben Robie, in the 13th year of his age.

Wednesday April 30, 1851 - Married - At Cameron 23d ult., by Rev. O. P. Alderman, Sebastian Young of Memphis, Michigan to Maria Royce of Starkey.
Died - In this village on 17th inst., Lucy Jane, wife of Anson Rowe, aged 28 years, 4 months & 12 days.

Wednesday May 7, 14, 28, June 4, 1851 - no deaths or marriages.

Wednesday May 21, 1851 - Married - In St. Thomas Church Bath Tuesday 20th inst., by Rev. George Morgan Hills of Lyons, Robert M. Lyon Esq., to Rebecca P. Brother, both of Bath.
Died - Dr. Samuel Watkins, of Jefferson, Chemung Co., died at his residence there Saturday 10th inst., aged 82 years.
Died - Hon. Samuel B. Thurston, delegate to Congress from Oregon Territory on the 9th ult., on board Steamer California, bound from Panama to San Francisco of dysentery.

Wednesday June 11, 1851 - Married - In Lindley, Steuben Co., on 28th ult., by Rev. S. Mills, John L. Sexton Jr. of Big Flats to Grace A., dau. of Benjamin Patterson Esq. of Lindley.
Died - In Avoca suddenly on 1st inst., Anna, wife of Henry Smith, in her 58th year.
Brief History - O. A. Bullard, distinguished artist whose panorama of New York City is being exhibited at the Methodist Church Liberty Corners today and at Avoca on Thursday, was born at Howard, Steuben Co., 25 February 1816. His parents came from Massachusetts, he was fourteen when his father died. In 1841 he married Angeline A. Olmstead, dau. of Augustus A. Olmstead, to whom Bullard was apprenticed for the purpose of wagon and sign painting. The panorama took four years to paint, was completed Nov. 1, 1850.

Wednesdy June 18, 1851 - Married - In Wayne, June 12, by Rev. A. C. Mallory, Alfred S. Woodruff of Urbana to Serepta Prindle of Wayne.
Died - At Stillwater, Saratoga Co., May 21st, in the 21st year of her age, Mary J., only dau. of Leonard & Janette Hodgman of measles.

Wednesday June 25, 1851 - Died - The Hon. C. C. Noble died suddenly at Owego last week. He was for some years, First Judge of Otsego County Courts.

Sudden death Albany, June 18th, James B. Weed, the only son of the senior editor of the *Albany Journal*.

Wednesday July 2, 1851 - Died - At her residence near Corning June 25th, Elizabeth, wife of Charles Wolcott, aged almost 89 years. She was a member of Baptist Church and one of earliest settlers of Painted Post.
Died - In this village on 5th ult., Mary Ellen, dau. of F. A. & Mary S. Fisk, aged 1 year 3 months.
Died - In Avon on Thursday last, Major Asa Nowlen, aged 62 years.

Wednesday July 9, 1851 - Married - In Savona July 6th, by Rev. J. C. Mallory, Charles French, late of California to Mary Read, of Campbell.
Died - In this town on 2d inst., Miss Lois Dudley, aged 58 years.

Wednesday July 16, 1851 - Married - In this village on 25th ult., by Elder Nutten, Edward B. Baker of Wilkes Barre, Pa. to Charlotte Ellis of Bath.
Married - In Avoca on 6th inst., by James Silsbe Esq., Warren Hunt to Elizabeth Brown, both of Bath.
Died - In this village on 9th inst., Fowler, eldest son of Robert Campbell Esq., aged 6 years 3 months 22 days.

Wednesday July 23, 1851 - Died - Anderson Dana Esq., died at Wilkes Barre, Pa. on 24th ult., aged 85 years. He was a boy at the time of the ever memorable Wyoming Massacre. His father & brother-in-law were killed there, then he fled with his mother, her family & others to Connecticut.

Wednesday July 30, 1851 - Married - In Bradford July 23, by Rev. J. C. Mallory, David O. Abel of Savona & Rhoda Stilts, of the former place.

Wednesday August 6, 13, 20, 27, September 3, 1851 - no deaths or marriages.

Wednesday September 10, 1851 - Arrest - Thurlow Weed Esq., editor & proprietor of the *Albany Evening Journal* was arrested yesterday & held to bail in the sum of $10,000 to respond in damages to Edwin Forrest Esq., the celebrated American Tragedian for some publication in the defendants paper, reflecting in an improper manner on Mr. Forrest's affairs. (*Herald*.)

Wednesday September 17, 1851 - Married - In this village on 10th inst., by Rev. Almon Gregory, David Woods, of the firm of Woods & Co., to Olive, dau. of Hon. Reuben Robie, all of Bath.
Died - At his residence in Hornellsville, on 11th inst., Comfort E. Beldin M. D., aged 46 years. He was a member of Arcanum Lodge #81 I.O.O.F.

Wednesday September 24, 1851 - Married - In Avoca, Steuben Co., Aug. 19th by Rev. J. Halsted, Francis H. Guiwitts (sic) of Wheeler to Sarah J. Clason of the former place.
Married - In Campbell Sept. 11th by Rev. J. C. Mallory, George A. Bronson of Beaver Dams, Chemung Co., and Margaret S. Benedict of the former place.
Married - In Bath, on 14th inst., by N. Sawyer Esq., Anson Rowe to Julia Ann Preston.
Married - Also on the same day, by the same, Lawrence Watson to Ann Welch.
Married - Also at the same time and place, Michael Stinser to Catherine O'Brien.
Married - In Cohocton Sept. 10th by Rev. Samuel Cross, A. Adams, attorney-at-law to Mary Raymond, both of Cohocton.

Wednesday October 1, 1851 - Married - In Howard Sept. 25th by Rev. A. Parcel, William H. Willis of Bath to Nancy Whiting of Howard.
Died - In Prattsburgh on 21st ult., Rev. James H. Hotchkin, aged 70 years.
Died - In Kennedyville, Steuben Co., Sept. 20, Henry Mesick in the 62d year of his age.

Wednesday October 8, 1851 - Married - In Hammondsport October 1st, by Rev. W. E. Pinder, John B. Foster of Prattsburgh to Hannah Elizabeth Fisher of Barrington.
Married - At Patchinville Oct. 2d, by Rev. D. Lantz, Freeman Howell of South Dansville to Tharessa (sic) Weidman of Cumingsville.
Married - At the same place on the same day by the same, Isaac S. White to Miss A. E. Covert, all of South Dansville.
Married - At Howard on 25th ult., by Rev. L. Rose, J. Rensselaer Decker of Bath to Hannah Ann, eldest dau. of Joel Bullard of the former place.

Married – Also by the same at the Presbyterian Church in Howard, 28th ult., Rev. Charles Kenmore of Andover, Allegany Co., to Sarah Elizabeth, adopted dau. of Eli Comfort of Howard.

Married – Also by the same at Howard on 1st inst., Mr. I. J. Haskins of Dansville to Amanda, dau. of Benjamin Bennet Esq., of the former place.

Married – Saturday evening Oct. 4th in St. Thomas Church Bath, by Rev. Almon Gregory, Phillip K. Shoemaker and Mary Gibbs.

Died – At Avoca on 23d ult., Catharine Pawling, relict of the late Henry P., aged 63 years. She was one of eight persons who constituted the Presbyterian Church at Howard at its organization July 5, 1815.

Died – In Prattsburgh on 21st ult., Rev. James H. Hotchin aged 70 years. Mr. Hotchkin lived to complete half a century of ministerial labor and thirty years of this time in our own county. The last few years of his life he devoted to writing the *History of the Settlement of Western New York and of the Planting & Present State of the Presbyterian Church Within its Limits.*

Died – In this village Oct. 1st of typhus fever, James Webster, formerly of Owego, aged 30 years.

Wednesday October 15, 1851 – Died – In Kennedyville on 12th inst., of consumption Elisha H. Evans.

Died – Mrs. Cornelia Van Zandt, wife of W. VanZandt Esq., of this city died yesterday of a brief illness. (Syracuse *Star* Oct. 4).

Change of Name – An act to authorize Myron Pond, a minor under the age of 21, of the village of Penn Yan, Yates Co., to assume the name of Myron Stanton, by which latter name he shall hereafter be known was passed July 9, 1851.

Married – In Avoca Oct. 14 by Rev. J. Halsted, William Dearlove to Polly Caster, both of Prattsburgh.

Wednesday October 29, 1851 – no deaths or marriages.

Wednesday November 5, 1851 – Married – By Rev. A. Gregory at the residence of Wm. Hamilton Esq. in Bath on 29th ult., Horace G. Donahe, merchant and Mary Helen Hamilton, all of Bath.

Married – In this village by Rev. E. G. Townsend, Ira H. Eggleston to Delilah Covell, both of Urbana, Steuben County.

Married – In Howard on 26th ult., by W. B. Rose Esq., Wm. H. Miller to Jerusha Graham, both of Howard.

Married - Also at the same time and place by the same, Samuel H. Allen of Cohocton, to Jane Howard of Howard.

Wednesday November 12, 1851 - Married - In Thurston on 30th ult., by Rev. E. G. Townsend, John A. Sinclair of Bath to Celinda Emerson of Thurston.
Married - In Thurston on 9th inst., by J. S. DePue Esq., Tunis Snook to Cynthia Gowers.
Married - In Bradford on 5th inst., by Rev. J. C. Mallory, Jacob H. Stilts and Sarah Ann Baker, both of Bradford.

Wednesday November 19, 1851 - Married - On 5th inst., by Rev. E. G. Townsend, Daniel A. Mills to Esther Eliza Eagleston, all of Bath.

Wednesday November 26, 1851 - Married - In Garretsville, Otsego Co., on 17th inst., by Rev. John Miller, William H. Miller of Howard to Elizabeth Miller of Garretsville.
Married - In Howard Oct. 12th, by N. Sawyer Esq., Israel Morris and Mrs. Eunice Willis of Bath.
Married - Nov. 23d by the same at the Eagle Hotel Bath, William Thomas & Maria Pierse (sic) of Bath.
Married - On 22d by Rev. E. G. Townsend, George Blakeley to Charlotte Dykins, all of Bath.

Wednesday December 3, 1851 - Married - In Howard on 12th ult., by Rev. L. Rose, John McAdam to Jane Stewart.
Married - Also John Sharp to Harriet Forester, all of Howard.

Married - On 16th ult., John Lood of Elgin, Ill. to Lucretia Bacon of Howard.
Married - On 20th ult., Otis N. Merrill to Lydia R. Bennett, all of Howard.
Married - On 26th Nov. by Rev. E. G. Townsend, John A. Freeman to Cynthia A. Covell, all of Bath.
Died - In this town November 25th, Sarah Wilhelm, wife of Joseph Wilhelm, aged 50 years 8 months 28 days.

Wednesday December 10, 1851 - Married - In Cohocton on 3d inst., by Rev. J. Strough, Henry R. May of Bath to Adaline Clayson of Cohocton.
Married - In Thurston on 3d inst., by Elder O. P. Alderman, Fenner S. Aldridge to Martha Morey, all of Thurston.
Married - In Savona Nov. 30th, by Rev. J. C. Mallory, Daniel L. Taylor and Esther Harvey, all of Savona.

Married - In Campbell Dec. 7th by the same, Edward J. Armstrong and Mary L. Wallen, both of Campbell.
Died - In this village on Sunday last, Frances Minerva, infant dau. of Edward and Mary Howell, aged 15 weeks.
Died - In Wheeler Dec. 4th, Col. Jonathan Barney aged 74 years.

Wednesday December 17, 1851 - Married - On Wed. 3d inst., in Lindley by Rev. S. J. M'Collough, Hon. Wm. E. Butts of Helena, Arkansas to Catherine Lindsley of Lindley, N.Y.
Married - In Bath, Dec. 9th, by Rev. B. R. Swick, Sylvester Miller and Caroline C. Aood (sic), all of Bath.
Married - By the same and in the same place Dec. 11th, James P. Harris of Bath and Prudence R. Butler of Prattsburgh.
Died - In East Pembroke Nov. 23d ult., Sarah E., wife of Dr. George Norton, aged 23 years.

Wednesday December 24, 1851 - Married - In Buffalo on 10th inst., by Rev. Doct. Thompson, John Q. Dudley to Helen M. Walker, all of Buffalo.
Died - In Prattsburgh on 10th inst., Hon. Ezra Chapin, lately one of the judges of Steuben County, aged 66 years.
Died - In Elmira on 8th inst., Caleb Lewis Gardner, aged forty-five years.
Died - At Statesburg, S. C. at his residence, Hon. Joel R. Poinsett on Fri. 12th inst., aged 73 years. He was appointed minister to Mexico by Gen. Jackson and held the post of Secretary of War in Mr. Van Buren's cabinet.

Wednesday December 31, 1851, January 21, 1852 - no deaths or marriages.

Wednesday January 7, 1852 - Married - In Cohocton on 13th ult., by W. W. Wait Esq., Daniel Stephenson to Mary E. Jones, both of Naples.
Married - Also on 21st ult., by the same, Henry St. John of Cohocton to Sarah Ann Smith of Prattsburgh.
Died - In Troy, N.Y., Col. Hooker of that city died Sunday morning at 3 o'clock, in the 64th year of his age.

Wednesday January 14, 1852 - Married - On the 6th inst., by Rev. A. Hull, Abram H. Miller of Spencer, Tioga County to Miss Vie, dau. of Thomas Maxwell Esq., of Southport.

Married - In Savona Dec. 21st by Rev. J. C. Mallory, Daniel Raplee of Starkey, Yates County and Catharine Beald (sic) of Bath.
Married - In Campbell Jan. 1st, by the same, Charles S. Bronson of Beaver Dams, Chemung County and C. Elizabeth Benedict of Campbell.
Died - In Saville, Pa. Jan. 7th John Rhodes, father of the editor (W. C. Rhodes) of this paper, aged 65 years, 5 months, 14 days.

Wednesday January 28, 1852 - Married - In this village on 22d inst., by Rev. E. G. Townsend, Elijah Wetmore of East Springwater, Livingston Co., N.Y. to Louisa Roth of Bath.
Married - January 26 by Rev. A. Parcel, Henry M. Snyder of Barrington to Fanny M. Barton of Bath.
Married - In Pulteney on 21st inst., by Rev. Waite, George M. Drew and Abbie Van Ness.
Married - At the same place and time by the same, Peter Van Ness and Caroline Pelton, all of the above place.
Married - In Pulteney on the same inst., by the same, Hiram Clark of Urbana and Laura Hyatt, of the former place.
Married - In Bath on 10th inst., John Fairfield of Urbana and Betsy McCarter of the former place.
Died - In Thurston on 21st inst., Emma, dau. of Elder O. P. Alderman, aged 10 months 28 days.
Died - At the residence of his father in Sugar Creek, Walworth County, Wisconsin on 29th ult., Simeon R. Nyce, formerly of Hammondsport, in the 27th year of his age.

Wednesday February 4, 1852 - Married - In Pulteney on 27th ult., by Rev. White, John L. Scofield to Frederika, dau. of John A. Prentiss, all of Pulteney.
Married - In this village on 29th ult., by Elder David Smith, George W. Bundy to Hannah Lane, of Cameron.
Married - In Howard on 21st ult., by Rev. J. Campbell, John Harris to Jane Stewart of the above place.

Wednesday February 11, 1852 - Died - In this town on 26th ult., William Graham Little, aged 25 years, 10 months 4 days.

Wednesday February 18, 1852 - Married - In this village on 15th inst. by N. Sawyer Esq., Nelson P. Barney to Polly Ann Van Duser.

Wednesday February 25, 1852 - no deaths or marriages.

Wednesday March 3, 1852 - Married - At Christ Church Oswego on 24th ult., by Rev. Stearns, Hon. Charles S. Benton, clerk of the Court of Appeals, to Elizabeth B., dau. of S. H. Reynolds Esq., of Oswego.
Married - At the Mansion House in this village on Monday last, by A. D. Read, Esq., David M. Chisom to Jane Brown, both of Cameron.

Wednesday March 10, 1852 - Married - At Avoca on 25th ult., by Rev. Nichols, James Erls, to Ortha A. Davis, all of Avoca.
Died - March 8, 1852, Martha P. Hess, wife of Hiram R. Hess, in the 35th year of her age.
Died - At Prattsburgh on 19th ult., Hester A. Pratt, wife of William B. Pratt, aged 29 years.

Wednesday March 17, 1852 - Died - In Wheeler on 10th inst., Hon. Grattan B. Wheeler, aged 68 years 6 months.

Wednesday March 24, 1852 - Married - On 16th inst. at residence of Geo. B. King Esq. in Bath, by Rev. G. D. Stewart, John F. Green of Penn Yan to Cynthia, dau. of Geo. King.
Married - In Bath on 18th ult., by Elder O. P. Alderman, Daniel Goodsell to Susan Hewlett, both of Bath.
Married - In Wheeler on 14th inst. by Rev. A. Parcel, James Neally to Eunice, dau. of L. Gray Esq., all of Wheeler.
Married - In Erwin Centre on 11th inst., Julius G. Morgan to Sarah L. Gridley, both of Erwin Centre.
Married - In Wayne on 28th ult., by Rev. Benjamin Russell, Robert L. Dorr, attorney & counselor-at-law of Dansville to Mary Tompkins, dau. of Rice Tompkins Esq. of Wayne.
Died - At his residence in this village on 16th inst. in the 73d year of his age, David Rumsey sen., father of Hon. David Rumsey, late member of Congress from this District.
Died - In Jasper on 15th inst., of congestion of the brain, David Woodard, aged 65 years. Mr. Woodard came to Jasper from Linesboro, N. H. among the early settlers of the town of Jasper. He was one of the founders and officers of the Presbyterian Church. (Amherst, N.H. papers please copy).

Died - In Bath on 18th inst. Samuel Benjamin, aged about 65 years. In this town on 18th inst., at the residence of her son, Mrs. Dorothy Mather, aged 81 years.
Died - In the Steuben County jail on 21st inst., Mrs. Rowland Avoca, aged about 65 years. Mrs. Rowland was committed to jail some two weeks since on the charge of poisoning her husband. Subsequent investigation proved she was entirely innocent of the charge. Last week she was attacked with a violent fever which caused her death.

Wednesday March 31, 1852 - Married - In Savona Jan. 10th, by Rev. J. C. Mallory, John Fairfield of Urbana to Elizabeth McCarty of Bath.
Married - In the same place Jan. 27th by the same, Alfred Wixom of Wayne to Thankful Bennett of Bradford.
Married - In the same place March 18th by the same, Emory T. Hulett, to Caroline Moore, all of Savona.

Wednesday April 7, 1852 - Married - In Savona on 31st inst., by Rev. J. C. Mallory, Jefferson Moore to Julia T. Wing, all of the above place.
Died - In Prattsburgh on Monday last, Chester Lamb, aged about 30 years.
Died - Of consumption in Howard on 23d March, Juliet E. Rice, dau. of W. B. Rice Esq., aged 15 years 7 days.

Wednesday April 14, 1852 - Died - In Howard April 4th of brain fever, Angeline Augusta, wife of Otis A. Bullard and dau. of Augustus A. Olmsted, aged 28 years.
Died - At Genesee Grove, Whiteside County, Ill. on 22d March of lung fever, Nancy Richardson, age 61 years.

Wednesday April 21, 1852 - Died - In Howard on 10th inst., of apoplexy, Richard Towle in the 59th year of his age. Mr. T. removed from Candia, N. H. in 1818 to Howard. (Manchester, N. H. papers please copy).
Died - On 11th inst., Amanda, youngest dau. of Thomas & Sarah Barton, aged 11 years 10 months.

Wednesday April 28, 1852 - Died - In Avoca March 22d, Nancy J. McClary, aged 17 years 1 month 4 days.
Died - In Towlesville on 11th inst., of consumption, Martha Hopper, wife of Mansfield Hopper, aged 34 years. She leaves a husband and two little daughters.
Died - Gen. Solomon Van Rensselaer yesterday afternoon at his residence at Cherry Hill, a short distance below the

city. He was in the 78th year of his age. (Albany Atlas 25th).

Wednesday May 5, 1852 - Died - In this village on 2d inst., Simon Sayles aged 75 years. Mr. S. was father-in-law of Jesse P. Brace Esq., of this village and father of Alexander Sayles of Painted Post.
Died - In Elmira, Wilson Densmore, aged 26 years 10 months.

Wednesday May 12, 1852 - Married - In East Ashford, N.Y. on 22d ult., by Rev. A. C. Andrus of East Ashford, Truman P. Purdy to Emily M. Hopkins, both of Bath.
Married - In Lindley on 4th inst., by E. Watson Esq., Richard Beagle to Mary Ann Louke, all of Lindley.
Married - In Cohocton on 5th inst., by Rev. J. J. Brown, Mr. J. J. Rosenkrans to Miss E. J. Wemple, all of the above place.
Married - In Bath on 15th ult., by Rev. Parker, Mr. B. F. Grant to Mary E. Benedict, all of Bath.
Died - At his residence in Wayne, on 8th inst., Samuel Turner, a native of Ireland, one of early settlers of Steuben County and for several years, a resident of this village, aged 71 years.

Wednesday May 19, 1852 - Married - In Hammondsport May 1st by Rev. W. E. Pinder, Richard Brown to Maria Wilson, both of Prattsburgh.

Wednesday May 26, 1852 - Married - In this town May 25th by Rev. D. Smith, William Lawton to Rosetta Higgins, both of Cameron.

Wednesday June 2, 1852 - Married - At St. Thomas Church in this village on 1st June, by Rev. Almon Gregory, Thomas J. Magee Esq., of Hornellsville to Ellen P. L. Whipple of this village.
Married - May 25th by Rev. E. G. Townsend, Charles D. Thomas to Emeline Southard, all of Bath.
Married - At the Mansion House in this village on 29th ult. by Rev. Townsend David Snow to Margaret Shults, all of Wheeler.
Died - At Hornellsville May 29th, at 11 a.m., John D., son of Benjamin and Abby Hallock of Bath, aged 15 years 4 months 19 days.

Wednesday June 9, 1852 - Died - In this village on 7th inst. Harriet, wife of Charles W. Campbell Esq., aged 27 years. She was dau. of Dr. Robert H. Hoyt, formerly of Painted Post and niece of Wm. S. & P. P. Hubbell Esqrs., of this village.

Died - With apoplexy in Howard June 6th, Nancy, wife of Hubbard W. Rathbone Esq., in the 68th year of her age.

Wednesday June 16, 1852 - Married - Tuesday June 1st at St. Paul's Church New York City by Rev. Dr. Haight, Charles K. Wilmer to Harriet Wheeler of New York.

Married - At the same time and place by Rev. Dr. Haight, James Arkell of New York to Christine Heloise Brown of New Haven.

Married - In Thurston on 8th inst. by Elder O. P. Alderman, Jason Ranger Esq. of Howard to Mrs. Janette Hickox of Thurston.

Died - In Rushford on 10th inst., of tubercular consumption, Rebecca M., wife of Dr. Wm. McCall and dau. of Hon. A. C. Smith of Erwin Centre, aged 29 years.

Wednesday June 23, 1852 - Married - In Hartsville on 17th inst. by C. C. Purdy Esq., Russell Carrington to Ellen Gilbert, both of Dansville.

Died - In Howard on 4th inst. Rev. Levi Rose, aged about 40 years. Mr. Rose was a Presbyterian clergyman and for the last eight years had been preaching in Howard.

Wednesday June 30, 1852 - Married - In St. Andrews Church Meriden, Conn. on 15th inst. by Rev. R. A. Hallam of New London, Edgar Munson of Bradford and Lucy Maria, only dau. of Amos Curtis Esq., of Meriden.

Married - On Saturday last at the residence of Capt. Wm. H. Stewart, near Penn Yan by Rev. B. C. Smith, Addison Chapin of Prattsburgh to Rachel Stewart.

Died - In this village June 9th Eleanor Nixon, aged 66 years 8 mos. 4 days.

Wednesday July 7, 1852 - Married - In Jerusalem, Yates County on 1st inst., by Rev. B. C. Smith, Mr. B. Vrooman Lewis of Prattsburgh to Esther A. Stoddard of Jerusalem.

Married - At the American Hotel in this village May 26th by N. Sawyer Esq., Mr. Smith Hurlburt of Oramel, Allegany Co., to Almira Lovell of Nunda, Livingston County.

Married - In Bath on 9th ult., by the same, George Minier of Thurston to Elvira Smith, dau. of Harlow Smith Esq.

Married - In avoca on 14th ult. by the same, George Patterson of Florida, Montgomery County to Susan Maxwell of Riga, Monroe County.

Married - In Bath on 4th inst. by the same, Jeremiah Knowles of Upper Gilmanton, N. H. to Sarah Jane Nash, dau. of Levi Nash of this town.

Married - At the Christian chapel in Thurston on 27th inst., by Elder O. P. Alderman, Mr. O. F. Burley of Cameron to Jane Hall of Thurston.

Married - In Cameron on 4th inst. by Rev. J. C. Mallory, Minor Swarthout of Wayne to Ann Eliza Horton of the former place.

Died - In Campbell on Friday last, Samuel Besley, aged 70 years. Mrs. Mary Besley, wife of the deceased, died 29th Dec. last, in her 68th year.

Wednesday July 14, 1852 - Married - In Bath on 7th inst. by Rev. James Parker, Robert F. Harris to Miss Seneca V. Brace, all of Bath.

Married - In Avoca July 4th by H. S. Rose Esq., Ransom G. Parker to Susan Hollis, all of Avoca.

Married - In Avoca July 5th at J. Cornue's Hotel by James Silsbe Esq., Levi Keyser to Margaret Cook, all of Avoca.

Married - At the same place by the same, John Cornue to Myanda Cooper, all of Avoca.

Married - In Avoca July 13th at the residence of Thomas Moore, by H. S. Rose Esq., David Tilton to James Moore, all of Avoca.

Died - In this village June 28th Mrs. Harriet Cooper, aged 75 years.

Wednesday July 21, 1852 - Married - In New York City at St. John's Chapel on Tuesday 5th inst. by Rev. Dr. Vinton of Grace Church Brooklyn, Henry H. Raymer to Henrietta A., dau. of the late John Sharpe Esq.

Died - In Geneva on 6th inst. at the residence of her mother, suddenly, Miss Janet Cameron, dau. of the late George Clark of Canandaigua.

Wednesday July 28, 1852 - Died - In Howard on 19th inst. Mrs. Rhoda Dolby, relict of Parden (sic) Dolby, aged about 90 years. Mrs. Dolby came with her husband, a soldier of the Revolution, to Howard 34 years since and was one of early settlers of that town.

Wednesday August 4, 1852 - Died - At Memphis, Tenn. on 9th ult., of typhoid fever, George W. Richardson, aged 23 years.

Wednesday August 11, 1852 - Married - In Bath on 4th inst., by Rev. Almon Gregory, Sebastian Holzmaier to Dorothea Funk.

Wednesday August 18, 1852 - Married - At Seneca Falls on 12th inst. by Rev. B. C. Smith, Horatio B. Eddy Esq., and Parmenas F. Olney M.D., both of Prattsburgh; the former to Mary Jane, the latter to Helen Mar (sic), daughters of Doct. M. B. Bellows, of the former place.
Married - In Prattsburgh on 9th inst. by Rev. B. C. Smith, Rev. William F. Purington, pastor of the Baptist Church to Rhoda Jane Smith, all of Prattsburgh.

Wednesday August 25, 1852 - Died - At the Elmira Water Cure on 17th inst. after an illness of six weeks, Mary Elizabeth, wife of George H. Bidwell of this village and sister-in-law of Rev. W. H. Frisbie of Westport, Ct., for some years resident of Hartford, Ct., aged 32 years 8 months & 23 days.

Wednesday September 1,8, 1852 - no deaths or marriages.

Wednesday September 15, 1852 - Married - In this village by Rev. A. Gregory Sept. 9th, John Casper Overhiser to Caroline Wraight, both of Wheeler.
Married - In Elmira on 8th inst., by Rev. C. N. Chandler, Henry H. Harman Esq. of Howell, Mich. to Esther Bancroft, dau. of R. Bancroft M. D.

Wednesday September 22, 1852 - Married - In St. Thomas Church Bath 16th inst. by Rev. Almon Gregory, Wm. Beach Pratt of Prattsburgh and Cornelia Pratt, eldest dau. of Henry Brother Esq., of Bath.
Married - In Thurston on 14th inst. by Elder O. P. Alderman, Wm. B. Harvy of Addison to Mary E. Barker of Thurston.

Wednesday September 29, 1852 - Married - In Thurston on 22d ult. by Rev. J. C. Mallory, David E. Benedict of Campbell to Mrs. Harriet Love, of the former place.
Married - In Savona on 26th inst. by the same, Lucien Billinghurst to Mary Jane Palmer, both of Corning.

Died – In Howard on 24th inst., Launcelot Dawson, a native of Billi S's (sic) County Cavan, Ireland, aged 49 years.

Wednesday October 6, 1852 – Married – In Avoca Sept. 19th by Rev. J. Halsted, Richard Leonard to Mrs. Mary E. Green, all of Avoca.

Married – In Avoca on 3d inst. by the same, Joel Salmon of Avoca to Mary Whitney, formerly of Burns, Allegany County.

Wednesday October 13, 1852 – Married – In Cameron Oct. 11th by Rev. J. C. Mallory, Rev. A. B. Chase of Townsend, Chemung County and Miss M. Cordelia Horton of Cameron.

Died – In Prattsburgh on 17th ult. of consumption, Ann Wixom, aged 17 years.

Wednesday October 20, 1852 – Married – In this village on 14th inst. by Rev. Fellows, Mr. M. C. Purdy to Betsey Bauter, all of Bath.

Married – In Greenwood on 7th inst. by Rev. Charles Penmore of Andover, D. A. Spicer M. D. to Miss A. J. McClay, both of Greenwood.

Died – At Cohocton on 14th inst. of consumption Mrs. Adeline, wife of Henry R. May of this village and eldest daughter of Hiram Clayson of of Cohocton, aged 22 years.

Wednesday October 27, 1852 – Married – By Rev. M. Skeller Oct. 21, James Spring of Towlesville to Lavina Johnston of the same place.

Died – Suddenly of heart disease on 8th inst., Mary McCay, sister of Wm. W. McCay of this village, aged 66 years 1 month two days.

Died – In this village on 17th inst., Sarah Emily, dau. of William and Elizabeth Crosby of typhus fever, aged 14 years 8 months 22 days.

Wednesday November 3, 1852 – Married – In Wheeler on Thursday last by Rev. B. C. Smith, Otis Shepherd Esq., of Prattsburgh to Lydia Ann, dau. of E. Aulls Esq. of Wheeler.

Married – In Prattsburgh on Friday last, by Rev. B. C. Smith, Thomas Early, to Betsy Jane Horr, all of Prattsburgh.

Died – In this town on Thursday 26th ult. Thomas Rutherford, aged 75 years.

Died - In Howard on 30th inst. of typhus fever, Emeline, dau. of Seth Rice, aged 13 years 10 months 8 days.

Died - On 31st ult. of consumption, Elizabeth, wife of Perry Topping and dau. of Nathaniel Bundy Esq. of Cameron, aged 28 years.

Wednesday November 10, 1852 - Married - In Elmira on 28th ult. by Rev. Dr. Murdoch, Jesse Cooley to Mary Stephens, of Elmira.

Married - In Hornellsville on 31st ult. by Rev. H. Pattengill, Homer Halliday, counsellor-at-law to Sarah Jane, dau. of Hon. Wm. M. Hawley, all of Hornellsville.

Married - In Kennedyville Oct. 27 by Elder J. Case, Erastus Olmsted of Avoca to Margaret Billinger of Wheeler.

Married - In Urbana on 25th Oct., Thomas Lake to Huldah Bailey, both of Urbana.

Wednesday November 17, 1852 - Married - On the 10th inst. by Rev. Edwin Benedict, George W. Breck to Mrs. R. E. Rutherford, all of Bath.

Married - By Rev. G. D. Stewart on Wednesday Nov. 10th at the residence of Mrs. N. Dudley in Bath, Charles G. Little to Susan Dudley.

Married - On the same evening by the same at the residence of John J. Smith in Bath, Chester Ellis to Elizabeth Smith.

Married - At the Hornellsville House in Hornellsville on 8th inst. by H. Bennet Esq., George F. Fisher of Wellsville, Allegany County to Mary Davis of Greenwood.

Married - In Hornellsville on 11th inst., by H. Bennet Esq., Gilbert L. Wilbur to Parmelia Phoenix, both of Addison.

Married - In the same place by the same on 14th inst. George F. Kinne of Addison to Catharine Jones of Rathboneville.

Married - On 7th inst. by G. A. Bennet Esq. of the town of Willing, Reuben Drake of Cameron to Elizabeth Moore, dau. of Aris Moore Esq., of Independence, Allegany County.

Wednesday November 24, 1852 - Married - In this village on Nov. 22d at the residence of Col. Wm. Gamble by Rev. George D. Stewart, Edward E. Erwin to Susan J. Gamble.

Married - In Bath 18th inst. by Rev. J. Parker, Dwight Warren to Angeline Grant, all of Bath.

Married - In Kennedyville Oct. 27th, by Elder J. Case, Erastus Olmstead of Avoca and Margaret Bellinger of Wheeler.

Married - In Urbana on 25th Oct., Thomas Lake to Hildah Bailey, both of Urbana.

Died - On Sept. 4th last at Plymouth, Wisconsin of cholera, William W. Chamberlain, formerly of this town, aged 22 years.

Wednesday December 1, 1852 - Married - In Prattsburgh Nov. 25 by Rev. B. C. Smith, Charles C. Smith to N. Margaret Swetman.

Died - In Wheeler on 12th Oct. last, Jane T., wife of Daniel D. Lewis and dau. of John Wheeler, aged 27 years.

The Voice Of The Nation
Addison, New York
January 10, 1855-December 19, 1855

Wednesday January 10, 1855 - Married - In this village Jan. 3d by Rev. C. M. Gardner, Zelotes Grinnell & Caroline Colwell, all of this village.
Married - In Addison Dec. 30th by the same, Otis Bridgeman and Ann E. Wright.
Married - In Corning on 31st ult. by Rev. D. Nuton, Charles Bliss and Ann Milligan, all of Corning.
Married - In the same place Jan. 2 by Rev. Thomas Cunningham, Luke Hickey of Oswego and Honora Barry of Corning.
Married - In the same place on the 1st inst. by Rev. Robert E. Wilson, Charles Wolcott 3d, and Hulda Jane Gillett, all of Corning.

Wednesday January 17, 1855 - Died - In Hornellsville Jan. 9th, Mrs. Jerusha, wife of Jacob Hartshorn, deceased in the 76th year of her age.
Died - In Susquehanna Jan. 8, Mr. S. B. Dennis, formerly of the Dickinson House, Corning.
Died - In Corning Jan. 7th, Ralph, son of Mr. R. Egbert, aged 4 years.
Died - In Corning Jan. 10, Mr. Oliver Arnold, aged 52 years.

Wednesday January 24, 1855 - Married - In this town Jan. 10th by C. W. Robinson Esq., Silas Chapman & Abigal (sic) Higgins, all of this town.
Died - In Hornellsville Jan. 14, Marinda, wife of Joseph Wallace aged 44 years 5 months.
Died - In Bath Jan. 17, John Richardson in the 78th year of his age.
Died - In Corning Jan. 17, Samuel Merrick, father of Mrs. D. A. Fuller, aged 73 years.

Died - In Bath Jan. 10th, Catharine A. Church, wife of Hon. Edwin F. Church.

Wednesday January 31, 1855 - Married - In Prattsburgh Jan. 18 by Rev. B. C. Smith, Edward C. Chase of Wayne and Mrs. Hannah M. Chase of Wisconsin.
Married - In Wayland Jan. 16th by Rev. W. C. Andrews, Harrison C. Miner and Ellen M. Hamlin, both of Wayland.
Died - In this village Jan. 24, Harriet M., only child of Henry J. and Marion F. Fonda, aged seven months.

Wednesday February 7, 1855 - Married - In Corning Jan. 30th by Rev. A. H. Starkweather, Oren D. Gray of Maine, Broome County, N.Y. to Margaret Wolcot of Corning.
Married - In Urbana on 26th ult. by Rev. J. C. Mallory of Savona, Mr. S. B. Norris of Kanona to H. Mariah Smith of Urbana.
Married - In Pultney on 24th ult. by Rev. Warren, Mr. G. R. Benton to Lydia A., dau. of Andrew Armstrong, all of Pultney.
Died - At Hornby Feb. 3d John M. Perry, only son of Nelson Perry of Woodhull, aged 21 years.
Died - At Painted Post Jan. 25th of heart disease, Alvah Redfield of Tunkhannock, Pa., aged 54 years 10 months 3 days.

Wednesday February 14, 1855 - Married - In Bath Jan. 28th by Rev. A. Sutherland, Henry G. Aber and Nancy L. Pangburn, both of Bath.
Married - In Bath Jan. 30th by the same, Andrew Loveless & Lucy Gustin, both of Bath.
Married - In Monterey Jan. 18th by Rev. Wm. R. Downs, Henry Cowell & Mary M. Dawson, all of Monterey.
Married - In Binghamton Feb. 3d by Rev. A. Starkweather, Thomas Van Atten of Newton, N.J. and Mary D. Struble of Union, N.Y.
Died - Near Monterey, of typhoid fever Jan. 20th, Joel aged 22; Jan. 25th William aged 26; Jan. 31st Michael aged 17; all sons of Mr. & Mrs. Joseph Minard.
Died - In Waymart, Wayne Co., Pa. Feb. 3d of congestion of the brain, Miss Sarah L. Courtright aged 26 years.

Wednesday February 21, 1855 - Married - At Liberty Corners Feb. 12 by Rev. W. E. Pinder, Inglehart Waggoner of Wheeler and Mary E. Shay of Italy, N.Y.

Died - In Bath Feb. 7th, William Hamilton, only son of Horace G. and Mary F. Donahe, aged 10 months 12 days.

Wednesday February 28, 1855 - Married - On 11th inst. by Rev. D. F. Brown, Lewis Rightmire to Elizabeth Emisse, all of Corning.

Married - In Orange, Schuyler Co., N.Y. on 11th inst. by Rev. Benjamin Russell, William Waugh and Margaret Hughey, dau. of Joseph Hughey Esq, all of Orange.

Married - At the Crooks House in this village Feb. 17th by Rev. George D. Stewart, James A. Waldo of Manitowoc, Wisconsin to M. Amelia Wheaton, dau. of John M. Wheaton of Prattsburgh.

Married - In Avoca Feb. 14th by Rev. W. E. Pinder, Mr. C. O. Weeks to Catharine Dillenback, both of Wheeler.

Died - In this town on 12th inst., Edward Rutherford Sr. in 89th year of his age. He was born in Northumberland County, England in the year 1766. In 1819 he emigrated to this country with his family.

Died - On the 1st inst. of congestion of the lungs at Strachan Place Halfmoon, Ahay (sic), wife of Hon. Zeba Leland and dau. of the late Dr. Elijah Porter of Waterford.

Wednesday March 7, 1855 - Married - In Kanona Feb. 20th by Rev. George D. Stewart, Andrew J. Brundage Esq., attorney-at-law to Frances A., dau. of Russell Kellogg.

Married - In Bath on 20th ult. by J. Lindsay Esq., Robert Fawcett of Livingston Co., Mich. to Mary Fawcett (sic) of Bath.

Married - In Elmira on Feb. 19th by Rev. C. N. Chandler, Mr. F. W. Woodward of Bath to Elizabeth Kelley of Elmira.

Married - In Avoca Feb. 22 by Rev. W. E. Pinder, Richard Loucks and Elizabeth Morse, both of Avoca.

Married - In Wheeler on the same day by the same, Andrew J. Maxfield and Miss Lany A. Dillenback, both of Wheeler.

Died - In Corning on 26th ult. Elizabeth, wife of Wellington Stewart, and dau. of Dexter Davis Esq., aged 23 years.

Wedneday March 14, 1855 - Married - In Prattsburgh on 5th inst. by Rev. B. C. Smith, Joseph H. Vandemark of Junius, Seneca Co., to Jane A. Hunt of Prattsburgh.

Married - In Corning March 1st by C. H. Thompson Esq., Nelson Pratt to Ann Abbott, both of Tioga, Pa.

Married - In Avoca Feb. 25th by Rev. W. E. Pinder, Oliver R. Towner to Sarah J. Squire, both of Avoca.

Died - In Elmira on March 6th, Dugold Cameron Maxwell, aged about 30 years.

Died - In Corning on 9th inst. Lucene, eldest dau. of Mr. Jesse May, aged 5 years four months 16 days.

Died - In Corning on 4th inst., Robert W. Foster, aged 67 years.

Died - In Caton March 7, Milicent Brown, wife of William A. Brown, in the 40th year of her age.

Wednesday March 21, 1855 - Married - In Ithaca, March 14 by Rev. D. A. Wheadon, Henry Sherwood Esq., of Addison & Eleanora Robinson of Ithaca.

Married - In Corning on 1st inst. by Rev. David Nutten, Rollin Farnum to Emily L. Doud.

Married - By the same at the Dickinson House on the 13th, John Wolcott to Phebe Berry.

Married - At the same time and place Henry D. Smith, Jr. to Elizabeth C. Westcott, all of Caton.

Married - On the morning of the 14th inst. in Christ Church Corning by the rector, James D. Myers of Waverly, N.Y. to Elizabeth A. Kress of Corning.

Married - In Bath March 7th by Rev. Campbell, John Walker of Howard to Elizabeth L. Marsh of the former place.

Married - At Canisteo on 16th inst. by P. Masten Esq., Henry P. Sawtell to Caroline Totten, all of the same place.

Died - In Addison on March 20, Ann Eliza, dau. of Abraham Dudley of this village, in the 19th year of her age.

Died - In Addison on March 16th, Adaline H., wife of E. Howard Ames in the 33d year of her age.

Died - At Deposit (sic) March 11 Mary Waxaville, only dau. of Francis R. E. and Eliza Cornell, aged 2 years 3 months.

Wednesday March 28, 1855 - Married - In Addison March 20 by Rev. A. H. Parmalee, John S. Munroe of Woodhull to Margaret Stephens of this place.

Married - In South Addison on 25th inst. by Chas. W. Robinson Esq., Eleazer Albee to Eunice Brooks, all of Addison.

Married - In Bath March 18th by Rev. George D. Stewart, Elmer C. Dicey of Grand Haven, Mich. to Emeline Lewis of Bath.

Married - At Savona Feb. 28 by Rev. Wm. R. Downs of Monterey, Leroy Gaylord to N. Caroline McElwee, both of Savona.

Married - In Avoca March 15 by Rev. W. E. Pinder, J. Sylvester Beales of Wheeler and Sophia Jones of Prattsburgh.

Married - In Thurston on 18th inst. by Elder O. P. Alderman, John H. Goodsell and Elizabeth S. Corbitt, all of Thurston.
Married - In Painted Post on 14th inst. by Rev. B. F. Balcom, Alvin Owen to Emily Remington.
Died - In this village March 16th, at the residence of Mr. J. N. Robinson, Mrs. Polly Stillson, aged 82 years.

Wednesday April 4, 1855 - Married - In Elmira on 26th inst. by Rev. H. Hickock, Daniel O. Rice to Leonora C. Miles, both of Elmira.
Died - In Elmira on Friday last, Adolphus Colburn, aged 55 years.
Died - In Bath on 21st inst., Myranda Goble aged 55 years.
Died - In Elmira Wednesday morning, Miss Sarah Cleeves, in the 62nd year of her age.
Died - On 22nd ult. Nelson Chapman killed by his brother William Chapman in a hunting accident (Hornellsville *Tribune*).
Died - On 27th ult. Judge Lazarus H. Read, late Chief Justice of Utah, at his residence in this village in the 40th year of his age.

Wednesday April 11, 1855 - Married - In Corning March 28th by Rev. S. M. Brockman, Griffin Beckwith of Tioga, Pa. to Margaret E. Cushion of Schuyler Co., N.Y.
Died - In this village on April 3d, Bradley Blakeslee 2d, aged 31 years.
Died - In Corning April 3d, Mary, wife of Joseph Robinson, aged about 40 years.

Wednesday April 18, 1855 - Married - In Hornby April 8th by Rev. Wm. R. Downs of Monterey, Joseph Pound' of Big Flats to Sarah Jane King of Hornby.
Married - In Prattsburgh April 5 by Rev. W. E. Pinder, Jacob Dillenback of Wheeler and Mrs. Kathline (sic) M. Upthegrove, of Prattsburgh.
Died - In Bath on 30th March, Mrs. Eleanora, consort of John Able, aged 43 years; she survived a second paralytic shock only five days.

Wednesday April 25, 1855 - Married - In Bath April 10th, by Rev. Almon Gregory, Ambrose F. Andrus of Addison to Permelia Flyn of Bath.
Married - In Savona April 8th by Rev. J. C. Mallory, Wm. R. Phipps of Jasper and Julia A. Pomerly of Woodhull.

Died - In this village on April 22d, Mrs. Theodora Adams, mother of Mrs. Wm. H. Smith, aged 75 years.
Died - In this town Saturday 21st inst. by drowning, Mrs. Toby Bean (?) and infant.

Wednesday May 2, 1855 - Married - In this village by Rev. R. P. Brooks of Cameron, Giles B. Thompson of Worcester, Mass. and Catherine Chase of Elkland.

Wednesday May 9, 1855 - no deaths or marriages.

Wednesday May 16, 1855 - Married - In Bath on 11th inst. by Rev. A. Gregory, Thomas A. Whittenhall of this village to Sarah Shoemaker of Bath.
Married - In this village May 3d by Rev. A. H. Parmale, George W. Wombough to Caroline E. Clark, all of this village.
Married - At South Addison May 12th by Chas. W. Robinson Esq., Austin S. Hatch to Julia Fairbanks, both of Addison.
Married - On 2nd inst. by Rev. M. Buttolph of Castile, Rev. Lafayette Dudley of Lakeville to Sarah Ann, dau. of Israel Willis Esq. of Castile.
Married - In Corning by Rev. D. Nutten, Anthony Stewart to Ann H. Sherwood. (No date given.)
Died - In Bath on Friday last, Antoinette Kasson, wife of Sheriff G. T. Harrower, and dau. of Ambrose Kasson Esq. of Utica, in the 41st year of her age.
Died - In Elmira on 7th inst., Phebe, wife of Riggs Watrous, aged 42 years.

Wednesday May 23, 1855 - Married - In this village on May 21st by Rev. C. M. Gardner, James Brong and Miss Silly (sic) Shearer, both of this town.
Died - In Bath on 9th inst. John D. Higgins M. D.

Wednesday May 30, 1855 - Married - In Prattsburgh on 15th inst. by Rev. B. C. Smith, George E. Bramble to Mary Robbins.
Married - On 16th inst. by the same, Harvey Hill to Susan Jane Wilson.
Married - In Starkey, Yates Co. on 22d inst. by Rev. Sidney B. Hewell of Painted Post and Isabell Swartwood of Starkey (sic).
Married - In Thurston on 19th inst. by E. P. Mulford Esq., Thomas J. Ottarson and Harriet Eliza Martin, both of Thurston.

Died - In Southport on 12th inst., Abbey, dau. of Chauncey and Mary Jane Smith, aged 3 years 7 months 2 days.

Died - In Knoxville, Tioga Co., Pa. May 16th Anna Melissa, infant dau. of Thos. H. and Melissa D. Johnson. (Philadelphia papers please copy).

Wednesday June 6, 1855 - Married - In this village on 26th inst. by Rev. H. Pattengill, Levi N. Call and Mary Guyon, both of Hartsville.

Married - By Rev. N. A. DePew on 27th ult. Albert S. Stephens and Sarah E. Hoag of Hartsville.

Died - In Painted Post on 29th ult. Hamilton Ward aged 21 years.

Died - In Columbia, Pa. on 23d ult. after a brief illness, Henry J. Hoyt Esq. of Cameron aged 37 years. Resident of Cameron last fifteen years, native of New England, leaves wife and one child, burial in Cameron.

Wednesday June 13, 27, 1855 - no deaths or marriages.

Wednesday July 11, 1855 - missing issue. July 25, 1855 - no deaths or marriages.

Wednesday June 20, 1855 - Died - In this village on 16th inst. James Baldwin aged 74 years.

Wednesday July 4, 1855 - Died - In this village Jan. 26, 1854 (sic), Ella, dau. of Seth Mullen, aged 3 years.

Died - In Big Flats June 27th, Asaph Rowley, aged 78 years.

Died - In Caton June 15, Wallace Rhodes, aged 21 years.

Wednesday July 18, 1855 - Married - In this village July 4th by Rev. C. M. Gardner, George McPherson of Jasper and Miss E. A. Towers of Addison.

Married - At the same time by the same, Mr. Burdice of Bainbridge and Miss L. McPherson of Jasper.

Married - In Bath July 15th by Rev. Almon Gregory, James Faulkner Howell and Lydia Shepard.

Married - In Prattsburgh on 4th inst. by Rev. B. C. Smith, Martin A. Rees and Ruby J. Edson.

Wednesday August 8, 15, 29, September 5, 12, 19, 26, 1855 - no deaths or marriages.

Wednesday August 1, 1855 - Married - At South Addison on July 22d by C. W. Robinson Esq., Whitman Gordon and Sarah McMinds, both of the same place.

Wednesday August 22, 1855 - Married - In this village Aug. 19 by Z. L. Webb Esq. William W. Gillan and Harriet O'Neil, all of Addison.

Wednesday October 3, 1855 - Married - At the residence of James F. Haskins in Addison on 29th ult., by John W. Dininy Esq., William Fortner and Martha Gee, all of Addison.
Married - Bath Sept. 19th by Rev. C. M. Gardner, R. B. Dawson of Addison and Miss Johnson of Bath.
Married - In Cameron Sept. 25th by Rev. C. M. Gardner, R. P. Hollenback of Corning and Nancy S. Dyer of Cameron.
Died - In this village Sept. 19, William Wright, aged 35 years, leaves a wife and family.

Wednesday October 10, 1855 - Married - In this village Oct. 10, by Rev. H. L. Grose, James Baldwin & Emma L. Cowley, dau. of C. Cowley Esq., both of Addison.
Married - In Hornby Sept. 20 by Rev. Wm. R. Downs, Alfred Roleson to Mary Knowlton, both of Hornby.
Married - In Prattsburgh Sept. 27, 1855 by Elder O. P. Alderman, James L. Whitaker & Nancy M. Mallory, both of Troupsburgh.
Married - On the same day by the same, Samuel W. Wheaton of Bingham to Betsy Ann Mallory of Troupsbourgh.
Married - In Urbana Sept. 27th by Rev. S. M. Day, Charles D. Stewart of Tecumseh, Mich. to Ro-Ella Read, of the former place.
Married - In Urbana Sept. 22 by Rev. S. Mills Day, George S. Bailey to Sarah Jane Wixom, both of Urbana.
Died - In this town Oct. 3d of dropsy, Mrs. Robert Rowley, aged 65 years.

Wednesday October 17, 24, 31, November 7, 19, December 12, 1855 - no deaths or marriages.

Wednesday November 12 (?), 1855 - Married - In Corning on 1st inst. by Rev. C. Norton, Mahlon H. Manderville of Columbia, South Carolina to Maria Arford of Corning.
Married - In Avon on 1st inst. by Rev. D. Nutten, William T. Rigby to Susan Pearce, both of Corning.

Died - In Canisteo on 5th inst., William Stephens, aged 78 years. Mr. Stephens was a member of the Masonic order and has lived on the same farm since 1799.

Wednesday November 28, 1855 - Died - In this village on 24th inst., Henry J. Fonda, aged 33 years. He leaves a wife and child.

Wednesday December 5, 1855 - Married - In South Addison on 25th ult. by Charles W. Robinson, William H. McCorlum of Farmington, Tioga Co., Pa. to Rachel Gee of Middleburg, Tioga Co., Pa.

Wednesday December 19, 1855 - Married - At the American Hotel in this village on 7th inst. by Z. Lewis Webb Esq., Sylvester S. Bailey and Sally Elizabeth Dalley, both of Woodhull.

The Steuben American
Bath, New York
January 2, 1856-May 6, 1857

Wednesday January 16, February 27, Maroh 26, 1856 - no deaths or marriages.

Wednesday January 2, 1856 - Died - William Chapman formerly of this place was killed at Corning Saturday night when attempting to couple the cars of a passenger train to the tender on the Buffalo, Corning and New York railroad.
Died - Lewis M. Waters of Addison aged 29, on Dec. 25th ult. Suicide by laudnum, depressed by death of wife a year ago.

Wednesday January 9, 1856 - Married - In Addison on 1st inst. by Rev. R. N. Parke, William Stradella to Pameta Wombough, dau. of Henry Wombough Esq., of Addison.
Married - In Woodhull on 1st inst. by Rev. Rosa, John Hibbard to Ellen Worden, all of Woodhull.

Wednesday January 23, 1856 - Died - In Bath Jan. 21st, Mrs. C. M. Lockwood of Wheeler, in the 45th year of her age.

Wednesday January 30, 1856 - Died - Killed by a falling tree, 19 year old son of Lewis Briggs on Saturday last in Wheeler.

Wednesday February 6, 1856 - Died - Froze to death January 8th in town of Broom, New York, Mrs. Joseph Thompson, nine-month old infant and seven-year old son.
Died - In Bath on 2d inst. of scarletina anginosa and cyanche parotidea, George E. only child of E. K. and Orilla L. Potter, age one year seven months.

Asylum - Sent to Lunatic Asylum at Utica from Steuben County, Abby Hallock of Bath, 29 Sept. last and Jane Brooks of Corning, 27 Oct. last.

Wednesday February 13, 1856 - Married - In Bath Feb. 5th by Rev. C. M. Gardner, John Boyd of Pultney and Eunice Hotchkin of Prattsburgh.

Wednesday February 20, 1856 - Died - At his residence in Bath, of erysepelas, Mr. E. K. Potter, age 30 years, native of Vermont in business here six years. His wife, the only remaining member of a family of three, which one month ago were in perfect health.
Married - On 14th inst. by Rev. E. Benedict, Myron K. Fletcher and Hannah Haven, all of this village.

Wednesday April 2, 23, 1856 - no deaths or marriages.

Wednesday March 5, 1856 - Married - On February 19, by Rev. C. M. Gardner, Charles Stratton of Hammondsport and Sophia Lyon of Bath.

Wednesday March 12, 1856 - Died - By suffocation, infant of Mr. & Mrs. Richard Towle of Towlesville, March 7th.

Wednesday March 19, 1856 - Married - In Addison Feb. 29th by Rev. Keyes of Painted Post, Mr. I. D. Sammons of Painted Post and Adelaide Whittenhall of Addison.
Died - In Prattsburgh, Rebecca, wife of the late Rev. J. H. Hotchkin, aged 75 years.
Died - In Addison March 15, George Smith, aged 25 years.

Wednesday April 9, 1856 - Died - On Friday last, John Perry at Millport. He was killed by train on railroad tracks. He was a widower and leaves three children to mourn his loss.
Married - At Addison April 8, by Z. Lewis Webb Esq., Peter Baxter and Louisa Welch, all of Addison.
Married - At the Church of the Redeemer Addison by Rev. R. N. Park, Josiah Curtis and Caroline Smith, all of Addison.
Married - In Corning on 2d by Rev. A. Wright, Peter Rhoda of Hornby and Mrs. Adaline Chapin of Campbell.
Married - Also on 10th inst. by the same, Reuben Stetson to Elsie Gifford, both of Corning.

Wednesday April 30, 1856 - Married - In Kanona April 9th by Rev. S. H. Aldrich, John Jay Laman Esq., of Toledo, Ohio to Caroline Rumsey of Kanona, formerly associate editor of *The Temperance Gem*.

Married - In Prattsburgh in Presbyterian Church April 28 by Rev. B. C. Smith, Mr. J. J. Hotohkin to Miss H. M. Lewis, all of Prattsburgh.

Wednesday May 14, June 4, 18, 25 July 2, 30, August 13, 20, 1856 - no deaths or marriages. Wednesday July 16, 1856 - missing issue.

Wednesday May 7, 1856 - Married - At the American Hotel in Kanona May 1st by Rev. S. H. Aldridge, Abram Overhiser to Alice Wraight, both of Wheeler.

Wednesday May 21, 1856 - Died - At her residence in Painted Post, on Friday last, aged 49 years, Sophia McCall, wife of Gen. Francis E. Erwin and dau. of the late Abel McCall Esq., of Painted Post.

Wednesday May 28, 1856 - Died - At his residence in this village on May 19th, suddenly from congestion of the lungs, John R. Gansevoort Esq., age 58 years. He came hither as early as 1817 from Albany.

Wednesday June 11, 1856 - Died - On 31st May last, at Cincinnati, Ohio by accidental drowning, Peter C. Gansevoort age 29 years. Called home a week ago on the death of his father, John R. Gansevoort.

Died - In Erie County, N.Y. June 3d, Abijah Sibley, father of Dr. J. C. Sibley of this village, of chronic gastritis, aged 66 years.

Wednesday July 9, 1856 - Married - In this village on 3d inst. by Rev. C. M. Gardner, James L. Brundage to Caroline Brundage (sic).

Died - In this village on 4th inst. of bilious remittent fever, James H. VanLoon of Steuben County, N.Y. aged 24 years. The affectionate wife is left a widow and the little one fatherless. (Livingston, Mich. *Courier* May 14).

Wednesday July 23, 1856 - Died - King Strang of Beaver Island, Michigan died at his former residence in Racine County, Michigan (sic) on Wednesday last. (compiler's note - Racine County is in Wisconsin).

Wednesday August 6, 1856 - Died - In this village on 3d inst., Lydia M. Fay, wife of Lewis D. Fay sheriff of this county, in the 33d year of her age.

Wednesday August 27, 1856 - Married - In this village on 21st by Rev. Stewart, A. J. McCall Esq., and Mary Ann Ellas.
Died - In this village on 22d inst., Miss Mary Lizzie, dau. of Hiram B. Hess, of this village.

Wednesday September 17, 24, October 1, 8, 22, 1856 - no deaths or marriages.

Wednesday September 3, 1856 - Married - In Urbana August 28th by Rev. C. M. Gardiner, Rev. L. D. Chase of E. G. Conference and Miss E. Larrowe, dau. of Judge Larrowe of Hammondsport.
Married - In Bath August 31st by the same, Mr. H. D. Manchester and Mrs. Elizabeth Daniels, both of Bath.
Married - At the parsonage in Avoca August 13 by Rev. W. Potter, Rev. Uria S. Hall of E. G. Conference and Elizabeth Parkhill of Avoca.
Died - In Corning, W. Franklin, only son of J. H. and A. J. Conner aged eight months.

Wednesday September 10, 1856 - Died - Mrs. N. E. Hotchkin, wife of James H. Hotchkin Esq. of Prattsburgh on the 28th ult. at age 47 years.

Wednesday October 15, 1856 - Married - At Hammondsport October 2d by Rev. E. Loveridge, William B. Powers M. D. and Lovina A., dau. of Seth W. Barrett Esq., all of Hammondsport.
Married - At Bath October 2d by Rev. George D. Stewart, at the residence of M. L. Billington, Alonzo W. Hewlezl (sic) to Sarah J. Billingeon (sic), all of Bath.
Married - At Thurston Sept. 21st by E. P. Mulford Esq., Philander J. Hall of Addison and Melissa R. Chase of Rathbone.
Died - At Prattsburgh of dysentery on 7th inst. after an illness of two weeks, James J. Hotchkin, merchant aged 25, an only son ... his death following so quickly that of his mother.

Wednesday October 29, 1856 - Died - In this village Sept. 30th, Mary Louise aged 11 months and Oct. 22d, Osa Kate aged 3 years 9 months, daus. of Charles and Elizabeth Lenhart.

Wednesday November 19, December 10, 17, 24, 31, 1856 - no deaths or marriages.

Wednesday November 12, 1856 - Died - Near Rocky Point, Greenbrier County, Virginia, Thursday week (Nov.6), George Fox about 15 years was killed by pet bear at residence of William T. Mann.
Died - Mr. Wood, brakeman, killed by train at Millport. (Elmira *Gazette* Oct. 30).
Died - Fifteen year old son of Alexander A. Race of this village (Hornellsville) Tuesday afternoon of this week was crushed by falling log.
Married - At Kanona on 22nd inst. by Rev. George D. Stewart, Franklin C. Foote to Frances L. Norton, both of East Pembroke, N.Y.
Married - In Prattsburgh on 20th inst. by Rev. B. C. Smith, Joseph K. Burnham of Buena Vista to Sarah Jane Cople of Prattsburgh.
Married - At Bath Sept. 30th by Rev. C. M. Gardner, Frank Hardenbrook and Miss M. J. McElwee, both of Bath.
Married - By Rev. G. D. Stewart on Nov. 5th at the residence of John J. Smith in Bath, his dau. Margaret J. to Menzer D. Donahe of Avoca.

Wednesday November 26, 1856 - Married - At the residence of the bride in Addison, Nov. 11th by Rev. R. D. Brooks, Mr. C. H. Edwards of Brown, Pa. to Miss A. A. Jones of Addison.
Married - In Hornellsville on 5th inst. by Rev. James A. Robinson, Henry Baldwin Esq. of Addison and Bella Bliss of Hornellsville.
Married - At the parsonage in Painted Post, Nov. 18th by Rev. J. Joralemou, Edwin P. Arnold of Lisle and Melissa Kinney of Painted Post.
Married - In Elmira on 18th inst. by Rev. J. C. Nobles, L. Baldwin Jr. to Helen Tillotson, dau. of D. L. Tillotson Esq., all of Elmira.
Died - Augustus S. Lawrence, formerly a merchant of Elmira, committed suicide at Canandaigua by taking opium one night last week. (Elmira *Advertiser*).

Wednesday December 3, 1856 - Died - Mary O'Connor, wife of James O'Connor of Thacher's Mill and her 18-month old son, killed by train Monday last. (Hornellsville *Tribune*).

Wednesday January 7, 1857 - Died - Mr. Swartwood of Owego fireman locomotive 115, New York & Erie railroad, by explosion of boiler on Dec. 27th at Addison.

Wednesday January 14, 1857 - Died - A colored person well known as "old George" died in this village on 2d inst., he was one of the oldest residents & was formerly held in bondage in this town. His age is not exactly known, but it is supposed that he was about 120 years old.

Wednesday January 21, February 4, 11, 18, March 11, 1857 - no deaths or marriages.

Wednesday January 28, 1857 - Died - Rev. E. P. Havens, a Wesleyan Methodist clergyman, his wife and three children living in "Dudley Settlement" about two miles south of this village were burned to death Wednesday last. Mr. Havens aged 36, Mrs. Havens aged 33, & the children 15, 5, and 2.
 Died - In Livonia Friday afternoon last, John Egan killed by a barn door hinge thrown by John H. Carter of South Livonia. Deceased age 37 years, leaves a wife and two children. (Livingston *Republican*).
 Died - Mr. Robinson died Monday last at Joe Rice's hotel in Kanona.
 Died - At Avon Friday evening last, John Laughlin, in the employ of C. H. Nowlen at Avon was gored to death by a bull. Deceased was about 50 years of age & employed by Nowlen for over 20 years. He leaves a wife and several children. (Livingston *Republican*).

Wednesday February 25, 1857 - Married - In Addison Feb. 15, by James Whittenhall (attorney) Esq., James H. Murray of Hornby and Alvira Thomas of Addison.
 Married - Also at the same place by the same on the 18th inst., Isaac N. Chase and Helen Bennett, both of Elkland, Pa.
 Died - In this village at the Crooks House Feb. 20th of typhoid fever, Frances M., wife of E. P. Barton of this village.

Wednesday March 4, 1857 - Died - Death of Dr. Elisha Kane, artic explorer of Philadelphia, has been fully confirmed by arrival of his remains at New Orleans. The Philadelphia *North American* of Monday evening says death was anticipated several months. He was born in 1822 and died at the untimely age of 34 years.

Died - In Prattsburgh Feb. 23d, James Edmund, infant son of Lester and Eliza Lockwood, age 1 year 9 months 12 days.

Died - In Prattsburgh March 2d at the residence of her brother, of scarlet fever, Ellen G., youngest dau. of James H. & Catherine M. Lockwood, aged 3 years 7 months 14 days.

Wednesday April 15, 29, May 6, 1857 - no deaths or marriages.

Wednesday March 18, 1857 - Married - Mary Ann Baker 22, dau. of John Baker of Tarrytown, N.Y. to John Dean March 11th by Rev. Hatfield at Tarrytown.

Married - In Merchantville on 1st inst. by Rev. Ezra Gleason, formerly of Luzerne, N.Y. to Sarah F., dau. of H. R. Clark Esq., now all of Thurston, Steuben Co., N.Y. (sic).

Wednesday March 25, 1857 - Died - Jedediah Grant, the Mormon's president, who died in Great Salt City on 1st Dec. was a native of Windsor, N.Y. He was a major general of the Nauvoo Legion and had been speaker of the House of Representatives of Utah: "St. Grant, we believe, left seven widows".

Wednesday April 1, 1857 - Married - In this village on March 30th by Rev. C. M. Gardner, Lewis D. Fay, sheriff and Nancy Zielley, all of Bath.

Died - At the residence of her brother in this village on March 27th, Margaret C., youngest dau. of the late John Brown, aged 15 years.

Wednesday April 8, 1857 - Died - On March 25th at the residence of her brother in Avoca, Betsy Ann, dau. of John and Lucy Donahe.

Died - In Bath at the residence of his son Rev. C. M. Gardner on 30th ult., Daniel Gardner aged 79 years. He was born in New York city and served in the War of 1812.

Died - In Bath on Wed. April 1st at the residence of his father, A. Eugene Staniford, aged 21 years 10 months.

Wednesday April 22, 1857 - Died - Drowned last Saturday, Mrs. Pepper from Gibson, whose husband is at work for Col. Balcom in Wisconsin. (Corning *Journal*).

Died - In Bath on Monday April 13th, Almon T., son of Daniel A. and Esther E. Mills, aged 4 years 4 months.

The Addison Advertiser
Addison, New York
March 3, 1858-February 16, 1859
and
March 6, 1861-March 18, 1868

Wednesday March 3, 1858 - missing issue. March 17, April 7, 14, 21, May 5, 1858 - no deaths or marriages.

Wednesday March 10, 1858 - Married - At Elmira College by Rev. A. Bradley of Olean, Theocrastus Bombastus Houghenstounten to Adrianna Augustina Van Ozzledozzle, both of Addison (sic).
Died - 3d inst. Commodore Mathew Galbraith Perry at his residence, No. 38 West Thirty-second St., N.Y.C. He was brother of Commodore Oliver H. Perry, hero of Lake Erie in the War of 1812 with Great Britain. (*New York Tribune* of 5th inst.).

Wednesday March 24, 1858 - Married - In Addison 12th inst. by J. Whittenhall Esq., Stephen Christjohn to Susan Barnes.
Died - Murdered on Friday evening last, Sidney Benham, bar keeper of the Franklin House in Canandaigua, and brother-in-law of the proprietor by Charles Merry. Merry and John Osborn were quarreling, Benham attempted to part them, whereupon Merry shot him in the head. Benham was 25 years of age, universally respected, and leaves a wife and child.

Wednesday March 31, 1858 - Married - In Addison March 30th by J. Whittenhall Esq., Nicholas Feith and Monika (sic) Krumhold, both of Corning.

Wednesday April 28, 1858 - Married - In Geneva on 15th inst. by Rev. R. N. Parke, rector of Christ Church Albion, Henry J. Higgins of Flint, Mich. and Augusta F. Taylor of Geneva.
Married - In this village April 23d by J. Whittenhall, Esq., Nathan Bishop of Warren County, N.Y., and Johanna Colburn of Addison.
Married - In Knoxville, Pa., April 3d by M. Comstock, Esq., George Spring of Elkland and Martha May of Knoxville.

Wednesday May 12, 1858 - Died - In this village May 6th, Albert H., son of Henry and Rachel Wombough, in the 17th year of his age.
Died - In this village May 7, Mr. Rulof S. Gile, in the 32 year of his age.

Wednesday May 19, 26, June 2, 16, 23, July 21, 28, August 4, 1858 - no deaths or marriages.

Wednesday June 9, 1858 - Married - In Elkland June 7th by Rev. D. F. Judson, Henry S. Jones of Addison to Maria R. Atherton, of the former place.
Died - At Otisville, Orange Co., N.Y. May 15th, Sarah A. Otis, youngest dau. of Galen Otis, aged 19 years 5 months.

Wednesday June 30, 1858 - Married - In Addison July 3d by Jas. Whittenhall, Esq., Luther S. Corse to Martha Marvin, both of Osceola, Pa.

Wednesday July 14, 1858 - Married - At Towanda, Pa., July 1st by Rev. DePew, Mr. J. M. Seamen to Charlotte Eaton.
Died - In this village June 29, at the residence of his father, Seth A. Merian, aged 31 years.
Died - In this village June 21st at the residence of Dr. F. R. Wagoner, Henry Searls, aged 27 years.

Wednesday August 11, 1858 - Died - In this village on August 9th at the residence of her father, Abram Dudley, Esq., Helen M. Higley, wife of H. M. Higley, aged 24 years.

Wednesday August 18, 25, September 1, 8, 15, 22, October 6, 13, 27, November 3, 10, 17, 24, 1858 - no deaths or marriages.

Wednesday September 29, 1858 - Married - At the residence of Joseph Powell, Sept. 26th by Rev. John H. Blades, Robert Short to Nancy King, both of Addison.

Wednesday October 20, 1858 - Married - At the residence of Simon S. Rial Sept. 30, by Rev. John H. Blades, William Mose and Rachel E. Rial, both of Addison.
Married - At the residence of James Blanchard Oct. 7th, by Rev. J. H. Blades, Lyman Elwood and Maria N. Blanchard, both of Addison.
Married - On the 13th inst. at the residence of the bride's parents by Rev. D. Chichester, James A. Parson and Mary E. Land, both of Corning.

Wednesday December 1, 1858 - Married - At the Methodist parsonage Oct. 19th by Rev. J. H. Blades, Edwin M. Reynolds and Freelove Smith, both of Addison Hill.
Married - At the residence of the bride's father E. J. Horn Oct. 22 by the same, Charles C. Young and Almira Horn, both of Addison.
Married - At the residence of Ira Z. Beckwith Oct. 24th by the same, Francis L. Crane of Addison and Mary A. McHenry of Covington.
Married - At the residence of A. Dudley, Esq., Nov. 19th by the same, George A. Evans of Rathbone and Sarah C. Willson of Addison.
Married - At the residence of Colby Teed Nov. 23d by the same, Charles O. Graves of Waverly and Phebe A. Seaman of Addison.

Wednesday December 8, 15, 22, 19, 1858 - no deaths or marriages. Wednesday January 5, 1859 - Married - In Addison Dec. 29th by Jas. Whittenhall, Esq., Daniel Weaver to Emma McBeath, both of Erwin, N.Y.

Wednesday January 12, 1859 - Married - At the Eagle Hotel in Bath Dec. 29th by Rev. N. N. Beers, Washington Vanderwarner to Hannah L. Leech, both of Cameron.
Married - On the 28th ult., by Rev. Norman Fox Jr., Alvin O. Sanford to Mary Ann Wilkes, both of Corning.
Died - Suddenly at Rock Stream Yates County Jan. 1st, Sally Wollage, widow of Rev. Elijah Wollage, and mother of Mrs. J. B. Pratt of Corning, aged eighty-six years.
Died - In Corning January 1st, Mrs. Eunice Dickerson, aged 75 years, 11 months.

Died - In Howard Dec. 30th of apoplexy, Rufus R. Palmer, aged 59 years.

Wednesday January 26, February 9, 1859 - no deaths or marriages. February 16, 1859 - missing issue.

Wednesday January 19, 1859 - Married - In this place Jan. 12th at the residence of the bride's father by Rev. D. F. Judson, David B. Winton of Chicago, Ill. and Frances J. Gillette, dau. of J. D. Gillett, Esq.
Died - At Burlington, Pa. on Jan. 9th Rev. R. D. Brooks, pastor of the M. E. church in this village for two years previous to the last annual conference meeting and was much esteemed as a minister and citizen.

Wednesday February 2, 1859 - Married - By Rev. A. Parcel on evening of the 23d inst., N. V. Manley to Miss E. C. Clinton, of this vicinity.

Wednesday March 6, April 17, 24, May 8, 15, June 5, 26, 1861 no deaths or marriages. Wednesday March 13, 20, May 22, 1861 missing issues.

Wednesday March 27, 1861 - Married - March 14th at the residence of John Y. Dates, Ramseys, N. J., by Rev. Wm. Demarest, Richard Graham of Ramseys to Julia Thorpe of Ellenville, N.Y.
Died - Another pioneer gone, Marcus Gaylord of Hornby, on 13th last, aged 82 years. He was one of early pioneers of Steuben Co. On the lot he took up at the land office 41 years ago, he has since resided.
Died - George Sherman of this town, while on a visit at his son-in-law's, E. T. Hollis, Esq., at Woodhull, Friday last and while conversing in a jovial manner with his dau., was taken with convulsion and almost instantly expired. He was buried on Sunday last. Cause of death is supposed to have been heart disease.

Wednesday April 3, 1861 - Died - On Friday March 29, the two daus. of Rev. W. A. Bronson of Canisteo, aged 9 & 12 respectively, when their clothing caught fire while filling a "bleached oil" lamp.

Wednesday April 10, 1861 - Married - In this village on 5th inst., at the house of the bride's mother, by N. S. Calkins, Esq., Cyrus B. Morse & Ada K. Barr, both of Addison.

Died - In Woodhull April 5th, Oscar B., infant son of E. T. & L. G. Hollis, formerly of this place.

Wednesday May 1, 1861 - Died - In this village on Mon. April 29th, George H. Weatherby, aged 35 years.

Wednesday May 29, 1861 - Married - On 25th inst., by S. D. Clinton, Esq., John M. Talles & Mrs. Susan Lackey, both of Tuscarora.

Wednesday June 12, 1861 - Married - At the Methodist parsonage in Addison June 2, by Rev. M. Wheeler. Charles Nettleton and Maria Gibson.
Married - Also June 2d by the same at the same place, Samuel Miller and Clarissa E. Crane, both of Addison.

Wednesday June 19, 1861 - Married - At the Methodist parsonage in Addison June 13th by Rev. M. Wheeler, Fayette F. Cook and Mary Wolever, both of Addison.
Married - At Kanona June 5th by Rev. O. R. Howard, Charles H. Young and Marion Kellogg, dau. of Russell Kellogg Esq.
Married - June 5th at Bath by the same, Thomas Campbell and Mrs. Mary Clyde, both of Cameron.
Married - May 27th at Eagle Hotel by the same, Robert C. Morey and Elizabeth A. Baker, both of Woodhull.
Married - At Pultney May 27th by Rev. D. D. Gregory, Edward Van Housen and Amanda Williams.
Married - In Pultney June 4th by the same, Elijah Allis and Emily O. Hayes.
Married - In Urbana June 6th by Rev. D. E. Leveridge, James M. Ordway of Addison and Elzina Bailey of Urbana.
Married - In Bath on 9th inst., by James Lindsey, Esq., Harmon Mills and Sarah Champlain of Savona.
Died - In Hammondsport May 30th, Margaret, infant dau. and only child of Ruth and Orlando Shepard.
Died - In Corning on 11th inst., Mary, dau. of John Talerday, aged 16 mos.

Wednesday July 3, 10, 17, 31, August 14, 21, 1861 no deaths or marriages.

Wednesday July 24, 1861 - Died - At his residence in Rathboneville the 17th inst., Gen. Ransom Rathbone, aged 81 years.

Died – In Jasper July 14th of dropsey of the heart, Don T. Winchell, nephew and adopted son of R. C. Twogood, aged 22 years 14 days.

Wednesday August 7, 1861 – Died – Patrick Quinlan of Rathboneville Saturday night by jumping off train. He leaves a wife and four children.

Wednesday August 28, 1861 – Married – At the Franklin House in Tuscarora on 22d by Charles W. Robinson, Esq., John Bullock of Tuscarora to Julia Froman of Jasper.
Died – At Belle Plain, Scott Co., Minnesota on Aug. 27th, James U. Whittenhall, aged 27 years.

Wednesday September 4, 1861 – Married – At the American Hotel in this village Aug. 24th by Rev. D. C. Loop, Joel Stone and Martha Ann Brotzman, both of Troupsburgh.

Wednesday September 11, 1861 – Died – In this village of cholera morbus Sept. 9th, Mary, wife of David Phillips, aged 26 years.
Died – In this village Aug. 15, Fred S., aged 9 months; Sept. 1, Edward S., aged 2 years 9 mos., sons of Dr. J. and A. D. Mitchell.

Wednesday September 18, 25, October 16, 30, November 6, 13, 27, December 4, 18, 1861 no deaths or marriages. October 9, 1861 missing issue.

Wednesday October 2, 1861 – Died – In Addison Sept. 28th, Gertrude B., aged 6 weeks 3 days; Sept. 29th, Clara Elsie, aged 2 years 7 months 6 days ; daus. of Wm. H. & Sarah Manners.

Wednesday October 23, 1861 – Married – At the residence of E. H. Buck, Esq. in Addison on Oct. 17, by Rev. D. F. Judson, Charles E. Montgomery and Emma E. Kellogg, formerly of Alba, Penna.

Wednesday November 20, 1861 – Married – At the Methodist parsonage in this village Nov. 18th by Rev. H. T. Giles, Teneyck Fluent of Rathbone, N.Y., to Amanda Rosencrance of Brookfield, Penna.

Wednesday December 11, 1861 – Married – At the residence of the bride's father in Addison Dec. 10th by Rev. H. T.

Giles, Rev. Francis Sherer of Bromont, N.Y., & Helen A. Hill.

Wednesday December 25, 1861 - Married - At the M. E. church in this place Dec. 22d by Rev. H. T. Giles, W. A. Warriner of Addison to Bertha J. Thompson of Knoxville, Pa.
Died - In this village on 20th inst., Mary Vivian, wife of Rev. D. C. Loop, aged 22 years 3 months.
Died - In this village on Sun. 15th inst. of diptherea croup, Esther A., dau. of John and Esther Peck, aged two years nine months.

Wednesday January 8, 1862 - Married - At the Methodist parsonage in this village Jan. 1st. by Rev. H. T. Giles, Judson D. Slade of Rathboneville, to Mary E. Wilson of Woodhull.
Died - In this village on 4th inst., of diptheria, Charlotte A., dau. of Andrus D. & Sarah M. Hoffman, aged 2 years 5 months 4 days.

Wednesday January 15, 1862 - Married - At Osceola, Tioga Co., Pa., Jan. 1st by Rev. Howe, James C. Van Orsdale to Emma A. Dunn, all of this village.

Wednesday January 22, 1862 - Married - In Virgil, Cortland Co., N.Y., Dec. 26th by Rev. P. Kinney, Franklin L. Hurdick of Addison to Mira E. Kingkade (sic) of Virgil.
Died - In this village of diptheria on Jan. 19th, Sarah E., dau. of Andrus and Sarah M. Hoffman, aged 12 years.
Died - John Stearns of Canisteo at his residence on 25th Nov., aged 96 years 3 months 15 days. He was born in Worchester, Mass., in 1765, was one of first settlers in Canisteo, having moved to that place in 1794. He was one of the first Grand Jurors in Steuben County.

Wednesday January 29, 1862 - Married - By Rev. Wm. E. Jones on 8th inst., R. W. Eddy of Towanda, Pa., to Fannie K., second dau. of Lewis Biles(?) Esq. of Bath.
Married - In Bath Jan. 14th by Rev. E. J. Scott, A. C. Yost to Mary O'Hare, both of Bath.
Married - Jan. 8th by Rev. S. Ottman, Mathew B. Hall to Sarah Caryell, all of Pulteney, N.Y.
Married - In Caton Jan. 10th by Rev. H. Wisner, C. E. Lewis to Jane O. Thurber, of that place.

Married - At the same place and time by the same, Jason R. Veazie to Phoebe A. Babcock, all of Caton.

Died - In Hornellsville on 10th inst., Samuel Adshead, aged 44 years.

Died - In Caton Jan. 17, Jesse Jaynes, aged 72 years.

Died - In Corning of measles, James M., son of John Doud & adopted son of Mrs. Sarah Jane Seward, aged ten months.

Wednesday February 12, 19, March 5, 19, 26, May 7, 1862 no deaths or marriages. Wednesday February 5, April 9, 23, 30, 1862 missing issues.

Wednesday February 26, 1862 - Married - At the parsonage Feb. 23d by Rev. H. T. Giles, George J. Sanders of West Addison to Anna Scutt of West Cameron, N.Y.

Died - In this village of diptheria on 12th inst., Lester A., son of Andrus D. and Sarah M. Hoffman, aged 10 months 27 days.

Died - In this village of diptheria on 19th inst., Mary J., dau. of Andrus D. and Sarah M. Hoffman, aged 10 years 2 months 26 days.

Died - In Jasper Feb. 22d, Mrs. Burnette Dennis, committed suicide by throwing herself into a well, wife of Rodney Dennis, Esq., school commissioner for this district. She leaves one child. (*Hornellsville Journal*).

Died - In Gaines township, Theron Boyd lost his life while cutting down a tree a week ago last Monday. He leaves a wife & 5 children. (*Tioga Agitator*).

Wednesday March 12, 1862 - Died - In this village on March 6, of diptheria, Miss Kitt, dau. of Benjamin J. & Julia Kinney, aged 16 years 11 months.

Died - In this village March 7th, Adelaide Weed, wife of Mason N. Weed of Havana, N.Y., & dau. of Almon & Almira Beeman of Addison aged 22 years.

Wednesday April 2, 1862 - Died - In this village on March 25th, Richard C. Twogood of Jasper, aged 53 years of apoplexy.

Died - In this village of consumption on March 25th, Wm. Becktal, aged 38 years.

Wednesday April 16, 1862 - Accident - A son of John Bebout of Carrtown, Tuscarora was scalped in a runaway accident April 7th. Dr. Brown sewed scalp in place and he is doing well.

Wednesday May 14, 1862 - Died - Fri. last John Hurley, native of Ireland, His skull was crushed by a timber from a building he was demolishing. He leaves a wife and family. (*Hornellsville Journal*).

Wednesday May 21, 1862 - Died - On 14th inst., Sarah Fulford committed suicide by taking strychnine. She was housekeeper for George H. Dates. (*Corning Journal*).

Wednesday May 28, 1862 - Died - Thomas Gould, son of Caton Gould, residing in Mt. Washington, Addisontown, as result of a hunting accident Thurs. last, aged 15 years.

Wednesday May 7, June 11, 18, 25 July 2, 9, 23, August 6, 13, 1862 no deaths or marriages. Wednesday June 4, 1862 missing issue.

Wednesday July 16, 1862 - Married - In this village at the house of Russell Dodge, by Rev. H. T. Giles, Wm. S. Ludington and Laura A. Jones, both of Addison.
Died - At Bemis Saw Mill Campbell, James Lynch, last week on Thursday.

Wednesday July 30, 1862 - Married - On July 13th at the residence of the bride's father, by Rev. D. F. Judson, Gilbert T. Sears of Freemansburgh & Alice N., dau. of Martin Wilbur of Addison.

Wednesday August 20, 27, 1862 missing issues. Wednesday September 10, 17, October 1, 8, 15, 22, 29, 1862 no deaths or marriages.

Wednesday September 3, 1862 - Married - In this village on 20th inst. by Rev. S. L. Congdon, Henry Chapman of Otisville, Orange Co., N.Y., to Frances C. Otis of the same place.
Married - In this village Aug. 3d, by Rev. H. T. Giles, Russell L. Fairbanks to Elizabeth Eygabroat, both of Addison.

Wednesday September 24, 1862 - Married - On Sept. 9th at the residence of M. O. TenEyck Esq. of Buffalo, by Rev. W. A. Niles, Frank B. Brown, editor of the Corning Democrat to Nellie M. DeVoe of Owasco.

Wednesday November 5, 1862 - Married - In this village Nov. 2d by S. D. Clinton, Esq., Levi V. Payne of Woodhull and Elizabeth A. Bolyen, of Rathbone.

Wednesday November 12, 1862 - Married - On Wed. 22d ult. at the residence of the bride's father by Rev. W. C. Mattison, George Heermans to Hattie C. Sedgwick, both of Bath.

Married - On the 21st inst. by James Lindsay, Esq., John M. Johnston to Lizzie D. McCann, both of Bath.

Married - At Corning Oct. 29th by Rev. H. F. Hill, C. B. Tift & Miss H. C. Hill, dau. of the officiating clergyman.

Died - In Caton Oct. 29th, Martha, dau. of Richard H. Smith, aged 15 years. This makes his fifth child that has died from diptheria, all within fifteen days, but one child is left and she is married.

Died - In Caton Oct. 31st of diptheria, Viola, dau. of Lewis Gridley, aged nine years.

Died - In Corning Oct. 15th, Frederick Barnard, aged 61 years. Near Perryville, Ky., Oct. 14th, Alonzo Gaylord of Co. B. 75th Illinois Volunteers, aged 24 years. He was a son of the late Willis H. Gaylord of Hornby.

Died - Near Tonica, Laselle(sic) Co., Ill. Sept. 30th Rev. Benjamin P. Wheat, aged 53 years. He was formerly a resident of Addison.

Died - On Tues. 4th inst. of diptheria, Theodore P. Badger, aged 39 years.

Wednesday November 19, 1862 - Married - In Knoxville by Rev. B. F. Balcom, Frederick Amey of Corning and Catherine Yale of Knoxville.

Married - In Hornellsville Nov. 1st by Rev. Milton Waldo, George A. Townsend and Louisa V. Brimmer of Hornellsville.

Married - In Hornellsville Nov. 9th by the same, Robert Harper Warren of Owego and Eliza Ann Van Campen of Hornellsville.

Married - Also at Hornellsville on the same day, Hamilton Van Campen and Maryette Edwards, both of Hornellsville.

Married - In Bath on 15th ult. by Rev. W. C. Mattison, Charles V. Carpenter of Dundee, Ill. and Huldah Sherman of Urbana.

Married - By the same at Bath on 15th inst. Abel Rarick and Emily Lake, both of Pultney.

Married - By the same on 9th inst. James E. Fisk and Henrietta Carr, both of Hammondsport.

Died – In Cameron on 31st Oct., Freddie H., son of Freeman and Jane Hemmenway, aged 8 months 7 days.
Died – At St. Louis, Missouri Oct. 31st aged 26 years, Lieut. Thomas W. Cooper, son of John Cooper Jr., of Coopers Plains.

Wednesday November 26, 1862 – Married – In Addison Nov. 20th at the residence of Henry Wombough, Esq., by Rev. D. F. Judson, Stephen A. Pierce of New York City and Mrs. Sarah E. King of Addison.
Married – On Nov. 10th at Governor's Island by Rev. Dr. J. Scudder, James Gansevoort and Mrs. Eliza E. Ogden.
Married – At Corning Nov. 9th by J. S. Robinson, Esq., Leroy Grant and Helen Woodward, both of Corning.
Married – At Corning Nov. 13th by Rev. W. A. Niles, James P. Smith and Sarah J. Cross, both of Caton.
Died – In Bath Nov. 10th, Hannah, youngest dau. of James F. and Lydia Howell, aged 5 months.
Died – In Bath on 16th inst., Ezekiel Palmer, aged 76 years.
Died – In Hammondsport Nov. 6th of diptheria, Lennie L., only child of R. L. and Susey(sic) J. Seeley, aged 3 years 6 months.
Died – In Hornellsville on 17th inst. of typhoid fever, Edward B. Sturtevant, aged 31 years.
Died – In Caton of diptheria Nov. 11th, Henrietta V., dau. of Lewis Gridley, aged seven years. This is his 4th dau. to die in 18 days.

Wednesday December 10, 24, 1862 no deaths or marriages.

Wednesday December 3, 1862 – Married – In Tuscarora Nov. 15th by Rev. Frank Mack, Byron G. Brown and Huldah A. Higgins, both of Tuscarora.
Married – At the home of the bride's father in Tuscarora Nov. 27th by Rev. H. T. Giles, Daniel R. Hurlburt of Addison to Adelaide D. Moore.
Married – In Woodhull Nov. 16th by J. P. Stroud, Esq., Hugh Tubbs to Jane Bullin, both of Woodhull.
Married – At Merchantville Nov. 23d by Elder O. P. Alderman, Uriah A. Carpenter of Cameron and Francis A. Merchant of Merchantville.
Married – At Bath Nov. 19th in First Presbyterian church by Rev. Wm. E. Jones, Oscar J. Averell of Bath to Helen C. Thomson of the same place.
Died – In Bath on 18th ult., William R. Beach, aged 64 years.

Wednesday December 17, 1862 - Married - In Tuscarora Nov. 25th by Rev. S. L. Congdon, Andrew J. Easterbrook of Hornby and Minerva R. Newman of Tuscarora.
Died - In Owego of diptheria, Fannie Bell, only dau. of J. E. and M. M. Stebbins, aged 6 years 5 months 20 days.

Wednesday December 31, 1862 - Married - In this village Dec. 24th by S. D. Clinton, Esq., Edmund Crocker of Addison and Sarah V. Marlatt of Woodhull.
Died - In this village on Christmas morning of diptheria, Clara Mabel, only child of Charles H. and Harriet E. Henderson, aged 13 years.

Wednesday January 6, 14, 21, 28, February 11, 18, March 18, 1863 no deaths or marriages. February 4, 1863 missing issue.

Wednesday February 25, 1863 - Died - In Addison Feb. 23d. of scarlet fever, Nancy E., dau. of Henry S. and Maria Jones, aged 2 years 2 months 23 days.

Wednesday March 4, 1863 - Married - At the residence of the bride's father Feb. 1st by Rev. O. R. Howard, Ten Eyck G. Swart and Ellen T. Abel, all of Bath.
Died - Eight-year old son of Jefferson Moore drowned in river Monday afternoon. (*Steuben Courier*).

Wednesday March 11, 1863 - Died - In Woodhull on Feb. 8th of typhoid fever, H. M. Baxter, aged nine years. He leaves a bereaved father and six sisters to mourn his loss; his mother died about ten months before.

Wednesday March 25, 1863 - Married - At the home of the bride's father in this village March 15th by Rev. H. T. Giles, Mr. A. J. Parker of Dryden and Miss M. C. Wilcox of Addison.
Married - In Tuscarora March 12th by C. W. Robinson, Esq., at the residence of the bride's parents, Alvin D. Carr and Harriet Spicer, both of Tuscarora.
Married - In Rathbone by E. H. Buck, Esq., Aruna(sic) Jones of Rathbone and Mrs. Sarah Crane of Addison.
Died - In Tuscarora on 17th inst. of scarlet fever, Mary, youngest dau. of Michael and Huldah Spicer in the 6th year of her age.

Wednesday April 1, 1863 - Died - At Woodhull two of the oldest residents of this county, a short time since, Samuel Stroud 90 years and David Edwards 76 years.

Wednesday April 22, May 13, 27, 1863 - no deaths or marriages. Wednesday April 29, June 3, 17, 24, 1863 missing issues.

Wednesday April 8, 1863 - Married - At the Episcopal church in Addison April 2d by Rev. Albert Wood, Rufus Bates of Ithaca and Flora Melissa Doolittle, dau. of Anson Doolittle of Addison.
Died - Cyrus Crosby of Jasper was killed by the railroad cars on Friday of last week, about one mile west of Canisteo depot.
Died - At his residence in Cincinnati March 24th, Henry D. Smead aged 56 years. Mr. Smead was for many years a resident of this village where he published the *Steuben Farmers Advocate*, founded by his father. (*Steuben Courier*).

Wednesday April 15, 1863 - Married - At the home of S. D. Clinton, Esq., April 11th, by Rev. H. T. Giles, Mr. S. A. J. Booth and Angie Smith, all of Addison.

Wednesday May 6, 1863 - Died - In Bath 27th April, Catherine F., wife of Honorable R. B. Van Valkenburgh, aged 40 years.
Died - In Prattsburgh, Mrs. Slighter, sister of Rev. D. D. Gregory with whom she resided, fell down cellar steps of a neighbor causing instant death.
Died - Daniel Kelsey of Delmar, Tioga Co., Pa., he became a resident in 1807, aged 85 years. (*Corning Journal*).

Wednesday May 20, 1863 - Married - In Lawrenceville, Tioga Co., Pa., May 16th by Rev. Sidney Mills, Horace Seaman and Mercena M. Fox, both of Addison.
Married - In Tuscarora May 13th by M. M. Manly, Esq., Charles Ball and Harriet Stoddard, both of Lawrence, Pa.

Wednesday June 10, 1863 - Married - In this village on 9th inst. by Rev. S. L. Congdon, James E. Jones and Betsey B. Brown, both of Addison.

Wednesday July 1, 8, 15, 29, August 5, 12, September 2, 23, 1863 no deaths or marriages. July 22, August 19, 26, September 16, 1863 missing issues.

Wednesday September 9, 1863 - Married - In this village Sept. 8th by Rev. H. T. Giles, John T. Jackson and Rachel Holmes of Addison.

Wednesday September 30, 1863 - Married - In this village at the parsonage Sept. 27th by Rev. C. S. Fox, John Fox and Ermina Hutchins, both of Addison.
Died - In this village Sept. 22d, Mrs. Bella Bliss, wife of Capt. Henry Baldwin late of the 34th Reg't. N.Y. V., aged 28 years.

Wednesday October 7, 1863 - Married - In this village Sept. 25th by Rev. L. C. Warriner, George Ferrow of Alexandria, Va., and Annie J. Stephens of Addison.
Died - In Bath on 23d ult., Catherine Sherwood of Woodhull, aged 70 years, mother of Hon. Henry Sherwood of Corning.

Wednesday October 14, 1863 - Died - In this village Monday, the three-year old dau. of Patrick Connors, fell into the cistern and drowned. (*Corning Journal*).

Wednesday October 21, November 25, December 16, 30, 1863 no deaths or marriages. November 18, 1863 missing issue.

Wednesday October 28, 1863 - Married - In this village on 22d inst. by Rev. Albert Wood, Augustus W. Lyon and Gertrude Berry, both of Addison.

Wednesday November 4, 1863 - Married - In this village on 28th Oct. by Rev. Albert Wood, Howard Ames 2d and Ruth E. Jones, both of Addison.

Wednesday November 11, 1863 - Married - At the parsonage in Cameron Nov. 2d by Rev. Wm. Sharp, Fernando Allen and Helen Church, both of Rathbone.
Died - At East Greene, Chenango Co., Nov. 10th of consumption, Thomas A. Kathan, formerly of this village, aged 46 years.
Notice - Whereas my wife Rachel has left my bed and board without just cause or provocation, I hereby forbid all persons harboring or trusting her on my account, as I shall pay

no debts of her contracting after this date. Addison, N.Y., Nov. 11, 1863 John T. Jackson.

Wednesday December 2, 1863 - Died - On Saturday Nov. 21st, Hon. Wm. J. Gilbert of Erwin at his residence, aged about 50 years.

Died - Jerome Gifford recently in the employ of A. J. Gilbert in blacksmith shop was accidentally shot at Osceola, Tioga Co., Pa., on 18th ult. and died the same night, aged 19 years. He was setting out muskrat traps and was shot by some boys who supposed it to be a muskrat. (*Corning Journal*).

Wednesday December 9, 1863 - Died - On Dec. 2d at the Dickinson House in Corning, Cornelia M. Brown, wife of F. B. Brown, editor of the *Corning Democrat*, aged 25 years.

Died - Lewis Jones was killed on Wed. of last week by being knocked off the lower railroad bridge below Corning by the Express going east. (*Corning Journal*).

Died - A fatal accident occurred at the depot in Hornellsville on Wed. night last to Jerome Percival of Cleveland, Ohio, who was on his way to New York City in company with his brother Capt. Percival to enlist in the 13th N. Y. heavy artillery. (*Hornellsville Tribune*).

Died - Poisoned, the three year old dau. of Rev. Kennedy of Osceola, Tioga Co., Pa., on 17th ult.; found some cobalt which had been obtained for fly poison and ate freely of it. Medical aid was immediately obtained without effect. (*Tioga Agitator*).

Wednesday December 23, 1863 - Old Resident - The oldest resident of Steuben Co., Mrs. Sarah Rowley, mother of J. W. Rowley of Tuscarora, has attained the age of 97 years. She is quite hale and hearty, always insists upon dressing and taking care of herself and until three months past has taken a daily walk out of doors. She remembers distinctly the incidents of the Revolution, was a married woman before Geo. Washington was president, and was mother of twelve children.

Wednesday January 13, February 3, March 2, 9, 1864 no deaths or marriages. Wednesday January 27, February 17, 1864 - missing issues.

Wednesday January 6, 1864 - Died - Mr. Asa Downs of Cameron died suddenly while sitting in his chair at the breakfast table, aged 84 years.
Died - Alonzo D. Lewis on 24th ult. while edging boards at Reynolds sawmill, a mile north of this village. (*Hornellsville Tribune*).

Wednesday January 20, 1864 - Married - In Addison on 13th inst. by Rev. Albert Wood Capt. Samuel Stone of 86th N.Y. V. and Anna M. Searles, niece of Mrs. Dr. Wagner(sic) of this place.
Died - At Jasper, N.Y., Jan. 11th of congestion of lungs, Mellie J., infant son of J. C. & Emma A. Van Orsdale, aged 3 weeks. J. C. was ass't. assessor of Jasper.
Died - On Jan. 1st, Albert Franklin Lynch of Co. E., 141st N.Y.S.V., aged 22 years 10 months.

Wednesday February 24, 1864 - Died - Seaman Simons, convicted of murder of Levi Van Geller in Avoca last summer, committed suicide by hanging himself in the jail at Bath Tuesday night last.

Wednesday March 16, 1864 - Died - At Washington, D. C., on March 6th, Major Edward F. Bates, Surgeon of the U.S. Volunteers, son of Mrs. L. D. Coburn of this village, aged 23 years. He leaves a young wife.

Wednesday March 23, 1864 - Married - At the residence of the bride's father in Woodhull March 10th, by Rev. C. S. Fox, John W. Hammond of Tuscarora to Adelaide M. Delamater.
Died - Fred Hart, son of W. E. Hart of Elmira, suffocated to death Fri. night last when First Presbyterian church burned.
Died - On Sunday last, M. M. Converse of Elmira died of burns received attempting to rescue a woman from the same fire.

Wednesday March 30, 1864 - Married - In Elmira March 27th by Rev. Levy, Isaac Rosskam formerly of Addison and Bertha Gerstly.

Wednesday April 6, 20, May 25, June 15, July 13, 1864 missing issues. April 27, May 4, June 22, August 3, 24, 1864 no deaths or marriages.

Wednesday April 13, 1864 - Died - In Addison March 28th of membraneous croup, Katie Dee, dau. of Oliver and Kate Horn, aged 5 years 20 days.

Wednesday May 11, 1864 - Married - At the residence of the bride's parents May 5th by Rev. C. S. Fox, Llewellyn M. Jones of Addison and Mary E. Erwin, dau. of Arthur Erwin Esq. of the town of Erwin.

Wednesday May 18, 1864 - Died - In Tuscarora May 4th, James, son of Homer Mandeville, age 19 years.

Wednesday June 2, 1864 - Died - On the 24th inst. in Corning, Mariah Windsor, youngest dau. of Rev. Ira Brown of diptheria, aged 21 years 1 month 17 days.

Wednesday June 8, 1864 - Died - Alonzo D. Hill, son of John Hill of Addison, wounded at Battle of Wilderness & died at Fredericksburg May 13th. He has a brother who is a Lieut. in 107th N.Y. Reg't. He was in 97th Reg't. as a draftee.

Wednesday June 29, 1864 - Died - At Hornellsville June 28 of diptheria, Georgie, son of Eugene T. and Loretta Hollis of this village, aged 1 year 8 months 19 days.

Wednesday July 6, 1864 - Died - In this village May 22 of dropsy, Mrs. James Baldwin, aged 64 years.
Died - In this village May 27 of consumption, Lieut. George L. Taggart, quartermaster of the 64th Reg't. N.Y.S.V., aged 42 years.

Wednesday July 20, 1864 - Died - In this village on July 17, Georgie, son of George S. and Eliza Shepard, aged 6 years 5 months 3 days.

Wednesday July 27, 1864 - Died - In this village on July 17, of whooping cough and congestion of the brain, Tommy P. infant son of Fred and Ann Harford of Lincoln, Placer Co., California, aged 1 year 3 months.

Wednesday August 9, 1864 - Died - In Addison Aug. 5th, Sally M., wife of Benjamin Colwell, aged 33 years 5 months 15 days.
Died - Ephraim Tuttle killed by the railroad cars Friday morning last, three miles south of Corning.

Wednesday August 17, 1864 - Died - At the residence of his father-in-law Wm. Curtis in the village of Addison, on 9th Aug. of wounds received at Battle of Wilderness May 10th, Capt. John Phinney. He was born 2d June 1836 Athens, Pa., enlisted as pri. July 1861 Co. K, 86th Reg't. N.Y.V., commissioned 2d Lt. 24 Nov. 1862, 1st Lt. Dec. 9th and Capt. of Co. K 2d July 1863, buried in Addison August 11, 1864.

Wednesday August 31, 1864 - Died - In this village Aug. 24th Catharine, wife of John T. St. John, aged 69 years.
Died - Of diptheria, Mr. Banks has lost 3 of 5 children. Joseph B. Hotchkin has lost 6 of 8; Lucius H. Hotchkin June 23, aged 17 years, Joseph Allen aged 2 years & Charles D. aged 7 years Aug. 2, Fannie D. aged 4 years Aug. 7, Maria L. aged 15 years & Agnes aged 9 years Aug. 15. The 2 children dying on Aug. 2d buried in same grave & 2 more on 15th buried same day. (*Steuben Courier*).

Wednesday September 14, October 5, 19, November 9, December 14, 21, 1864 no deaths or marriages. October 12, 26, December 28, 1864 missing issues.

Wednesday September 7, 1864 - Married - At the residence of the bride's father Sept. 1st by Rev. E. V. Wales, Charles W. Gillet of Addison and Augusta R., dau. of Wm. Comstock, Esq., of Laurens, N.Y.
Died - In the General Hospital in Louisville, Ky., Oscar Roat of Co. F. 107th Reg't.

Wednesday September 21, 1864 - Died - In this village on Friday last, Elijah Keyes, aged 68 years.
Died - In Campbellton Sept. 8th, Samuel Cook, aged 85 years 7 months 8 days. Mr. Cook was one of the pioneer settlers in the early settlements of Bath, Hammondsport and Painted Post.

Wednesday September 28, 1864 - Died - In the U. S. General Hospital at Natchez, Miss., Sylvester Lynch of Co. G., 2d N.Y. Cavalry of chronic diarrhea, aged 16 years.

Wednesday November 2, 1864 - Married - In this village Oct. 9th by Rev. S. L. Congdon, Charles Peck of Elmira and Josepha B. Bonham of this village.

Wednesday November 16, 1864 - Died - On Wednesday of last week, Orren Wells of Tuscarora was instantly killed while getting out logs.

Wednesday December 7, 1864 - Died - At Pontiac, Mich. Nov. 20th, Pamelia Baldwin of this village aged 65 years. She came to this place with her father, Wm. Wombough in 1802, married Rufus Baldwin who died in 1843, soon after followed two sons and but a week prior to her death, the death of her dau. Pamelia whose obituary we copy from the *Pontiac Jacksonian.*
Died - At Pontiac, Mich., on Fri. Oct. 28th, Pamelia W., wife of Hon. Byron G. Stout of Pontiac, aged 25 years.
Died - In Tuscarora Oct. 9th, Harriet M., wife of Charles W. Robinson, Esq., aged 32 years.

Wednesday January 4, 11, 25, February 1, 8, 15, 22, March 1, 8, 1865 no deaths or marriages. January 18, March 15, 1865 missing issues.

Wednesday March 22, 1865 - Married - At Addison on 27th ult., by Rev. S. S. Sturges, Jonathan W. Anson to Emily Curran, all of Addison.
Married - By the same on 19th inst. at the residence of the bride's father in Addison, Thomas C. Davis of Brookfield, Pa., to Mary E. Wilber.

Wednesday March 29, 1865 to Wednesday March 18, 1866 missing. (This volume would have contained news of Lincoln's assassination and the end of the war).

Wednesday March 28, 1866 - Married - In this village March 23d by Rev. C. S. Fox, Thomas Ward of Rathbone and Mary Stroud of Woodhull.
Married - In this village March 22d by Rev. C. S. Fox, John H. Minard of Troupsburgh to Cornelia P. Olmsen, of the same place.
Died - In this village March 25th, Marcia M. Shepard, eldest dau. of J. K. Shepard, aged 21 years 4 months 29 days.

Wednesday April 4, 1866 - Married - In church at the close of service in Knoxville, Pa., March 25th, William B. Smith of Knoxville, Pa., and Sarah H. Shove of Farmington, Pa.

Wednesday April 11, 1866 - Married - In this village April 6th, Orvel Brewster and Helen Eastwood, both of this village.

Wednesday April 18, 1866 - Married - At the Eagle Hotel in this village April 12th by Rev. D. F. Judson, Wm. W. Richardson and Emma Smith, both of Beecher's Island, Pa.
Married - By Rev. D. F. Judson at his residence in this village April 17th, Thomas R. Atherton of Osceola, Pa. and Margaret M. Gordon of Tuscarora.

Wednesday April 25, May 2, 9, 16, 23, 30, June 13, 27, July 4, 25, August 1, 1866 no deaths or marriages.

Wednesday June 6, 1866 - Married - In Hornellsville on 26th inst. by H. Bennett, Esq., Charles Austin to Hannah Bovier of Canisteo.
Died - At LaCrosse, Wisconsin March 18th of dropsey, James Tutton, formerly of this village, aged 31 years.
Died - April 12th, twin infants of Mary Morse of Savona.
Died - April 16th, twin infant daus. of Caroline Butler of Canisteo.
Died - May 15th, John Cronan of Corning.
Died - May 17th, John Schank of Bath, aged 85 years.
Died - May 21st, Samuel Brink, aged 103 years. (Bath papers).

Wednesday June 20, 1866 - Married - In Towanda, Pa., on May 31st, Rev. E. P. Hammond to Eliza, dau. of Edward Overton, Esq., of that place.

Wednesday July 11, 1866 - Married - On 3d of July by Rev. C. S. Fox, Walter Crandal to Mary Crane, both of this village.
Married - On July 4th by the same, William Walty of Lindley to Rachel Ward of Erwin.

Wednesday July 18, 1866 - Married - At the residence of the bride's father in Rochester on 12th inst. by Rev. Albert Wood of Addison to Sarah Ames of Rochester. (No groom named.)
Married - At Tuscarora July 4th by George W. Webb, Esq., George W. Crowl to Catherine M. Albee, dau. of Stephen T. Albee, all of Tuscarora.

Married - On July 11th at the house of the bride's father in Knoxville by Rev. W. A. Niles, Lieut. Isaac P. Clark to Sarah A. Cask, all of Corning.

Married - At Painted Post July 4th by Rev. P. P. Sanderson, Albert V. Gibbs of Addison to Lovina Gibson of Gibson.

Wednesday August 8, 1866 - Married - In Bath on 28th ult., at the residence of Dr. A. DeWolfe by Rev. A. F. Morey, Frank Z. Jones of N.Y. to Mara E. DeWolfe of Bath.

Died - In this village Aug. 6th of scarlet fever, Julia, dau. of Ransom R. and Susannah Phillips, age 4 years 4 months.

Died - In Hornellsville July 25th of congestion of the brain, Mrs. Sarah M. Logan, eldest dau. of Moses and Melissa Stevens, aged 41 years.

Wednesday August 15, 1866 - Married - At the residence of the bride's parents in Bath July 28th by Rev. S. M. Merritt, Jacob C. DeWitt and Emily J. Gay, both of Bath.

Married - In Corning August 5th, by Rev. J. K. Tuttle, Mr. T. E. Hardie of Syracuse and Miss M. Bennett of Corning.

Married - In Corning July 30th by the same, Mr. M. P. Cook and Jennie Coddington of Elmira.

Married - At the same place and time, Mr. H. H. Peters and Miss E. A. Coddington of Elmira.

Married - By the same July 1st in Caton, Mr. H. H. Davis and Louisa J. Castor, dau. of William Castor.

Married - By the same July 4th in Corning, Jacob Koon and Alma L. Moore of Lawrenceville, Pa.

Wednesday August 22, 1866 - Married - By Leonard Aldrich, Esq., at his residence in Thurston, August 5th, James H. Boatwright to Catharine A. Clements, both of Rathbone.

Died - In this village Aug. 14th of dysentery, Lizzie, dau. of Isaac and Cecelia Craft, aged 1 year 1 month 14 days.

Died - In Hornellsville on 8th inst. of typhoid fever, Mrs. Sarah E. Nicholson, aged 18 years 5 months 16 days, eldest dau. of J. B. and M. A. Shurbin of Avoca.

Died - In Bath Aug. 2d of inflammation of the bowels, Mary E. Brooks, dau. of William Brooks, aged 22 years 2 months 21 days.

Wednesday August 29, 1866 - Married - At Addison Aug. 20th by Rev. D. F. Judson, Ross S. Jones and Miss Allen(sic) E. Mullen, dau. of Seth Mullen of this village.

Married - On the 20th inst. by Rev. J. K. Tuttle, Eugene Jaynes to Julia F. Brown, all of Corning.

Married - August 13th by Rev. D. McDougal at the residence of the bride's father, Henry J. Elder of Fulton, Oswego Co., to Martha L. Rice of Gibson, Steuben Co., N.Y.

Wednesday September 5, 1866 - Married - At Addison Aug. 30th by Rev. D. F. Judson, Wm. H. Edwards to Helen E. Shepherd, dau. of J. K. Shepherd, Esq., both of Addison.
Married - Aug. 25th by Rev. J. M. Harlow, John D. Armstrong of Bath to Sarah Ann Polmateer of Avoca.
Married - In Bath Aug. 22d by Rev. A. F. Morey, Samuel Hall of Almond to Levica Page of Bath.
Married - At the residence of Mr. H. Miller in Bath Aug. 17th by Rev. J. C. Mallory, Joseph B. Loghry to Emma N. Chapman, both of Bath.
Died - At Albany, Nemoka Co., Kansas on 23d ult. of cholera, Eliza A., wife of Elihu and mother of Capt. D. S. Whittenhall of St. Louis, in the 57th year of her age. Mrs. W. was formerly of Oxford, N.Y., and long a resident of this place. Mr. Whittenhall left Addison with his family ten years ago to live in Albany, Kansas. There, as here, they united with other Christians in the formation of the First Presbyterian Church.
Died - In Cameron Aug. 27th of consumption, Duran Knapp, aged 27 years.

Wednesday September 12, 1866 - Died - Ex-sheriff Allen at his residence in Canisteo on 15th inst., aged 60 years. He was demented for over a year before his death, caused by a disease of the brain. (*Hornellsville Vidette*).

Wednesday September 19, 26, October 31, November 21, 28, December 12, 1866 no deaths or marriages. December 19, 1866 missing issue.

Wednesday October 3, 1866 - Died - At Addison Sept. 29th of chronic diarrhea, George B., son of Wm. J. and Jennie E. Newhall, aged 4 months.

Wednesday October 10, 1866 - Married - In Jasper Oct. 3d by Rev. A. F. Countryman, Rufus Park and Catherine C. Countryman.
Married - At the same time and place, by the same, Charles A. Van Orsdale and Helen C. Countryman, both daus. of Solomon Countryman, Esq., of Jasper.

Married - At Lawrenceville, Pa., Sept. 30th by Rev. S. Mills, Hugh J. Magee and Mrs. Mary Eldridge, both of Lawrenceville.

Wednesday October 17, 1866 - Died - At Woodhull, Mr. Nye Blyn, Fri. last while coon hunting. Buried on Sunday last.

Wednesday October 24, 1866 - Married - In this village on 17th inst. by Rev. A. Wood, Obed Nye of West Union to Eliza Ann Boardman of Clymer, Pa.
Died - In Hornellsville on Monday of last week, James Whitford, son of L. D. Whitford lost his life.
Died - Willie Brewster, son of Gilbert B. Brewster, died on Monday evening last of injuries.

Wednesday November 7, 1866 - Married - At Lawrenceville, Pa., at the residence of the bride's uncle on Oct. 31st by Rev. Thomas Cullen, Wm. B. O'Connell of Dunkirk to Mary S. Depuy, dau. of Mrs. C. Cowley of Addison.

Wednesday November 14, 1866 - Died - Jerry Deland of this place was killed at Osceola, Pa., on Monday last by the felling of a tree. He was there getting out lumber for George Bonham. He was promoted to Lieut. during an engagement in the recent war. He leaves a wife and children.
Died - Mr. J. D. Hendershot of Corning died on Sunday of last week from the injuries he received in a train accident.

Wednesday December 5, 1866 - Died - In this village on Fri., Nov. 30th of dropsy, Mrs. David Smith, in the 69th year of her age.
Died - On Sunday Nov. 25th on Addison Hill, Cora Agnes, infant dau. of Charles C. and Roby Brown, aged 2 months 13 days.
Died - In Tuscarora Oct. 10th of chronic diarrhea (contracted in the service) Sergt. Amos Carr Jr. 2d N.Y.V. Cavalry, aged 23 years 6 months 11 days. He was mustered into service at Saratoga Springs Oct. 10, 1863. Mustered out with his company and arrived home in Dec. 1865.

Wednesday December 26, 1866 - Married - In Addison Dec. 19th by Rev. David F. Judson, assisted by Rev. Joel Wakeman D.D., Wm. A. Waldo of Prattsburgh to Gertrude L., dau. of the officiating clergyman.
Married - On Dec. 2d by J. P. Stroud, Esq., at his residence, Harlow J. Howard and Nettie Clark, both of Woodhull.

Married - By the same on 6th inst. at the house of Luther Newton, Willett C. Newton and Julia Fuller, both of Woodhull.

Married - At the residence of the bride's brother in Penn Yan Dec. 18th by Rev. David Magee, Hon. Thomas A. Johnson of Corning to Sarah W. Parker, dau. of Hon. Henry Wells of Penn Yan.

Married - In Hornby Dec. 19th at the residence of the bride's father, by Rev. Isaac Easterbrooks, Sylvester B. Hilton to H. Louisa Dickinson, all of Hornby.

Married - On Dec. 12th at the residence of D. S. Magee, Esq., in Watkins by Rev. D. C. Mann, Mr. S. Stewart Ellsworth of Penn Yan and Phebe P., only dau. of Hon. John Magee of Watkins.

Married - In Corning Dec. 10th by Rev. W. A. Niles, John Wilson of Jackson, Pa., to Mrs. Emma E. Buchanon of Corning, N.Y.

Married - In Hornby Dec. 2d by Rev. H. W. Bixby, Richard H. Rogers to Delphine Backer of Dix, Schuyler Co., N.Y.

Married - At Savona Dec. 9th by Rev. J. C. Mallory, Albert J. Perry of Galesburg, Ill., to Albina S. Hughes of Savona.

Married - Dec. 12th by Rev. J. M. Harlow, James S. Harlow, M.D., to Sarah Dudley, all of Bath.

Married - Dec. 2d by Rev. F. Wilbur, Josiah Townsend to Diantha Angel, all of Urbana.

Married - Dec. 5th by the same, Horace Exlls(sic) to Anna E. Smith, all of Bath.

Wednesday January 2, 16, 23, February 6, 13, 20, 27, March 6, 13, 20, 27, April 3, 10, 17, May 1, June 5, 12, 1867 no deaths or marriages.

Wednesday January 10, 1867 - Married - At Addison Jan. 2d by Rev. D. F. Judson, Mr. H. G. Spaulding of Corning to Jennie E. Brown, dau. of John N. Brown, Esq., of Addison.

Died - At his step-father's in Addison Dec. 27th, Sgt. Charles Vine DePue, brother of Mrs. Wm. Ambridge and nephew of Mrs. Levi Bishop of Detroit.

Wednesday January 30, 1867 - Married - At the residence of Moses Finch Jan. 19th by J. F. Stroud, Esq., John Finch to Mrs. Rebecca M. Mead, both of Woodhull.

Wednesday April 24, 1867 - Married - Feb. 9th by Rev. D. F. Judson, James Morris of Williamsport, Pa., to Harriet A. Holmes of Addison.

Married - Also by the same March 21st, Wm. H. Templer of Schenectady to Elizabeth Stewart of Addison.

Married - Also by the same April 4th James Wright to Mary Derand, both of Addison.

Married - Also by the same April 10th Llewellyn A. Swartwood of Cameron to Harriet Lanphear of Addison.

Married - Also by the same April 23d James H. Park to Miss E. A. Reynolds, both of Addison.

Wednesday May 8, 1867 - Married - April 26th by Rev. J. M. Harlow at the residence of the bride's father, Mr. A. C. Waggoner of Wheeler to Miss C. C. Wagner, both of Bath.

Died - In Hornellsville on 30th ult. of paralysis of the brain, Thomas J. Reynolds, aged 66 years.

Wednesday May 15, 1867 - Married.- At Addison on April 30th by Rev. D. F. Judson, Wm. A. Falkner to Julia Fraser, both of Knoxville, Pa.

Died - At Avoca April 30th of heart disease, Anna M., wife of Ira C. Williams and mother of Francis Williams, Esq., of Corning, aged 54 years.

Died - In Masonville, Delaware Co., N.Y., on 3d inst. Darius Smith, Esq., father of Justin M. Smith of Corning, aged 85 years.

Wednesday May 22, 1867 - Married - By Rev. W. L. Rogers April 23 at the bride's residence in Greene, Chenango Co., N.Y., Cyrus J. Reynolds of Addison and Jennie Gray.

Wednesday May 29, 1867 - Married - In Bath at the parsonage of the M. E. church by Rev. A. F. Morey, May 16th Francis A. Dickinson of Thurston to Minerva Jack of Risingville.

Married - At the residence of the bride's parents near Kanona on 1st inst. by Rev. J. T. Canfield, John D. Beecher of Avoca and Ellen Case.

Wednesday June 19, 1867 - Married - At Addison on 16th inst. by Rev. D. F. Judson at his residence, John Tracy and Lucilla Young, all of Addison.

Married - In Painted Post on June 18th by Rev. S. Nichols, James T. Dudley, Elmira and Ida, dau. of A. H. Bronson, Esq., of the former place.

Died - At Somerville, Tioga Co., Pa., June 8th Capt. Thomas Murray, formerly of Corning, aged about 60 years.

Died - In Corning June 7th, Mr. David Lane, aged about 60 years.

Wednesday June 26, 1867 – Married – In Hornellsville on 18th inst. by Rev. C. M. Gardner, Wm. F. Hyde and Helen M. Anderson, all of Hornellsville.
Married – In Fredonia on 12th inst. by Rev. Charles Arey, A. H. Judson, Esq., of Fredonia and Sarah A. Fairman, dau. of S. B. Fairman of Elmira.
Married – In the Presbyterian church at Painted Post June 13th by Rev. Dr. Wakeman, Albert R. Sayles, of the firm of Howell & Sayles, and Fanny McMullen, dau. of James McMullen of Corning.
Died – In Penn Yan June 6th, C. Adell Welles, wife of S. H. Welles, P. M., aged 34 years 8 months 23 days.
Died – In Corning June 15th Charles H. Austin (formerly of Co. E. 141st Regt. N.Y. Vols.), son of Richard Austin, aged 22 years.

Wednesday July 10, 24, August 14, October 2, 16, December 4, 11, 1867 no deaths or marriages. November 20, 1867 missing issue.

Wednesday July 3, 1867 – Died – Thomas Phillips Saturday morning last in a wood sawing accident at the Erie Railway Company depot, in his 67th year. He reared a large family, of whom four daus. and two sons are in California.

Wednesday July 17, 1867 – Married – In Bath July 8th by Rev. S. F. Colt of Troy, Pa., Augustus S. Hooker, editor of *The Northern Tier Gazette*, Troy, Pa., and Anna Donahe, adopted dau. of P. S. Donahe, Esq., of Bath.
Died – In Addison July 12th, Rosa Belle, infant dau. of Wm. H. and Mary J. Orr, aged 7 months 28 days.

Wednesday July 31, 1867 – Married – In this village on 18th inst. at the residence of the bride's mother by Rev. A. Wood, Oliver S. Robinson of Corning and Katie M. Bliss of Addison.
Married – In this village on 4th inst. by the same, Stephen H. Sales of Bath and Eliza Ann Wright of Thurston.
Married – At the residence of Sally Concord in Thurston July 7th by Rev. S. M. Merritt, James Johnson of Bath and Mary Calkins of Thurston.
Married – On Saturday July 13 by Rev. Isaac Easterbrooks, Orva Hendrick, Esq., and Bella Clark, all of Hornby.

Married - In Caton June 30th by Rev. S. D. Merrick, Henry D. Cram of Meadville, Pa., late of Caton and Eva A. Veazie, dau. of Stephen Veazie, Esq.

Married - At Caton July 3d by Wm. D. Gilbert, Esq., George W. Harris of Southport, Chemung Co., N.Y., and Samantha Widger of Caton.

Died - In Knoxville (in the town of Corning[sic]) July 18th, Wm. D. Rutherford, aged 48 years 2 months 22 days.

Died - In Middleville, Mich. July 8th of whooping cough, LeBlanche, dau. of Dr. G. W. and A. A. Matteson (late of Knoxville, Pa.) aged 1 year 3 months.

Wednesday August 7, 1867 - Died - Monday July 29th, Enos G. Willard, of Cameron Mills. He leaves a wife and children. He was buried with Masonic honors.

Wednesday August 21, 1867 - Died - In this village Aug. 20th of heart disease, Martha H., wife of Rollin B. Smith, aged 34 years.

Wednesday August 28, 1867 - Died - Albert Smith of Hornellsville was killed by a train at Santee's Switch, three miles west of Cameron on Saturday last.

Wednesday September 4, 1867 - Married - In this village Aug. 28th at the residence of Dr. F. R. Wagner by Rev. Albert Wood, Lawrence B. Millington of Glenns Falls, N.Y., and Susan Amelia _____ (bottom of paper missing).

Wednesday September 11, 1867 - Married - At Woodhull Sept. 7th by Elder Brooks, Albert Colgrove and Clara Leach, dau. of I. C. Leach, Esq.

Wednesday September 18, 1867 - Married - At the Baptist parsonage Corning Sept. 7th by Rev. J. D. Barnes, Wm. W. Nicholson and Cora Pratt, both of Bath.

Married - At Centreville (town of Corning[sic]) by Rev. T. K. Beecher on 9th inst., John K. Ford of Campbell and Marilla A. Whitenack of Centreville.

Married - In Prattsburgh August 25th by J. Partridge, Esq., Amos Eldridge of Italy, Yates Co., and Huldah Johnson.

Married - Sept. 4th in St. Thomas Church, Bath, by Rev. O. R. Howard, Charles Frederick Carrington of Philadelphia and Mary Somerville, dau. of Rev. O. R. Howard.

Married - In the M. E. church in Bath Sept. 4th by Rev. A. F. Morey, Rev. David W. Gates, pastor of the M. E.

church in Merchantville, to Marian H. Purdy, dau. of Charles Purdy of Bath.

Died - In Bath Aug. 23, Mrs. Peggy Sharp, aged 56 years.

Died - In Bath Aug. 27, Bertha Shults, aged six months.

Died - In Bath Aug. 29, Emma Webster, aged 15 months.

Died - In Bath Aug. 30, Carrie B. Perkins, aged 4 years.

Died - In Bath on 2d inst., Caroline, wife of S. D. Hunter, aged 41 years.

Died - In Bath Sept. 3d, Charlotte, wife of D. M. Coss, aged 48 years.

Died - In Bath Sept 2d, Minnie Coss, aged 6 years.

Died - In Bath Sept. 5th, John Magee, only child of A. S. and Mary Howell, aged 14 months.

Died - In Bath Sept. 5th, Rose Williamson, aged 4 years.

Died - In Bath Sept. 8th of consumption, Elizabeth Simmons, aged 19 years.

Wednesday September 25, 1867 - Married - In this village on 19th inst. by Rev. Albert Wood, Robert Richards of Caton and Helen Howe of Beechers Island, Pa.

Wednesday October 9, 1867 - Died - In Lincoln, Placer Co., California on 13th Sept. of Cholera morbus, Louisa L., wife of Henry Whittenhall, formerly of this place.

Wednesday October 23, 1867 - Died - In Binghamton Oct. 10th at the residence of her son, Claudius B. Pratt, Cynthia W., wife of Joel B. Pratt and mother of the editor of the *Corning Journal*, aged 73 years.

Wednesday October 30, 1867 - Died - At Belle Plain, Minnesota, Aug. 23d of consumption, Fannie M. (Smith) Hyde, former preceptress of Union School at Bath until her marriage, and preceptress of Addison Academy until her health failed. She & her husband left for Minnesota July last. She graduated in the class of 1860 from the college. She will be interred at Addison.

Died - At Whitesville, N.Y., on Oct. 15th of gastric fever, Anna True of Addison, aged 21 years.

Wednesday November 6, 1867 - Married - On the 29th Oct. at the residence of the bride's father in Rathbone by Rev. Albert Wood, John E. McCaig(sic) of Penn Yan, Yates Co., and Sarah Jane Ward of Rathbone.

Wednesday November 13, 1867 - Married - At the Episcopal Church in this village on 13th inst. by Rev. Albert Wood, Edward Ransom Wheeler and Mary Isabel Murray, both of Beloit, Wisconsin, Oct. 30th by Rev. J. Harlow, Henry Braught and Sarah Hotchkiss, all of Bath.

Married - Oct. 31st by Rev. A. F. Morey at Mrs. Fletcher's, Eugene C. Allen to Rachel Havens, all of Bath.

Married - In Hornellsville on 16th inst. by Rev. Fillmore, Robert B. Dawson to Sarah Amidon, both of that village.

Died - Mr. David Turk of this village on Monday afternoon last, of consumption.

Wednesday November 27, 1867 - Married - At the residence of Isaac Jacobus in Bath Oct. 30th by Rev. H. F. Cochrane, Mr. E. Clinton VanGelder and Julia A. Jacobus.

Married - Also in Bath Oct. 31st by the same, Jeremiah Fagens and Sarah Gardner, all of Bath.

Married - At Bath Nov. 14th by Rev. J. N. Harlow, Cyrus Ballard of Tyrone, to Catharine A. Knickerbocker of Orange, Schuyler County.

Married - At Bath Nov. 13th by Rev. A. F. Morey, W. H. Baker of Corning to Jennie Van Zine of St. Louis.

Married - At the residence of the bride's father Nov. 5th by Rev. M. Barker, F. D. Robbins Jr. editor of the *Dansville Express* to Miss M. L. Knapp, dau. of H. T. Knapp of Ossian.

Married - At the residence of the bride's father in Avoca Oct. 10th by Rev. N. N. Beers, Willis J. Walters to Lisetta Griswold.

Married - At the residence of the bride's father Nov. 12th by Rev. Oliver Crane, S. H. Ferenbaugh, foreman of the Corning Journal office to Miss Tena E. Patchin, dau. of D. L. W. Patchin of Carbondale, Pa.

Died - At Hornellsville on 8th inst., of scarlett fever, Lizzie, only dau. of Jacob and Lizzie Schue, aged 6 years 9 months 21 days.

Died - At Hornellsville on 9th inst. of consumption, Caroline S., wife of Hon. Horace Bemis, aged 43 years.

Wednesday December 18, 1867 - Married - In this village Dec. 14th by Rev. Sutherland, Mr. J. S. Reynolds of DeKalb, Illinois, and Matilda Jones of this village.

Married - In Bath Dec. 5th by Rev. A. F. Morey, Wm. H. Vunk of Avoca and Maggie Spraker of Bath.

Married - At Coopers Plains Nov. 24th by J. A. Shults, Esq., Wm. A. Benedict to Matilda A. Crane, all of this village.

Married - In Italy, Yates County on 5th inst. by Rev. J. Knapp, Byron Hayes of Prattsburgh to Margaret Kennedy of Italy.
Married - In Hornellsville Nov. 23d by Rev. Waldo, Albert S. McGowan and Adelaide E. Stainer of Hornellsville.
Died - In Arkport on 25th ult., Jabish Lampheare, age 74 years.
Died - In Pultney on Dec. 1st, Noah Hill in the 25th year of his age.

Wednesday December 25, 1867; January 1, 22, February 5, 12, 19, 26, March 18, 1868 no deaths or marriages.

Wednesday January 8, 1868 - Died - In this village Dec. 30th, Elizabeth, wife of Simon Brown aged 75.

Wednesday January 15, 1868 - Died - On Jan. 8th at his residence in Nelson, Tioga Co., Pa., Harvey Andrews in the 67th year of his age.
Died - In Janesville, Wisconsin, Dec. 1, 1867, of typhoid fever, E. DeWitt Bostwick formerly of this village in the 22d year of his age.

Wednesday January 29, 1868 - Died - John Jacob Astor in New York City Friday a week last, aged 65 years.

Wednesday March 4, 1868 - Married - At the residence of the bride's father at Covington, Chenango Co., by Rev. A. J. Bael(sic), Charles H. Jones of this village to Helen L. Miles of Covington.
Married - At the church of the Incarnation, New York City, Col. Fiziot(sic) F. Sheapard formerly of the 51st N.Y.V. and of Gov. Morgan's staff, and Maggie Louise Vanderbilt, eldest dau. of Wm. H. Vanderbilt, Esq., and granddau. of Commodore Vanderbilt, all of this city, yesterday.
Died - In Rathbone Feb. 28th, William Barron in his 78th year.
Died - In Rathbone March 2d, Mrs. Isaac Mowger.

Wednesday March 11, 1868 - Married - In Bath Feb. 24th at the U. S. Hotel by Rev.A . F. Morey, James P. Welton to Amanda Smith, both of Cameron.
Married - By the same at the Park Hotel Feb. 26th, Charles L. Bailey of Hammondsport to Lydia Backus of Savona.

Married - By the same Feb. 28th at the house of John Lagross, Thomas Griffin to Ann E. Jones, both of Rathbone.

INDEX

---ARNEE, Mary B 21
---AY, John 21
ABBOTT, Ann 91 Ann D 57
   Caroline 45 Martha Matilda 45
   Moses 45
ABEL, David O 74 Ellen T 118
   Hannah 6 Rhoda 74 Sarah F 70
   Wm H 70
ABER, Aaron 62 Elizabeth Ann 62
   Henry G 90 Jane 39 Nancy L
   90 Samantha B 63 T J 63
ABLE, Eleanora 93 John 93
ABNER, Jane 35
ADAMS, A 58 75 Mary 75 Samuel
   H 54 Theodora 94
ADSHEAD, Samuel 114
ADSIT, Esther Jane 27 Martin 27
AIKEN, Daniel 37
AINSWORTH, Dewit C 38 Isaac
   19 Sarah L 29 Willard 26
ALBEE, Catherine M 126 Eleazer
   92 Eunice 92 Stephen T 126
ALDEN, Benjamin 54 Jane 65
   Lewis 54 S W 43 46 51 55
ALDERMAN, Emma 79 Janett 40
   O P 71 73 77 79 80 83-85 93
   96 117
ALDRICH, June 14 Leonard 127
   Rev 18 S H 100
ALDRIDGE, Fenner S 77 Martha
   77 S H 101
ALEXANDER, Susan M 47
ALLEN, Ann 8 Asaph 71 Caroline
   16 Catherine 48 Eugene C 135
   Ex-sheriff 128 Fernando 120
   Helen 120 Hubart 8 Jane 77
   Lydia 8 Marietta 71 Rachel 71
   135 S W 51 Samuel 8 Samuel
   H 77 Samuel T D 48 Stephen
   16 Vestus D 71
ALLERTON, Ann 5 Townsend 5

ALLIS, Elijah 111 Emily O 111
   Josiah 53
AMBRIDGE, Wm (Mrs) 130
AMES, Adaline H 92 E Howard 92
   Howard 2d 120 Sarah 126
AMEY, Catherine 116 Frederick
   116
AMIDON, Betsey Maria 66 Lucy
   55 Sarah 135 Shepherd 55 66
ANDERSON, Helen M 132
ANDREWS, Harvey 136 W C 90
ANDRUS, A C 82 Ambrose F 93
   Catharine 60 Permelia 93
ANDRUSS, F 12 W 12
ANGEL, Diantha 130
ANSON, Emily 125 Jonathan W
   125
ANTHONY, Charles E 49 Miss 52
AOOD, Caroline C 78
AREY, Charles 132
ARFORD, Maria 96
ARKELL, Christine Heloise 83
   James 83
ARMSTRONG, Ackerson 29
   Andrew 90 Edward J 78 Eliza
   29 John D 128 Lydia A 90
   Mary L 78 Sarah Ann 128
ARNOLD, Edwin P 103 Lyman 60
   Mary Jane 60 Melissa 103
   Oliver 89 Phebe C 7 S H 21
ASER, Elizabeth 18
ASHLEY, Harriet M 39
ASHWORTH, J 67
ASPELL, Phebe 57 Richard 57
ASTOR, John Jacob 136
ATHERTON, Margaret M 126
   Maria R 108 Thomas R 126
ATKINS, Rev 15
ATWATER, Rev 21
AULLS, E 86 Ephraim 68 Hannah
   56 Lydia Ann 86 Mary 68

AULLS (continued)
Sophia 24
AUSTIN, Charles 126 Charles H 132 Hannah 126 Richard 132
AVERELL, Helen C 117 Oscar J 117
AVOCA, Rowland (Mrs) 81
BABBITT, Rev 16
BABCOCK, Brayton 21 Caroline E 11 Catherine 43 Esq 56 Eunice 21 James 43 John C 11 Phoebe A 114 William 10 Wm 10
BABCOOK, William 17
BACKER, Delphine 130
BACKMAN, Edmund 16 Mary 16 Sarah 16
BACKUS, Lydia 136
BACON, Angeline 5 Edward 4 Lucretia 77 Mary 4 45 Noah B 25 Ruth Amy 25 Simeon 5
BADGER, Theodore P 116
BAEL, A J 136
BAILEY, Charles L 136 Eliza 5 Elzina 111 George S 96 Hildah 88 Huldah 87 Lydia 136 Sally Elizabeth 97 Sarah Jane 96 Sylvester S 97
BAILY, Lorinda 61 Richard 61 Thomas 61
BAIN, David 35 Eliza 35 36
BAKER, Charlotte 74 Edward B 74 Elizabeth A 111 Franklin 42 Hannah 40 Jennie 135 John 105 Julia 15 Mary 42 Mary Ann 105 Miss 48 Noah 48 Samuel 15 Sarah Ann 77 W H 135
BALCOM, B F 93 116 Col 106
BALDIN, Helen 103
BALDWIN, Bella 103 Bella Bliss 120 Catherine 22 Emma L 96 Henry 103 120 James 95 96 James (Mrs) 123 L Jr 103 Lydia 8 Pamelia 125 Rev 8 Rufus 125 William J 22
BALL, A M 54 Charles 119 Harriet 119
BALLARD, Alpheus R 61 Catharine A 135 Cyrus 135 Emeline 61
BANCROFT, Esther 85 R 85
BANKS, Mr 124

BARBER, Lucinda 25 Melancton 25
BARDEEN, Mary C 40
BARKER, M 135 Mary E 85 Robert 6
BARNARD, Frederick 116 Mary 5
BARNES, J D 132 Susan 107
BARNEY, Clarence S 14 Jonathan 78 Nathan 14 Nelson 68 Nelson P 79 Philance T 68 Polly Ann 79
BARR, Ada K 110
BARRET, Cornelius 49
BARRETT, Harriet 49 Lovina A 102 Seth W 102
BARRON, William 136
BARROWS, L A 27
BARRY, Honora 89
BARTHOLOMEW, Justus 25 Nancy E 70
BARTLETT, Julius 65 Montgomery R 10 Sarah E 10
BARTON, Amanda 81 E P 104 Fanny M 79 Frances M 104 Polly 34 Sarah 81 Thomas 81
BASSETT, Rev 8
BASSIER, P M 34
BATCHELDER, Demaris 29 Edwin J 25 Joseph 29 Sally 25
BATES, Edward F 122 Flora Melissa 119 Rufus 119
BAUTER, Betsey 86
BAXTER, Caleb 30 H M 118 Louisa 100 Peter 100 Sophia 30
BEACH, R M 65 William R 117
BEACHER, Susan 50
BEAGLE, Mary Ann 82 Richard 82
BEALD, Catharine 79
BEALES, J Sylvester 92 Sophia 92
BEAN, Isaac 46 Toby (Mrs) 94
BEBOUT, John 114
BECKTAL, Wm 114
BECKWITH, A B 22 Caroline 33 Griffin 93 Hannah 11 Ira Z 109 Joseph 11 Margaret E 93 Martha C 22
BEEBE, Almira 24 Daniel D 24 Rev 21

BEECHER, Ellen 131 John D 131 T K 132
BEEMAN, Adelaide 114 Almira 114 Almon 7 114 Elizabeth 53 Elmira 7 William M 53
BEEMER, Maria E 48 Thomas F 48
BEERS, N N 109 135
BEGOLE, Devan 58 M C 58
BELDIN, Comfort E 75
BELL, Polly 15
BELLAS, George 35 Jane 35
BELLINGER, Margaret 87 Nancy 68
BELLIS, George C 39 Jane 39
BELLOWS, Helen Mar 85 M B 85 Mary Jane 85
BEMIS, Caroline S 135 Horace 135 Rev 14
BENEDICT, C Elizabeth 79 David E 85 E 100 Edwin 87 Harriet 85 Margaret S 75 Mary E 82 Mary Jane 70 Matilda 135 Wm A 135
BENHAM, Sidney 107
BENJAMIN, Maria 40 Samuel 40 81
BENNET, Amanda 76 Benjamin 76 G A 87 H 87
BENNETT, Ann 8 48 Eliza 64 Elizabeth S 65 H 58 126 Helen 104 Hiram 64 Huldah A 59 Jeremiah 8 Lydia R 77 M 127 Thankful 81 Trumbull L 65 71
BENNITT, D N 20 Marilla 20
BENTON, Charles S 80 Elizabeth B 80 G R 90 Lydia A 90
BERKY, A 37
BERRY, Chas H 69 Gertrude 120 Phebe 92
BESLEY, Mary 84 Samuel 7 84 Susan T 7
BETTS, Thaddeus 20
BIDDLE, Nicholas 33
BIDWELL, E R 54 Eli Jr 38 Eli Sr 59 George H 85 Harriet 54 Louisa 38 Mary Elizabeth 85 Sarah M 68 William E 68
BIGELOW, Jacob 64
BILES, Fannie K 113 Hezekiah S 37 L 27 Lewis 113 Olive S 37 38

BILLINGEON, Sarah J 102
BILLINGER, Margaret 87
BILLINGHURST, Lucien 85 Mary Jane 85
BILLINGTON, M L 102
BIRD, George J 55 Nancy 55
BIRDSALL, H H 16 Maria D 21 Ransom 21
BISHOP, Charity 13 Charles 13 Johanna 108 Levi (Mrs) 130 Lucrietta 21 Mary 62 Nathan 108 Robert H 21
BIXBY, Alanson 11 Cornelia 11 H W 130 Phebe T 56 Simon 56
BLADES, J H 109 John H 109
BLAKELEY, Charlotte 77 George 77
BLAKESLEE, Bradley 93
BLANCHARD, James 109 Maria N 109 Samuel S 67
BLATCHFORD, John 5
BLISS, Ann 89 Bella 103 Charles 89 Katie M 132
BLODGET, Mary 29
BLOOD, Allen 11 Amelia I 40 Asa 37 57 Capt 57 59 Charles 46 66 Charles B 46 Ellen 66 Indiana 37 59 Lucretta 15 Rebecca P 57
BLOODGOOD, Francis 19
BLYN, Nye 129
BOARDMAN, Eliza Ann 129
BOATWRIGHT, Catharine A 127 James H 127
BODINE, John C 60
BOGARDUS, Mary Jane 27 Richard 27
BOLYEN, Elizabeth A 116
BONHAM, Charles 9 Eliza 24 Josepha B 124 Mary B 9 Robert T 48 Sarah 27 William 24
BOOTH, Angie 119 S A J 119
BORDEN, George Isaac 26 Isaac 26
BOSTWICK, E DeWitt 136 Elmira 7 H W 57 Mercy 57 Rev 6 11 13 W W 15 18
BOVIER, Hannah 126
BOWEN, Ira 27 Malvina 27
BOWLBY, James 36 Katurah D 36

BOWLSBY, Catherine 19
BOYD, Eunice 100 John 100 Joseph 14 Theron 114
BRACE, Alvira 55 Jesse P 82 Seneca V 84 Wm B 55
BRACKER, Susan 50
BRADFORD, James 9
BRADLEY, A 107 Sturges 59 Wm 67
BRAMBLE, Ezra C 33 George E 94 Lydia G 33 Mary 94 Samantha B 63
BRAUGHT, Henry 135 Sarah 135
BRAUNSCHWEIG, Maria E 37
BRECK, A Y 65 Elizabeth 65 George W 49 87 Joseph 65 71 Marcia Ann 49 R E 87
BREWSTER, Gilbert B 129 Helen 126 Orvel 126 Willie 129
BRIDGEMAN, Ann E 89 Otis 89
BRIGGS, Alanson E 63 Betsey E 63 Cecelia B 9 Lewis 99 Mr 36 Wm 9
BRIGHAM, A 58 Eugene 46
BRIMMER, Louisa V 116
BRINK, Harriet A 38 James L 38 Samuel 126 Susannah C 68
BRINKERHOFF, Caroline C 18 Jacob 18
BROCKMAN, S M 93
BRONG, James 94 Silly 94
BRONSON, A H 131 C Elizabeth 79 Charles S 79 E 36 George A 75 Ida 131 Ira 15 Margaret S 75 Phebe 61 Rev 38 W A 110
BROOKS, A L 69 Birdsey 43 Elder 132 Elizabeth 62 Eunice 92 Henry 43 Jane 100 Mary E 127 Mary J 12 R D 103 110 R P 94 William 127
BROTHER, Cornelia Pratt 85 Henry 85 Rebecca P 73
BROTZMAN, Charity 13 Martha Ann 112
BROWN, A C 23 Alva E 68 Betsey 16 Betsey B 119 Byron G 117 Calcina E 70 Charles C 129 Christine Heloise 83 Cora Agnes 129 Cornelia M 121 D F 91 Dr 114 Elizabeth 74 136 Elnathan G 16 F B 121 Frank B 115 Hannah C 51 Huldah A 117

BROWN (continued)
Ira 35 123 J J 82 Jane 80 Jane E 23 Jennie E 130 John 50 105 John N 130 Julia F 127 Lucius M 7 M 17 Margaret C 105 Maria 82 Mariah Windsor 123 Milicent 92 Myron W 70 Nellie M 115 P E 38 Philander 47 Rachel Elizabeth 50 Richard 82 Roby 129 S S 36 Sarah H 68 Sarah M 68 Simon 136 Susan T 7 William A 92 Wm 47
BROWNAL, Rev 28
BROWNELL, John 17
BROWNSON, Elisha 6
BROWNWELL, Sally Ann 17
BRUNDAGE, Andrew J 91 Caroline 101 Caroline E 50 Emily 72 Frances A 91 James 17 James L 101 Mary 42 Salina 34 Wm 42
BRYANT, Caroline E 11 Dr 11 Mary 68
BUCHANON, Emma E 130
BUCK, Catherine A 16 E A 16 E H 112 118
BUCKINGHAM, Harriet 13
BULL, Harvey 13 Lucinda 13
BULLARD, Angeline A 73 Angeline Augusta 81 Hannah Ann 75 Joel 75 O A 73 Otis A 81
BULLIN, Jane 117
BULLOCK, John 112 Julia 112
BUNDY, Charlotte J 41 Elizabeth 87 George W 79 Hannah 79 Harriet O 57 Nathaniel 57 87 Peter 41
BURDETT, John 32
BURDICE, L 95 Mr 95
BURGHER, Benjamin 18
BURK, Horace 39 Sarah Ann 39
BURKIRK, W 12
BURLEY, Jane 84 O F 84
BURNHAM, George W 72 Joseph K 103 Sarah Jane 103
BURNSIDE, James F 19
BURR, Aaron 34
BURROUGHS, Stephen 19
BURTON, Mary 16 William 16
BUSH, Gideon D 19 Huldah A 59 John 59
BUTLER, Caroline 126

BUTLER (continued)
Caroline L 28 Joseph 28 Laura
B 53 Prudence R 78
BUTTOLPH, M 94
BUTTS, Catherine 78 D B 10 17
Wm E 78
BUZZLE, Rev 8
CAHILL, Mrs 71
CAIN, Joseph L 60 Nancy 60
CALKINS, Abigail 50 Emily 48
John C 50 John K 39 Mary 132
N S 110 Philander 48 Ripley 12
CALL, Levi N 95 Mary 95
CAMERON, Charles 24 Christina
8 Eliza 56 Jane 24
CAMP, Abigail 8
CAMPBELL, Charles W 55 83
Fowler 74 George 15 Harriet 83
J 79 Laura 39 Mary 111 Rev 92
Robert 74 Robert Sr 55 Sarah
33 Thomas 111
CANFIELD, J T 131
CAREY, S 59
CARPENTER, Charles V 116
Francis A 117 Huldah 116
Uriah A 117
CARR, Alvin D 118 Amos Jr 129
Asaph 38 C C 55 Cordelia 38
Harriet 118 Henrietta 116 Rev
55
CARRINGTON, Charles Frederick
133 Ellen 83 Mary 133 Russell
83
CARRUTHERS, Cameron 36
Katurah D 36
CARTER, John H 104
CARYELL, Sarah 113
CASE, Adaline 41 Ellen 131
George 64 Harriet 64 J 37 87
John Jr 41
CASK, Sarah A 127
CASTER, Catharine 58 Polly 76
CASTOR, Louisa J 127 William
127
CHADWICK, Jabez 33 34
CHAMBERLAIN, Angeline 5
Henry W 5 Joshua 52 William
W 88
CHAMBERS, John 38
CHAMPLAIN, Sarah 111
CHANDLER, C N 85 91

CHAPIN, Adaline 100 Addison 83
Ann 5 Elizabeth 65 Ezra 78
Joseph 65 Lucy 61 Rachel 83
CHAPMAN, Abigal 89 Amanda M
67 Andrew F 38 Emma N 128
Frances C 115 Geo H 67 Henry
115 J 69 J S 13 Laura 42 Mary
E 38 Nelson 93 Rev 40 Ros-
well R 59 Silas 89 Wm 93 99
CHARLES, Esther Jane 27
CHASE, A 18 A B 68 86 Catherine
94 Charles 57 E 102 Edward C
90 Elizabeth B 68 Frances 69
Hannah M 90 Harriet O 57
Helen 104 Isaac N 104 L D 102
M Cordelia 86 Melissa R 102
Peter 22 Polly 45 Sarah 22
Solomon 13 Tripheny 13
CHATMAN, Rev 36
CHEESEMAN, Maria 13
CHEEVY, Louisa 61 Walter S 61
CHENEY, Sarah L 29 Walter S 29
CHICHESTER, D 109
CHISOM, David M 80 Jane 80
CHRISTJOHN, Stephen 107 Susan
107
CHRISTLER, Mariah 21
CHUBBUCK, Frances B 37 John
37
CHURCH, Catharine 60 Catharine
A 90 Edwin F 60 90 Helen 120
CLARK, Bella 132 Caroline E 94
Clarissa 36 Climena 14 Daniel
4 Elder 24 George 84 H R 105
Hannah Mariah 36 Hiram 79
Hiram C 40 Isaac P 127 Janet
Cameron 84 Laura 79 Mary C
40 Mr 28 Nettie 129 Phebe 57
Sarah A 127 Sarah F 105
Thomas Sr 57 Wm C 38
CLARKE, Eliza A 62 Jas C 62
Theodore F 62
CLASON, G W 12 Harriet 10 17
Henry P 10 17 N 12 Sarah J 75
CLAYSON, Adaline 77 Adeline 86
Hiram 86
CLEEVES, Sarah 93
CLEMENTS, Catharine A 127
CLEVELAND, Henry 37
CLINTON, E C 110 S D 111 116
118 119

CLISDELL, Elisa 47 Hannah 72 William 72
CLIZBE, Joseph 54 Phebe 54
CLYDE, Mary 111
COATS, Leonard 70 Leonard G 40 41 Nancy W 41 Nancy Whiting 70
COBB, Julia 15 Rev 33 Zenos 15
COBURN, L D (Mrs) 122 Phebe 58
COCHRANE, H F 135
CODDINGTON, E A 127 Jennie 127
COLBERT, George 31 Peter 31 Thomas 31 William 31
COLBURN, Adolphus 93 Johanna 108
COLCORD, Emily 48
COLE, C 38 Caleb 8 Franklin 36 Hannah Maria 36 Hezekiah M 20 Sophronia 20
COLGROVE, Albert 132 Clara 132
COLLIER, Catharine V 71 Jane M 12 Mary 71 Richard 70 71
COLLINGWOOD, Elizabeth 54
COLLINS, Margaret 45 Martin 41
COLT, S F 132
COLWELL, Benjamin 123 Caroline 89 Sally M 123
COMFORT, Eli 76 Sarah Elizabeth 76
COMSTOCK, A L 4 Augusta R 124 M 108 S E 4 Wm 124
CONCORD, Sally 132
CONGDON, S L 115 118 119 124
CONKLIN, Ambrose 67 Lucy E 67 Mary 22 Mary Elizabeth 35 Wm 29
CONNER, A J 102 Alexander M 27 J H 102 James 50 W Franklin 102
CONNERS, Patrick 120
CONNOR, Elizabeth 6
CONTARANAN, Samuel 5
CONVERSE, M M 122
COOK, C 46 Constant 25 32 Edwin 4 Eliza 24 Elizabeth 26 Ellen C 29 Fayette F 111 George 27 Henry H 47 Jennie 127 John M 32 M Adaline 39 M P 127 Margaret 84 Mary 47 111 Robert W 60 Samuel 124

COOK (continued) Sarah 27 William A 29
COOLEY, Jesse 87 L J 64 Mary 87 Mary Walbridge 64
COOPER, Daniel 41 Emeline 61 Hannah R 50 Harriet 84 John Jr 117 Myanda 84 Thomas W 117
COPLE, Sarah Jane 103
CORBITT, Elizabeth S 93
CORIELL, Luke 26 Martha 26
CORNELL, D B 11 Eliza 92 Elizabeth 10 Francis R E 92 H 12 Mary Waxaville 92
CORNING, Alexander 37 Alexander H 37 Erastus 37 Indiana 37
CORNUE, J 84 John 84 Myanda 84
CORNWELL, Elizabeth Ann 62
CORRELL, Elder 9
CORRY, W 35
CORSE, Luther S 108 Martha 108
CORSEN, Rev 46
CORSON, L H 47 51 58 M 43 Rev 42 56 57
CORT, Sarah A 36
COSS, Charlotte 134 D M 134 Harriet 8 Minnie 134 Minor 8
COSTEN, Frederick 13 Nancy 13
COTTON, Edward 54 Henry G 4 Mary 4 Phoebe 54 Wm Henry 54
COUNTRYMAN, A F 128 Catherine C 128 Helen C 128 Solomon 128
COURTRIGHT, Sarah L 90
COVEL, Jacob 26 Mary Ann 26
COVELL, Cynthia A 77 Delilah 76
COVERT, A E 75
COVIL, Mary 41 Willis 41
COWELL, Henry 90 Mary M 90
COWLEY, C 96 C (Mrs) 129 Emma L 96
COY, Hannah A 10 Levi 10
CRAFT, Cecelia 127 Isaac 127 Lizzie 127 Rachel 31
CRAM, Eva A 133 Henry D 133
CRANDAL, Mary 126 Walter 126
CRANE, Clarissa E 111 Francis L 109 Helena Ann 59 Joseph N 59 Mary 126 Mary A 109

CRANE (continued)
  Matilda A 135 Oliver 135 Sarah 118
CRAWFORD, Emily 72 Harriet 38 Nathaniel 72
CRESSY, Rev 23 25
CROCKER, Edmund 118 Jane R 66 72 Sarah V 118 Wickham R 66 72
CRONAN, John 126
CROSBY, Cyrus 119 Elizabeth 86 Lucinda 52 Mary 71 Sarah Emily 86 William 86
CROSS, Asa 19 Catherine 19 Samuel 75 Sarah J 117
CROUCH, Caleb 21 Mary 21 Richard 21
CROWL, Catherine M 126 George W 126
CRUTTENDEN, Eunice 37
CULLEN, Thomas 129
CUNNINGHAM, Thomas 89
CURRAN, Emily 125
CURRY, W F 39
CURTIS, Alvin H 70 Amos 83 Caroline 100 George W 42 Isabelle 42 Jane M 28 Josiah 100 Lucy Maria 83 Sophrona 70 Wm 124
CURTISS, Elmira 37 Wm 37
CUSHING, Martha 26
CUSHION, Margaret E 93
CUSTO, Mary 41
DABOLL, Auren 29 Mary 29
DAGGART, Nancy 55
DALLEY, Sally Elizabeth 97
DANA, Anderson 74 Ann Eliza 71 Brazilla 71
DANFORTH, Rev 26
DANIELS, Catharine A 24 Elizabeth 102 Kendrick 67 Norman 24 Sarah H 67 T W 46
DARLING, Mr 52
DATES, George H 115 John Y 110
DAVENPORT, Eliza 56 Ira 56
DAVIDSON, David 63 Eliza 59
DAVIS, Cornelius 12 Dexter 91 Elizabeth 91 H H 127 John 12 Louisa J 127 Mary 87 Mary E 125 Ortha A 80 Rev 27 51 Thomas C 125

DAWSON, Launcelot 86 Mary M 90 R B 96 Robert B 135 Sarah 135
DAY, Mary 28 S M 96 S Mills 96
DEAN, John 105 Mary Ann 105
DEARLOVE, Polly 76 William 76
DECK, Betsey 13 Daniel I 12 Eliza 12
DECKER, Hannah Ann 75 Hezekiah 58 J Rensselaer 75 Jane 58 Sidney S 57
DEGOLIA, Frances 53
DELAMATER, Adelaide M 122
DELAND, Jerry 129
DELEVAN, Emilie W 3 George D 3
DELONG, Harry 22 Mary Ann 22
DEMAREST, Wm 110
DENHAM, Francis 58 Martha O 58
DENNIS, Burnette 114 Fidelia Jane 11 Franklin 6 Martha 37 Martha E 6 Rodney 114 S B 89 Samuel F 10 Sarah S 10
DENNISTON, Judge 61
DENSMORE, Wilson 82
DEPEW, N A 95 Rev 108
DEPUE, Charles Vine 130 J L 48 J S 14 26 77
DEPUY, Mary S 129
DERAND, Mary 131
DERVEL, Daniel 37 Lucia Ann 37
DEVOE, Arvilla 6 Nellie M 115
DEWEY, Harriet Y 23 L H 23
DEWITT, Daniel 36 Eliza 36 Emily J 127 Harriet 8 Jacob C 127
DEWOLFE, A 127 Mara E 127
DICEY, Elmer C 92 Emeline 92
DICKER, R E 52
DICKERSON, Eunice 109
DICKINSON, A B C 52 Angeline 24 Charles Wesley 6 David 24 Francis A 131 H Louisa 130 Lucy V 43 Minerva 131 Renald 43 Samuel 6 Walter 63
DILLENBACK, Catharine 91 Jacob 93 Kathline M 93 Lany A 91
DILLISTON, Laura 31
DININNY, Attia 50 Ferril C 50

DININY, John W 96
DISBROW, Angeline 38 Caleb R 33 Electa 33
DODGE, J 57 Russell 115 Warren 57
DOER, Jas D 42 Louesa M 42
DOLBY, Parden 84 Rhoda 84
DOLLY, Christopher 54
DONAHE, Anna 132 Betsy Ann 105 Horace G 76 91 John 105 Lucy 105 Margaret J 103 Mary F 91 Mary Helen 76 Menzer D 103 P S 132 William Hamilton 91
DONALDSON, Elder 71
DOOLITTLE, Anson 119 Flora Melissa 119
DORR, Mary 80 Robert L 80
DOTY, Christopher 34 Eliza 64 Lucinda 34 Lydia 34
DOUD, Emily L 92 James M 114 John 114
DOW, Catherine 22
DOWNEY, Eleanor 71 Robert 71
DOWNS, Asa 122 Catherine B 64 Wm R 90 92 93 96
DRAKE, Allen 40 Amanda P 40 Catharine 58 Deacon 64 Elizabeth 87 Joseph H 58 Peter 71 Reuben 87 Ruhama 64 Susan 71
DREW, Abbie 79 George M 79
DUDLEY, A 109 Abraham 92 Abram 108 Ann Eliza 92 Benjamin F 38 Clarissa R 34 Helen M 78 108 Ida 131 James R 34 James T 131 Jennette 12 Jeremiah 11 John Q 78 Lafayette 94 Lois 74 Louisa 38 N (Mrs) 87 Sally Ann 33 Sarah 130 Sarah Ann 94 Susan 87 T J 12
DUNCAN, Cathia 63 Charles 63 Emma 63 Lydia 63
DUNN, Betsey 1 Emma A 113 Robert 1
DUNNING, Desiah 33
DURKEE, Adeline 68 John 68
DUTCHER, Mary B 18 19 William A 18
DYCKMAN, Mrs 14 Oliver 14
DYER, Mary 38 Nancy S 96 Patrick 38
DYGERT, Aurissa V 70 Charlotte 45 John 70 Rhoda 69 Sylvenus 45 Walter 69
DYKINS, Charlotte 77
EACKER, Elizabeth 72 John G 72
EAGLESTON, Esther Eliza 77
EARLY, Betsy Jane 86 Jackson 32 Patricia 32 Thomas 86
EASLING, Dayton 9 Emeline 9
EASON, Hart 42 Mary 42
EASTERBROOK, Andrew J 118 Minerva R 118
EASTERBROOKS, Isaac 130 132
EASTWOOD, Helen 126
EATON, Benjamin 40 42 Charlotte 108 Mary 42 Mercy 69 Thomas 69
EDDY, Betsey Ann 17 18 Daniel 18 Fannie K 113 Horatio B 85 John S 14 June 14 Mary Jane 85 R W 113
EDGAR, Huldah Maria 24
EDSON, Martha 40 Ruby J 95
EDWARDS, A A 103 Alexander 58 C H 103 Clarissa R 34 David 119 Elizabeth 58 George C 33 Helen E 128 Jesse 58 Maryette 116 Mason 33 William 72 Wm H 128
EGAN, John 104
EGBERT, R 89 Ralph 89
EGGLESTON, Delilah 76 Harriet 58 Helen Cornelia 64 Ira H 76 John 58 Keziah 25
ELDER, Henry J 128 Martha L 128
ELDRIDGE, Amos 132 Huldah 132 Mary 129
ELLAS, Amanda D 26 Francis S 7 George H 61 George S 26 Julia Ann 58 Mary Ann 102 Phebe 61 Sarah E 7 28
ELLIOTT, Temma 51
ELLIS, Amelia Alexandrina 7 Charlotte 74 Chester 87 Elizabeth 87 Ella 57 Eugene 57 George 29 George Washington 7 Jane 57 John 29 Martha 71 Sophia 51

ELLISON, George F 70 Mary E 70
ELLSWORTH, Joshua 4 Martha 4 Phebe P 130 S Stewart 130
ELWOOD, Lyman 109 Maria N 109
EMERSON, Amos 64 Celinda 77 Clarissa 18 Harriet 26 38 58 Helen Cornelia 64 Joseph 38 53 Mary Ann 26 Roxana 18
EMISSE, Elizabeth 91
EMMONS, Carlos 43 Caroline 43
ENGLISH, Rev 50
ERIS, James 80 Ortha A 80
ERWAY, Ira 52 Peter Henry 52
ERWIN, Adeline 68 Arthur 123 Edward E 87 Francis 16 Francis E 101 Mary E 123 Rachel A 17 Samuel 17 Sophia 101 Susan J 87
EVANS, Elijah 49 Elisha H 76 George A 109 Sarah C 109
EVEREST, G T 39 Rev 37
EVERETT, E 6 9
EWERTS, Mary 15
EXLLS, Anna E 130 Horace 130
EYGABROAT, Elizabeth 115
FAGENS, Jeremiah 135 Sarah 135
FAIRBANKS, Elizabeth 115 Julia 94 Russell L 115
FAIRFIELD, Betsy 79 Elizabeth 81 John 79 81
FAIRMAN, S B 132 Sarah A 132
FALKNER, Julia 131 Wm A 131
FALLS, Louisa 61
FARNAM, Caleb 17 Clarissa 17
FARNUM, Emily L 92 Rollin 92
FASSETT, John 9
FAULKNER, Angeline 3 Catherine 46 James 1 John 3 46 Richard 46
FAWCETT, Mary 91 Robert 91
FAY, A 46 Helen W 62 Lewis D 102 105 Lydia M 102 Nancy 105 Sarah M 46
FEITH, Monika 107 Nicholas 107
FELLOWS, Rev 86
FERENBAUGH, S H 135 Tena E 135
FERIS, Lewis G 18 Sophronia 18
FERRIS, A P 43 Ann 12 Catherine 43 Eliza Ann 62 George 12 Lemuel H 62 Lewis G 71

FERROW, Annie J 120 George 120
FIELD, Darius 58 Maria 58
FIFE, Hiram 55 Matilda 55
FILLMORE, Rev 135
FINCH, John 130 Moses 130 Rebecca M 130
FISHER, Arvilla 6 Coonrad 6 Elizabeth 27 53 George F 87 Hannah Elizabeth 75 John 39 Mary 87
FISK, F A 74 Henrietta 116 James E 116 Mary Ellen 74 Mary S 74
FLEET, Abram 16 Daniel 16
FLEMING, Hannah C 51 John B 51
FLETCHER, Hannah 100 Mrs 135 Myron K 100
FLUENT, Amanda 112 Boanerges 22 Fanny 42 Fanny E 42 John 20 Joseph 42 Lucy E 67 Maria Jane 14 Mehitabel 14 Rufus 14 Teneyck 112
FLYN, Permelia 93
FONDA, Harriet M 90 Henry J 90 97 Marion F 90
FOOTE, Frances L 103 Franklin C 103
FORD, Electa 63 Eli 54 Eliza 54 Henry 63 James 41 John K 132 Marcus 8 Maria 41 Marilla A 132
FORDYCE, Seymour 47 Susan M 47
FOREST, Edwin 50
FORESTER, Harriet 77
FORREST, Edwin 74
FORTNER, Martha 96 William 96
FOSSETT, Martha 13
FOSTER, Hannah Elizabeth 75 Helen W 62 John B 75 Robert W 92 William S 62
FOWLER, Christina G 46 Hannah 66 John 25 John W 5 25 46 66 P H 64
FOX, C S 120 122 123 125 126 Ermina 120 George 103 John 120 Mercena M 119 Norman Jr 109
FRACE, Calvin 61
FRANCIS, Harriet E 35 John M 35

FRANCIS (continued)
Martha 4
FRANKLIN, Albert 122 Charles 63 Mrs 55 Olive 49 Roswell 49
FRASER, Agnes Jane 27 James 27 Julia 131
FRAZIER, O 27 Oris 25 26
FREEMAN, Cynthia A 77 John A 77
FRENCH, Charles 74 Charlotte J 41 J P 33 J W 54 Jefferson 46 John 55 John F 57 Mary 8 46 55 74 Theodore 33
FRINK, R Robie 41
FRISBIE, Phidelia 29 W H 85
FROMAN, Julia 112
FROST, Jacob 62 Nancy 62
FULFORD, Sarah 115
FULLER, D A (Mrs) 89 E B 39-41 Julia 130
FULSOM, Sally Ann 7
FUNK, Dorothea 85
GALPIN, Amos 32
GAMBLE, Amelia 47 Susan J 87 William 47 Wm 87
GANSEVOORT, Conradt 60 Eliza E 117 Elizabeth 60 James 117 John R 60 68 101 Mary L 68 Peter C 101
GARDINER, C M 102
GARDNER, C M 89 94-96 100 101 103 105 132 Daniel 105 Lewis 78 Sarah 135
GARLINGHOUSE, John 70 Mary Jane 70
GATES, David W 133 Marian H 133 134
GAY, Emily J 127
GAYLORD, Alonzo 116 F S 29 Leroy 92 Marcus 110 N Caroline 92 Rev 14 26 Willis H 116
GEE, Martha 96 Rachel 97
GELSON, Rev 28
GELSTON, Rev 26
GEORGE, Rev 71 Sarah 6
GERSTLY, Bertha 122
GIBBS, Albert V 127 Lovina 127 Mary 76
GIBSON, Lovina 127 Maria 111
GIFFORD, Elsie 100 Jerome 121 Mary 26 Ruth E 5

GILBERT, A J 121 Ellen 83 Rachel A 17 Wm D 133 Wm J 17 121
GILE, Margaret A 9 Rulof S 108 William 9
GILES, H T 112-115 117-120
GILLAN, Harriet 96 William W 96
GILLET, Augusta R 124 Charles W 124 James 51
GILLETT, Anna 15 Hulda Jane 89 J D 110 Joseph 47 Samuel 15
GILLETTE, Frances J 110
GILMORE, Nelson G 3 Peres 3
GLASS, Franklin 9 39 Lydia Ann 39
GLEASON, Ezra 105 Nancy M 15
GLOAD, Charles W 39 John 39
GOBLE, Myranda 93
GOFF, Martha Ann 63
GOODALL, Wm 26
GOODELL, Wm 16
GOODON, Jane E 40
GOODRICH, A M 69 Amanda C 69 James 15 Polly 15 Rhoda 67
GOODSELL, Daniel 80 Elizabeth S 93 George 7 Hannah A 10 John H 93 Sally Ann 7 Susan 80
GOODWIN, Mary B 9
GORDON, Margaret M 126 Sarah 96 Whitman 96
GORTON, Hannah 11
GOULD, A R 13 Azel R 43 Caton 115 Jane A 70 John W 70 Louisa H 47 Maria E 26 Mary 13 Ralph F 43 Rev 29 Thomas 115
GOWERS, Cynthia 77
GRAHAM, George P 20 Hannah 67 Hellen Marr 56 Henry A 23 Jerusha 76 Julia 110 Richard 110 Samuel 67
GRAMES, Jane 5
GRANT, Angeline 87 B F 82 Helen 117 Jedediah 105 Leroy 117 Mary E 82 Nancy W 41 Nancy Whiting 70 Stephen 70
GRAVES, Charles 49 53 Charles O 109 Dorcas M 62 Elizabeth 63 Harriet 64 Horace 62 Mrs 53 Phebe A 109 Randall 63

GRAY, Eunice 80 Jennie 131 L 80 Margaret 90 Oren D 90
GREEN, Cynthia 80 John F 80 Mary E 86
GREENFIELD, Jerome 26 Mary 26
GREGG, John 27
GREGORY, A 76 85 94 Almon 68 75 76 82 85 93 95 D D 111 119 David 21 Eleanor 29 Julia 21 Meribah 51 Rev 29
GRIDLEY, Henrietta V 117 Lewis 116 117 Sarah L 80 Viola 116
GRIFFIN, Ann E 137 Thomas 137
GRIFFITH, John 36
GRINNELL, Caroline 89 Zelotes 89
GRISWOLD, C M 16 Electa 33 Lisetta 135 Sophronia 16
GRISWOULD, Olive S 38
GROCE, William P 52
GROSE, H L 96
GUIWITS, Mary 47 Mary J 66 William H 66
GUIWITTS, Francis H 75 Sarah J 75
GULICK, Spence 59
GUSTIN, Gardner 3 Lucy 3 90
GUSTINE, Fannie 10 Major 10
GUYON, Mary 95
HAIGHT, Maria 13 Rev D 83 Samuel S 13
HALL, Aaron C 52 Ambrose 54 Clarissa 54 Elizabeth 102 Jane 84 Levica 128 Maria 22 Mathew B 113 Melissa R 102 Rphilander J 102 Samuel 128 Sarah 113 Uria S 102
HALLAM, R A 83
HALLET, Harriet 69 Nehemiah 69
HALLETT, Dellevan 18 Harriet 18 Moses 10
HALLIDAY, Emma 48 Homer 87 Sarah Jane 87
HALLOCK, Abby 82 100 Benjamin 82 Geo W 42 John D 82 Mary H 42
HALSEY, Lucia 7 Peter 7
HALSTED, J 75 76 86
HAMILTON, Annis S 70 Daniel 20 56 Harmon M 70 John 37 Keziah 56 Lester 37

HAMILTON (continued) Marilla 20 Mary Helen 76 Sarah H 68 William 6 Wm 7 68 76
HAMLIN, Ellen M 90 Hester 19
HAMMOND, Adelaide M 122 E P 126 Eliza 126 Elizabeth 38 James R L 24 John W 122 Samuel H 24
HANDY, Cordelia 38
HANKS, Brigham 17 28 Ellen 28
HARDENBROOK, Frank 103 M J 103
HARDIE, M 127 T E 127
HARDINBROOK, J K 57 Lois 57
HARDING, Oliver 7
HARE, Elizabeth E 9 Wilber C 9
HARFORD, Ann 123 Attia 50 Fred 123 Tommy P 123
HARKINSON, Joseph 47
HARLOW, J 135 J M 128 130 131 J N 135 James S 130 Sarah 130
HARMAN, Alexander G 58 Esther 85 Henry H 85 Martha O 58 Philip 58
HARRINGTON, D 35
HARRIS, Edward N 6 George W 133 Hiram 51 James P 78 Jane 79 John 79 Joseph H 64 Maria 13 Mary Walbridge 64 Prudence R 78 Robert F 84 Sally Ann 51 Samantha 133 Sarah 6 Seneca V 84
HARRISON, Robert 33 William Henry 25
HARROWER, Antoinette 94 B 61 David 24 G T 94 Levi B 61 62 Mary 62
HART, Fred 122 Lucy 49 W E 122
HARTMAN, John 71
HARTSHORN, Jacob 62 89 Jerusha 89
HARVEY, Esther 77 Harriet 38 Holms 54 John 38 Sarah 54
HARVY, Mary E 85 Wm B 85
HASKELL, Abel 69
HASKINS, Amanda 76 I J 76
HASKMNS, James F 96
HASTINGS, Edward 9 George H 10 Hannah 6 Lemuel 5 Mary 5 Sarah E 10 Timothy 6 Wm 9
HATCH, Austin S 94 Heman 32

HATCH (continued)
Julia 94 William 35
HATFIELD, Rev 105
HAUSE, Alvin G 28 Fidelia 28 Joseph 11
HAVEN, Hannah 100
HAVENS, E P 104 Rachel 135
HAVERLING, Adam 26 Elizabeth 26
HAWKENBURY, Eliza 11
HAWLEY, Sarah Jane 87 Wm M 87
HAY, Rev 5
HAYES, Byron 136 Emily O 111 Margaret 136 Simeon 27
HAYS, Brayton 72
HEAD, Ann 48 James 48
HECKMAN, Betsey 13 Elizabeth 13 Robert H 13
HEERMANS, George 116 Hattie C 116
HELIKER, Mary 16
HELM, Capt 66
HELMER, Andrew 48 52 Charlotte 48 Daniel 48 Thankful 52
HEMMENWAY, Freddie H 117 Freeman 117 Jane 117
HEMPSTEAD, Mary 23
HENDERSHOT, J D 129
HENDERSON, Charles H 118 Clara Mabel 118 Harriet E 118
HENDRICK, Bella 132 Orva 132
HENDRYX, Jane Ann 25
HENRY, David 15 Rev 60
HENSLEY, John 20
HERRINGTON, Alonzo 70 Nancy E 70
HESS, Alexander 23 67 Hiram B 102 Hiram R 80 Martha 67 Martha P 80 Martha T 23 Mary 67 Mary Lizzie 102
HEWELL, Sidney B 94
HEWLETT, Susan 80
HEWLEZL, Alonzo W 102 Sarah J 102
HIBBARD, Ellen 99 John 99
HICKEY, Honora 89 Luke 89
HICKMOTT, Mary H 22
HICKOCK, H 93
HICKOX, Janette 83
HICKS, Mary E 38

HIGGINS, Abigal 89 Augusta F 108 Charles 67 Henry J 108 Huldah A 117 James G 20 John D 3 5 94 Loana 67 Rosetta 82
HIGLEY, H M 108 Helen M 108
HILL, Alonzo D 123 Alvah 71 Geo H 58 H C 116 H F 116 Harriet 58 Harvey 94 Helen A 113 John 123 Noah 136 R W 24 Susan Jane 94 Yankee 58
HILLS, George Morgan 73
HILTON, Angeline 38 Betsey E 63 H Louisa 130 Sylvester B 130
HINCKLEY, John 14 Sophia 14
HOAG, N 21 Nelson 20 Rev 18 Sarah E 95
HOAGLAND, Abraham 72 Eunice A 72
HOBARD, Albert M 28 29
HOBART, Almira M 24 Mary 29
HODGMAN, Janette 73 Leonard 73 Mary J 73
HOFFMAN, Andrus 113 Andrus D 113 114 Charlotte A 113 Chauncey 43 John S 30 Lester A 114 Lydia 30 Mary J 114 Sarah E 113 Sarah M 113 114
HOGELAND, Harriet 65 Jacob 65
HOLLENBACK, Nancy S 96 R P 96
HOLLIDAY, Eliza 25 Harvey 25
HOLLIS, E T 110 111 Eugene T 123 Georgie 123 L G 111 Loretta 123 Oscar B 111 Susan 84
HOLMES, Harriet A 130 Rachel 120
HOLMS, Simeon 18 Sophronia 18
HOLTON, Elisha 69 Mary A 69
HOLZMAIER, Dorothea 85 Sebastian 85
HOOD, Geo 61 Rev 71
HOOKER, Anna 132 Augustus S 132 Col 78 Horace 4
HOPKINS, Charlotte 48 Climena 14 Emily M 82 Erastus 14 Horatio 25 John C 53 Laura B 53 Norman 48 Rev 23
HOPPER, Mansfield 81 Martha 81
HORN, Almira 109 E J 109

HORN (continued)
  Kate 123 Katie Dee 123 Oliver 123
HORR, Betsy Jane 86
HORTON, Ann Eliza 84 M Cordelia 86
HOTCHIN, James H 76
HOTCHKIN, Agnes 124 Ann Eliza 24 Charles D 124 Desiah 33 Eunice 100 Fannie D 124 H M 101 J H 9 33 100 J J 101 James H 23 24 75 76 102 James J 102 Joseph Allen 124 Joseph B 33 124 Lucius H 124 Maria L 124 N E 102 Rebecca 100 Rev 7 William H 24
HOTCHKISS, E 40 Sarah 135
HOUCK, Abel 38 Angeline 38
HOUGHENSTOUNTEN, Adrianna Augustina 107 Theocrastus Bombastus 107
HOUSE, Betsey 8 George I 10 Mary 47 P R 47 Sally Rodela 10
HOVEY, Jacob R 72 Mary E 72
HOWARD, Harlow J 129 Harriet A 37 Jane 77 Mary Somerville 133 Nettie 129 O R 111 118 133
HOWE, Helen 134 John 32 Rev 113 S S 26
HOWELL, 132 A S 134 Edward 78 Edward Jr 68 Frances 47 Frances Minerva 78 Freeman 75 Hannah 117 James F 117 James Faulkner 95 John Magee 134 Lydia 95 117 Mary 78 134 Mary L 68 N W Jr 47 Robert 11 Tharessa 75 William 11
HOYT, Harriet 83 Henry J 95 Robert H 83 Samuel 42 Sarah E 7
HUBBARD, Robert 49
HUBBELL, Frances 69 Mary H 42 P P 83 W S 42 Wm S 83
HUDINOT, Ann 12
HUDSON, C W 58 Julia Ann 58 Tripheny 13
HUFF, Hannah 1
HUGHES, Albina S 130 Mary 8 Thomas Pancost 8

HUGHEY, Joseph 91 Margaret 91
HULBERT, Silas 58 Sophira 58
HULETT, Caroline 81 Emory T 81
HULL, A 64 78 Clara 66 Henry H 66 Louisa E 68 Luther 68
HUNT, Elizabeth 74 Ezekiel 54 55 Jane A 91 Levina 55 Warren 74
HUNTER, Caroline 134 Catherine 54 Eleanor 12 Fanny 54 Hannah 43 James 54 Mariah 42 S D 134 Wm 12
HURD, Bryant R 42 Rev 13
HURDICK, Franklin L 113 Mira E 113
HURLBURT, Adelaide D 117 Almira 83 Daniel R 117 Smith 83
HURLEY, John 115
HUSTED, W H 43
HUTCHINS, Ermina 120
HUTCHISON, Jemima 16
HYATT, Laura 79
HYDE, Fannie M 134 Helen M 132 Rev 63 Wm F 132
INGERSOLL, Sally Ann 51
INSLEE, Joseph 1 Nancy 1
IRVING, John T 6 Washington 6
JACK, Minerva 131
JACKSON, Cordelia 20 D 20 Gen 78 H M 70 J C 70 John T 120 121 Rachel 120 121
JACOBUS, Isaac 135 Janett 40 John D 40 Julia A 135 Sophrona 70
JAMEISON, Capt 17 Mary 17
JAMESON, John 24
JAMISON, Louis T 5 Mary E 5
JAQUAY, Harriet 38
JAYNES, Eugene 127 Jesse 114 Julia F 127
JENKS, Eliza Ann 46 Keziah 25 Waterman 25 Watermore 46
JEROME, Clarissa 54 Leonard Walter 54
JOHNSON, Anna Melissa 95 Cath 54 Elmira 37 Harriet 13 Helen 37 Henrietta 26 Huldah 132 J T 67 James 132 James C 36 37 Jane 27 Joel 63 John 13 Lucia 7 Lucretia 67 Mary 132 Mary B 9 Melissa D 95 Miss 96

JOHNSON (continued)
Nancy K 34 O 28 S A 26 37
Samuel A 51 Samuel C 36
Sarah B 67 Sarah W 130 Sophia
L 51 Thomas A 130 Thos H 95
William H 27
JOHNSTON, John M 116 Lavina
86 Lizzie D 116
JOLLEY, Hannah 40 James 40
JONES, A A 103 Allen E 127 Ann
E 137 Aruna 118 Betsey B 119
Catharine 87 Catherine A 16
Charles H 136 Frank Z 127
Helen L 136 Henry S 108 118
James E 119 Laura A 115
Lewis 121 Llewellyn M 123
Mara E 127 Maria 118 Maria R
108 Mary E 78 123 Matilda 135
Nancy E 118 Ross S 127 Ruth
E 120 S R 24 Sarah 118 Sophia
92 Wm E 113 117
JORALEMOU, J 103
JUDD, Rev 47
JUDSON, A 29 A H 132 D F 108
110 112 115 117 126-128 130
131 David F 129 Sarah A 132
KANE, Betsey 16 Elisha 104
James 72
KASSON, Ambrose 94 Antoinette
94
KATHAN, Thomas A 120
KATNER, Harlow P 19
KAUSH, Christian 37 Maria E 37
KAYLOR, Jacob Jr 35
KEATS, Isabel R 31 John 31
KEEHLER, Joseph 15 Lucretta 15
KEELER, David 32
KELL, Nancy 1 Patrick N 1
KELLEY, Elizabeth 91
KELLOGG, Ashbel 56 Emma E
112 Frances A 91 Marion 111
Russell 91 111 William 56
KELLY, Elizabeth 9 John 45
Manning 9 Margaret 45 Mary
64 Mary J 66
KELSEY, Daniel 119
KENDALL, Zebedee 16
KENMORE, Charles 76 Sarah
Elizabeth 76
KENNARD, John 3 Mary 3
KENNEDY, Margaret 136 Rev 121

KETCHAM, Jonathan 6 8 Ruth E
5 William R 5
KETCHUM, J R 18
KEYES, Elijah 124 Rev 100
KEYSER, Levi 84 Margaret 84
KING, Cynthia 80 Geo 80 B 80
Nancy 109 Sarah E 117 Sarah
Jane 93
KINGKADE, Mira E 113
KINGSBURY, Elizabeth 38 Heman
W 38
KINNE, Catharine 87 George F 87
KINNEY, Benjamin J 114 C D 34
45 Catherine 13 Elizabeth 72
Julia 114 Kitt 114 Melissa 103
P 113 Theodore B 72
KIP, Dyer S 29 Jane A 29
KNAPP, Duran 128 H T 135 J 136
John 40 M L 135 Martha 40
KNICKERBOCKER, Catharine A
135 Maria 58
KNIGHT, Daniel 8 Emily 8 John
56
KNOWLES, Jeremiah 84 Sarah
Jane 84
KNOWLTON, Mary 96
KNOX, Adah Zillah 51 Fannie 10
Jno 49 John 10 Levi 51 Mrs 49
W D 14
KOON, Alma L 127 Jacob 127
KRESS, Elizabeth A 92
KRUMHOLD, Monika 107
LACKEY, Susan 111
LAFURGE, Mary Jane 63
LAGROSS, John 137
LAKE, Helen 26 Hildah 88 Huldah
87 Phebe T 56 Rarick 116
Thomas 87 88
LAMAN, Caroline 100 101 John
Jay 100
LAMB, Charles 81
LAMBERT, M J 64
LAMPHEARE, Jabish 136
LAMSON, Charles E 26 Elizabeth
26 Martha E 6 Syrena 23
LANCASTER, Joseph 11
LAND, Mary E 109
LANDERS, Frederick B 64 Sarah
W 64
LANE, David 131 Hannah 79
LANGFORD, James 36

LANPHEAR, Harriet 131
LANTZ, D 75
LARE, David 43 Maria 43
LARROWE, E 102 Jacob 29 Judge 102
LATTA, Nancy 13
LAUGHLIN, John 104
LAWRENCE, Augustus S 103 James 17 Maryann 17
LAWTON, Rosetta 82 William 82
LEACH, Clara 132 I C 132
LEE, Leicester 34 Salina 34
LEECH, Hannah L 109
LEGRO, Elmira 33 John 15 Lois M 38 Nancy M 15 Samuel 33
LEIGH, A M 17 28
LELAND, Ahay 91 Charles 25 Z A 25 Zeba 91
LEMON, Michael 38
LENHART, Charles 103 Elizabeth 103 Mary Louise 102 103 Osa Kate 102 103
LEONARD, Richard 86
LEVERIDGE, D E 111
LEVY, Rev 122
LEWIS, Abraham Q 64 Alonzo D 122 B Vrooman 83 Barbara 36 C E 113 Daniel D 88 Eliza Forbes 15 Emeline 92 Esther A 83 H M 101 Helen Ann 35 James 15 19 Jane 11 Jane O 113 Jane T 88 John V 35 Mary Frances 61 Morgan 34 Patty 42 Sarah Jane 65
LILLY, Harriet 10 17
LINDSAY, J 91 James 116
LINDSEY, James 111
LINDSLEY, Catherine 78 Edward 9 Judge 41 Lydia G 33 Maria 41 Mary B 9
LINSLEY, Abial 12 Levinia 12 Melissa E 61
LITTLE, Catherine 41 Charles G 87 James 24 Susan 87 William Graham 79 Wm 41
LIVINGSTON, Edward P 31
LLOYD, A 70 Julia Ann 18
LOCKE, Rev 15
LOCKWOOD, C M (Mrs) 99 Catherine M 105 Eliza 105 Ellen G 105 James Edmund 105 James H 105 Lester 105

LODER, Elisha 30 Jane 65 Job 65
LOGAN, Lydia 30 Sarah M 127
LOGHRY, Emma N 128 Joseph B 128
LONG, Nancy 52 William 52
LONGWELL, David 39 Elizabeth 51 James 51 Laura 39 Lewis 23 Rachel 23
LOOD, John 77 Lucretia 77
LOOK, J B 46 Sarah M 46
LOOMIS, Amanda D 26 Ann Eliza 57 Chester 26 Ellen 28 Gelina F 68 Henry 49 57 68 Julina F 49 Lucinda A 62 Nathaniel S 51 Theron 28
LOOP, D C 112 113 Mary Vivian 113
LOSIER, John P 47 Louisa H 47
LOUCKS, Adam 12 Amanda 58 Elizabeth 91 Jane M 12 John 36 Nancy C 36 Richard 91
LOUKE, Mary Ann 82
LOVE, Harriet 85
LOVELESS, Andrew 90 Lucy 90
LOVELL, Almira 83
LOVERIDGE, E 102
LOZIER, Abram 22 Mary 22
LUDINGTON, Laura A 115 Wm S 115
LUDLOW, Jehial 15
LYMAN, William 4
LYNCH, Albert 63 Henry C 63 James 115 Mary C 63 Sylvester 124
LYON, A P 61 Abner P 35 38 Augustus W 120 Gertrude 120 Helen Ann 35 Laura 38 Mary Jane 27 Rebecca P 73 Robert M 73 Sophia 100
M'BEATH, James 27 Sarah 27
M'CLURE, George 5 Mary E 5
M'COLLOUGH, S J 78
MACK, Abigail 50 Elisha 38 Frank 117 Hannah 38
MADALE, John 49
MADISON, Ex-President 56 Mrs 56
MAGEE, Ann Eloise 3 Arabella 46 Calvin 22 Charles 24 D S 130 David 130 Ellen P L 82 Harriet 22 Hugh J 129 Jane 69 John 3 24 46 130 Mary 129

MAGEE (continued)
  Phebe P 130 Thomas J 69 82
MAKER, Archillus 11 Mary Ann 11
MALLORY, A C 52 60 70 72 73 Betsy Ann 96 Elder 65 J C 62 68 70 71 74 75 77 79 81 84-86 90 93 128 130 John 20 Minerva 20 Nancy M 96 S C 42
MANCHESTER, Elizabeth 102 H D 102
MANDERVILLE, Mahlon H 96 Maria 96
MANDEVILLE, Homer 123 James 123
MANLEY, E C 110 N V 110
MANLY, M M 119
MANN, D C 130 Sophia 30 William T 103
MANNERS, Clara Elsie 112 Gertrude B 112 Sarah 112 Wm H 112
MARKHAM, Charles 24 Olive 24
MARLATT, Sarah V 118
MARSH, Elizabeth L 92
MARSHALL, Eliza Ann 11 Mr 10 Otto F 11
MARTIN, Elisha 65 Harriet Eliza 94
MARVIN, Martha 108
MASON, Eliza H 14 Elizabeth 54 Elliott 69 George W 54 Jemima 69
MASTEN, Christina 8 Joseph G 8 P 92
MASTERS, Emeline 9 Nehemiah 9
MATHER, Dorothy 81
MATHEWS, Mary 29 Vincent 29
MATHEWSON, Jane E 31 John 46 John M 31 Mary 46 Phoebe 46
MATTESON, A A 133 G W 133 LeBlanche 133
MATTISON, W C 116
MAXFIELD, Andrew J 91 Lany A 91
MAXWELL, Dugold Cameron 92 Eliza P 56 Jane 65 Susan 84 Th 56 Thomas 78 Vie 78
MAY, Adaline 77 Adeline 86 Chas 10 Hannah 23 Henry R 77 86 Jesse 92 Joseph Adams 12

MAY (continued)
  Lucene 92 Martha 108 Mary 12
MCADAM, Jane 77 John 77
MCBEATH, Emma 109
MCBETH, Charlotte 43 James 43
MCBURNEY, Jane A 21 Thomas 21
MCCAIG, John E 134 Sarah Jane 134
MCCALL, A J 102 Abel 101 Dr 52 Mary Ann 102 Rebecca M 83 Sophia 101 Wm 83
MCCALLA, Nancy 62
MCCANN, Lizzie D 116
MCCARTER, Betsy 79
MCCARTY, Elizabeth 81
MCCAY, Frances 47 Hester 19 James Stuart 19 Mary 47 86 W W 19 47 Wm W 86
MCCHESNEY, Hannah 72
MCCLARY, Nancy J 81
MCCLAY, A J 86
MCCLURE, Charles H 14 Finla 14 George 17 Mary 17
MCCOLLUM, Sarah 22
MCCORLUM, Rachel 97 William H 97
MCCURDY, Elizabeth 58 James 58
MCDOUGAL, D 128
MCDOWELL, C J 48 Eliza Ann 62
MCELHANA, T 38
MCELWAIN, Elizabeth 60 John 60
MCELWEE, Henry 60 M J 103 N Caroline 92 Nancy 60
MCGLURE, Finla 43 George 43
MCGONEGAL, Ira 61 Mary 61
MCGOWAN, Adelaide E 136 Albert S 136
MCGRAW, Caroline E 50 Daniel 50
MCHENRY, Mary A 109
MCKENNEY, I J B 11
MCKENNY, J B 67
MCMINDS, Sarah 96
MCMULLEN, Fanny 132 James 132
MCNAUGHTON, Jane 17
MCNEIL, Mary Jane 60
MCNULTY, Mary E 64

MCNUTT, Gov 48
MCPHERRONS, Amy 67
MCPHERSON, Agnes Jane 27 E A 95 George 95 L 95
MCQUHAE, John 57
MEAD, Alvin 50 Rebecca M 130
MEEKS, Caroline 16
MEGRADY, Biny 37
MELONY, Mary 67 W Francis 67
MERCHANT, Francis A 117
MERIAN, Seth A 108
MERRELL, George H 51
MERRIAM, Eliza 12 Harriet Y 23
MERRICK, S D 133 Samuel 89
MERRILL, Aurissa V 70 Lydia R 77 Otis N 77
MERRITT, S M 127 132
MERRY, Charles 107
MESICK, Henry 75
MESSENGER, George 45 Rosanna Mary Theresa 45
MESSLER, Cornelius 32
METCALFE, Charlotte 6 Franklin 4 John 4 Nancy 62 Ose 4 Thomas 6
MILES, Helen L 136 Leonora C 93
MILLEN, Grenville 27
MILLER, Abram H 78 Caroline C 78 Clarissa E 111 Eleanor 29 Elizabeth 77 H 128 H M 70 Harry 9 Henry 18 Jane F G 9 Jerusha 76 John 77 Julia 21 L M 46 54 57 58 68 L Merrell 37 38 L Merrill 36 42 47 49 50 63 72 Mark 9 Merrill 43 Mrs 32 Rev 70 Samuel 111 Sarah 9 18 Sylvester 78 William H 77 Wm H 29 76
MILLERD, Elizabeth 10 Josiah 10
MILLIGAN, Ann 89
MILLINGTON, Lawrence B 132 Susan Amelia 132
MILLS, Almon T 106 Amelia I 40 Daniel A 77 106 Elisha T 21 Esther E 106 Esther Eliza 77 Harmon 111 Jane 13 Jane A 21 John H 40 Lydia 66 Mrs 50 68 S 73 129 Sarah 111 Sidney 119
MINARD, Cornelia P 125 Joel 90 John H 125 Joseph 90

MINARD (continued) Joseph (Mrs) 90 Michael 90 William 90
MINER, Ellen M 90 Harrison C 90 Rev 10
MINGAS, Henry 21 Mariah 21
MINIER, Elvira 83 George 83
MITCHELL, A D 112 Catherine 32 Edward S 112 Fred S 112 Helena Ann 59 J 112 J B 8 John B 59 John D 5 Mary Ann 5 Thomas 8 Walter 32
MOFFIT, Frances 47 J N 47
MONELL, Mary Ann 41 Oliver 41
MONELY, Edward 36
MONTGOMERY, Charles E 112 Emma E 112
MOORE, Adelaide D 117 Alma L 127 Aris 87 Azilla 34 Caroline 81 Elizabeth 27 87 Elizabeth M 16 Eunice 4 Francis Jr 16 James 84 Jefferson 81 118 Julia T 81 Thomas 84 Wm 27
MOREY, A F 127 128 131 133 135 136 Elizabeth A 111 Martha 77 Robert C 111
MORGAN, Cordelia M 52 Gov 136 Jane A 70 Julius G 80 Sarah L 80 William 52
MORGEWORTH, John 37
MORRIS, Eunice 77 Harriet A 130 Israel 35 77 James 130 John 35
MORSE, Ada K 110 Cyrus B 110 Elizabeth 91 Jane 5 Mary 126 Philip 5 Sarah 26
MORTON, Eber L 3 Lucy 3
MOSE, Rachel E 109 William 109
MOSIER, Sophronia 16
MOWGER, Isaac 136
MULFORD, E P 94 102
MULHOLLON, Sarah W 64
MULLEN, Allen E 127 Ella 95 Seth 95 127
MULLHOLLEN, Jane 50 William S 50
MULLIKEN, Albert 47 Alfred 47 John W 47 Sarah Jane 47
MUNDY, Esq 48
MUNROE, John S 92 Margaret 92
MUNSON, Edgar 83 Lucy Maria 83

MURDOCH, Rev Dr 87
MURPHY, Clarissa A 5 Jeremiah 5
MURRAY, Alvira 104 James H 104 Mary Isabel 135 Thomas 131
MYERS, Elizabeth A 92 James D 92
MYRTLE, Angeline 3 Phillip 62
NASH, Jane E 31 Levi 84 Sarah Jane 84
NEALLY, Eunice 80 Harriet 15 James 80 Samuel 15
NEALY, Saml 26 William 26
NEGRO, Daniel 32 Old George 104
NEILY, Daniel S (Mrs) 52
NETTLETON, Charles 111 Hannah 31 Maria 111
NEWCOMB, George 34
NEWHALL, George B 128 Jennie E 128 Wm J 128
NEWMAN, Minerva R 118
NEWTON, Julia 130 Luther 130 Willett C 130
NICHOLDS, Adeline 51
NICHOLS, Elizabeth 49 Rev 80 S 131
NICHOLSON, Ambrose 51 Cora 132 Sarah E 127 Sophia 51 Wm W 132
NICHOSON, James 39 John 71
NILES, Elizabeth G 20 Hannah 28 38 Mary 16 Noah 16 21 Simeon P 28 W A 115 117 127 130
NIPHER, Hannah 8 Michael 8
NIXON, Eleanor 83 Harriet 57
NOBEL, Sarah Ann 39
NOBLE, C C 73 Fidelia 28 Harvey 67 Lucy V 43 Mary W 40 Sophia 67 W O 40
NOBLES, Emeline 56 J C 103
NORRIS, H Mariah 90 Henry 63 Lucy 63 S B 90
NORTHROP, Eli 31 Rachel 31
NORTHRUP, Amanda 23
NORTON, C 96 Frances L 103 George 28 78 Sarah E 28 78
NOTT, Lois 57 Thomas 57
NOWLEN, Asa 74 C H 104
NUTON, D 89

NUTTEN, D 64 65 94 96 David 92 Elder 74
NYCE, Simeon R 79
NYE, Eliza Ann 129 Obed 129
O'BRIEN, Catherine 75
O'CONNELL, Mary S 129 Wm B 129
O'CONNER, Mary 104 James 104
O'HARE, Mary 113
O'NEIL, Harriet 96
OGDEN, Eliza E 117
OLIVER, Charles 37 Sally 37
OLMSEN, Cornelia P 125
OLMSTEAD, Aaron 72 Amanda 51 Angeline A 73 Angeline Augusta 81 Augustus A 73 81 Erastus 87 John 51 Margaret 87 Mary E 72 Melvifa 51
OLMSTED, Charlotte 45 Erastus 87 Jeremiah 45 Margaret 87
OLNEY, Helen Mar 85 P 42 Parmenas F 85
ONGLEY, Mary H 22 Wm H 22
ORDWAY, Elzina 111 James M 111
ORR, Mary J 132 Rosa Belle 132 Wm H 132
OSBORN, John 107
OSTERHOUT, John C 64 Mary 64 Susan 39
OTIS, Frances C 115 Galen 108 Mary 9 Ralph 9 Sarah A 108
OTTARSON, Harriet Eliza 94 Thomas J 94
OTTMAN, S 10 12 13 113
OVERHISER, Abram 101 Alice 101 Caroline 85 John Casper 85 Mary 55
OVERTON, Edward 126 Eliza 126
OWEN, Alvin 93 Emily 93 Mary 61
PAGE, Adelaide R 43 Hannah 31 James 62 John 43 Levica 128 Lucinda A 62 Thomas O 31
PAINE, E L 65 Elizabeth S 65
PALMER, Anna 15 Azilla 34 Elizabeth M 35 Ezekiel 117 Joseph E 35 Mary Jane 85 Milo 34 Rufus R 110
PANGBURN, Catherine 65 Edward S 65 Nancy L 90

PARCEL, A 75 79 80 110
PARK, Catherine C 128 E A 131 Henri 64 James H 131 Mary E 64 R N 100 Rufus 128
PARKE, R N 99 108
PARKER, A J 118 Allen J 39 Ansel 20 Elizabeth G 20 Harriet M 39 J 87 James 84 Jane A 29 M C 118 Ransom G 84 Rev 82 Sarah W 130 Susan 84
PARKHILL, Elizabeth 102
PARKMAN, Francis Jr 64 Geo 64
PARKS, Amos 63 Mary Jane 63
PARMALE, A H 94
PARMALEE, A H 92
PARMELEE, Rev 52
PARMER, Elias 56 Hannah 56
PARMETER, Rozilla 36
PARSON, James A 109 Mary E 109
PARSONS, Darwin A 60 Harriet 65 Lucy Sane 60
PARTRIDGE, J 132
PATCHIN, D L W 135 E W 15 Mary 15 Myron 36 Rozilla 36 Tena E 135
PATRICK, Benjamin D 56 Eliza P 56
PATTENGILL, H 64 87 95
PATTENT, Alexander 41
PATTERSON, Benjamin 73 George 84 Grace A 73 Robert 52 Sarah 56 Susan 84
PAWLING, Catharine 76 Henry 42 Henry P 76
PAYNE, Arnold 7 Elizabeth A 116 Levi V 116 Niles 42 Patty 42 Phebe C 7
PEABODY, Rev 6
PEAK, Esq 69
PEARCE, Susan 96
PECK, Adam L 19 Charles 124 Charles Andrew Roof 19 Esther 113 Esther A 113 John 113 Josepha B 124 Lucius 28 Mary 28
PELLET, Malvina 27 N 27
PELTON, Caroline 79
PENMORE, Charles 86
PEPPER, Mrs 106
PERCIVAL, Jerome 121

PERINE, Elizabeth S 42 Henry W 42 Marietta 71 P S 50 Rachel Elizabeth 50
PERKINS, Ann Eliza 24 Carrie B 134 James H 53 John 53 63 Rev 9
PERRY, Alanson 51 Albert J 130 Albina S 130 Gilbert N 71 John 100 John M 90 Martha 71 Mathew Galbraith 107 Nelson 90 Oliver H 107
PERSONS, Amy 67 Hannah 8 Lucinda H 67 Wm 67
PETERS, Charles 48 52 E A 127 Elizabeth 48 H H 127 Lucinda 52
PETRIKIN, David 71 Helen 71
PHELPS, Charlotte 14 Milo 14
PHILLIPS, A S 48 Amanda E 55 David 112 Julia 127 Mary 112 Ransom R 127 Samuel 55 Susannah 127 Thomas 132
PHINNEY, John 124
PHIPPS, Julia A 93 Wm R 93
PHOENIX, Parmelia 87
PICKLE, Clarissa 36 Peter 36
PIER, H 15 Henry 13 14 18 22
PIERCE, Judge 47 Sarah E 117 Stephen A 117
PIERSE, Maria 77
PIKE, Helen 26 John 26
PINDER, W E 75 82 90-93
PINNEO, James R 61 Melissa E 61
PLATT, Elizabeth 65 I W 34 Isaac W 27 Rev 5 6 13 14 16 18 19 28
POINSETT, Joel R 78
POLMATEER, Rachael 71 Sarah Ann 128
POMERLY, Julia A 93
POMEROY, Jemima 16 Nelson 16
POND, Myron 76
POPE, Rev 61
PORTER, Ahay 91 Elijah 91 Olive L 28 Rev 33 Robert D 28 Robert L 7 S 33 Wm G 56 Wm L 28
POTTER, Bradford A 61 E K 99 100 George E 99 Gifford 28 Orilla L 99 W 102

POTTS, Amelia Alexandrina 7
POUND, Joseph 93 Sarah Jane 93
POWELL, Joseph 109
POWERS, Caroline 43 Charles H 39 Cyrus 8 J 16 Lovina A 102 Nancy 8 P 31 34 Philander 43 William B 102
PRATT, Ann 91 Claudine B 134 Cora 132 Cynthia W 134 Elisha 24 Elizabeth 65 Harriet A 38 Hester A 80 J B (Mrs) 109 Joel 7 24 25 Joel B 134 Nelson 91 William B 80 Wm Beach 85
PRENTISS, Frederika 79 John 22 John A 79
PRESTON, Amos 8 Julia Ann 75
PRICE, W B 62
PRINDLE, Serepta 73
PROCTOR, Mr 52
PUFFER, Rosina 66 Tisdale 66
PUNCHIS, George W 37 Martha 37
PURDY, Betsey 86 C C 66 83 Charles 46 134 Emily M 82 M C 86 Marian H 134 Truman P 82
PURINGTON, Rev 53 Rhoda Jane 85 William F 85
QUICK, Elizabeth 7 James 12 Lucy 12
QUINLAN, Patrick 112
RACE, Alexander A 103
RANDALL, Alford 10 17 Sally Ann 10 17
RANDLE, Hannah R 45 Wm 45
RANGER, Janette 83 Jason 83
RAPLEE, Catharine 79 Daniel 79
RARICK, Abel 116 Emily 116
RARRICK, Anthony H 33 Sarah 33
RATHBONE, Hubbard W 83 Nancy 83 R 39 Ransom 111
RATHBUN, Chauncey 17 Frances B 37 Hiram 59 Jane 17 Louisa 59 Lucinda 25
RATTAN, Rachel 23
RAYMER, Henrietta A 84 Henry H 84
RAYMOND, John C 36 Mary 75 Sarah A 36 Wm G 41
RAZEY, Betsey Maria 66

READ, A D 39 45 56 80 Elizabeth L 6 Elizabeth S 42 James 42 67 71 James H 67 Lazarus H 93 Lazarus Hammond 6 Mary 74 Ro-Ella 96
REASER, S 15
RECTOR, Adaline 41
REDFIELD, Alvah 90
REED, Amanda C 69 Capt 43 Catherine 43 Sarah C 64
REES, Martin A 95 Ruby J 95
REMINGTON, Emily 93
REYNOLDS, Cyrus J 131 E A 131 Edwin M 109 Elizabeth B 80 Freelove 109 J S 135 Jennie 131 Julius A 35 Mary Elizabeth 35 Matilda 135 S H 80 Thomas 33 Thomas J 131
RHODA, Adaline 100 Peter 100
RHODES, B K 71 Helen 71 John 79 W C 79 Wallace 95
RIAL, Rachel E 109 Simon S 109
RICE, Anna Maria 36 Burrage 25 C A 66 Caroline L 28 48 Daniel O 93 Emeline 87 Joe 104 Joel H 28 48 66 Juliet E 81 Leonora C 93 Martha L 128 Orrin 26 Samuel 25 Sarah 26 Seth 87 W B 36 59 81 Wesson B 63
RICHARDS, Helen 134 Robert 134
RICHARDSON, Abel 32 E G 56 Eliza Ann 46 Emma 126 George W 85 John 89 Mary Ann 56 Miss 71 Nancy 20 81 Wm W 126
RICHMOND, Nancy 8
RIDER, Elizabeth 6 Olive 24 Samuel 6
RIGBY, Susan 96 William T 96
RIGHTMIRE, Elizabeth 91 Lewis 91
RIOE, Loana 67 Seth 67
RIPLEY, Christina G 46 Francis 46
ROAT, Oscar 124
ROBBINS, Edward 24 F D Jr 135 M L 135 Mary 94
ROBERTS, Catherine 41 Charles 63 Huldah Maria 24 Ira 24 Joseph 41 Rachel 15

ROBIE, James W 72 Jonathan 42 Lydia 46 Olive 75 Reuben 46 72 75
ROBINSON, Angeline 18 C W 89 96 118 Charles W 97 112 Chas W 92 94 Daniel 15 Eleanora 92 Harriet M 125 J N 93 J S 117 James A 103 Joseph 93 Katie M 132 Mary 93 Mr 104 Oliver S 132
ROCKWELL, Joseph G 59
ROGERS, Delphine 130 G A 68 Richard H 130 Samuel 68 Sarah S 68 W L 131
ROLESON, Alfred 96 Mary 96
ROLLET, Rev 12
ROLLETT, James 8
ROOT, D M 57 Elder 8 Russell 16
ROSA, Rev 99
ROSE, Daniel H 63 Eliza Ann 11 Eliza H 14 H S 84 John 14 L 37 38 47 64 68 75 77 Levi 83 Mahala G 6 Martha Ann 63 Martin H 11 Sherman 6 W B 76
ROSENCRANCE, Amanda 112
ROSENKRANS, E J 82 J J 82 Simeon 27
ROSS, James 14 Maria Jane 14 Mehitabel 14 Sarah C 64 William 64
ROSSKAM, Bertha 122 Isaac 122
ROTH, Louisa 79
ROULETTE, James 31
ROW, William 23
ROWE, Anson 30 52 75 Anthony 73 Cornelia 11 30 John S 26 Julia Ann 75 Lucy Jane 52 73 Rachel 26 Rev 15
ROWLAND, Hannah 34 Norman 34
ROWLETT, James 22 28 Mary Ann 5 Rev 5
ROWLEY, Asaph 95 J W 121 Moses 22 Rev 23 Robert (Mrs) 96 Sarah 121
ROYCE, Maria 73
RUDD, John C 48
RUGAR, Jane 65 John 65
RUMSEY, Caroline 101 David 47 80 David Jr 23 47 Jane E 23
RUSH, Christopher 27
RUSS, L M 59 L W 35 36 42 67

RUSSELL, B 42 55 Benjamin 80 91 Daniel 42 F 12 Mariah 42 Rev 9 10 72
RUTHERFORD, Andrew 18 Edward 40 Edward Sr 91 Nancy 60 R E 87 Roxana 18 Thomas 86 Turzah E 40 Wm 54 Wm D 133
RYERSS, John P 14
SAINT JOHN, Catharine 124 Henry 78 John T 124 Sarah Ann 78
SALES, Eliza Ann 132 Stephen H 132
SALMON, Joel 86 Mary 86 Mary Ann 60
SALSBURY, Charles Andrew 61 Mary 61 Tobias 61
SAMMONS, Adelaide 100 I D 100
SANDERS, Anna 114 George J 114
SANDERSON, Mary E 70 P P 127
SANDFORD, Laura 42 Russell 42
SANFORD, Alvin O 109 Mary Ann 109
SARGEANT, Laura 31 William 31
SARGENT, James R 39 Parker 64 Permelia 39
SATTLE, William 5
SAVAGE, Rev 23
SAWTELL, Caroline 92 Henry P 92
SAWYER, Jude 32 N 65 67 69 75 77 79 83 Rev 38
SAYER, Sally Ann 10 17
SAYLES, Albert R 132 Alexander 82 Fanny 132 Simon 82
SAYRE, Whittington 57
SCHANK, John 126
SCHENCK, Ellen 36
SCHERMERHORN, Matthew 17 Robert Campbell 17
SCHMIDT, Jacob 37
SCHUE, Jacob 135 Lizzie 135
SCOFIELD, Frederika 79 John L 79 Rev 16
SCOTT, E J 113
SCUDDER, J 117
SCUTT, Anna 114 Sally 34 Uriah 34
SEAMAN, Horace 119 Mercena M 119 Phebe A 109
SEAMEN, Charlotte 108 J M 108

SEARLES, Anna M 122
SEARLS, Calvin 16 Henry 108
SEARS, Alice N 115 Gilbert T 115
SEAVER, H N 55
SEDGWICK, Hattie C 116
SEELEY, Lennie L 117 Martha T 23 R L 117 Samuel S 23 Susey J 117
SELDEN, Eliza 59 J F 59 Manda C 15
SELMSER, Jno 68
SELOVER, John R 61 Mary Frances 61
SELSMER, J 41
SEWARD, B J 17 Maria 17 N 12 S S 57 Sarah Jane 114 Wm H 17 57
SEXTON, Grace A 73 John L Jr 73
SEYMOUR, Eugene 46 Mr 46
SHADDUCK, Daniel 26 Harriet 26
SHANNON, James 41 45 Martha 13 Mathew 13 Samuel 52
SHARP, Harriet 77 John 77 Peggy 134 Sally 25 Wm 120
SHARPE, Henrietta A 84 John 84
SHAUT, Clarinda 22 Jane Ann 25 Joseph 22 25
SHAVER, Amanda 58 Elizabeth 72 Henry 72 John H 58
SHAY, Mary E 90
SHEAPARD, Fiziot F 136 Maggie Louise 136
SHEARER, Louisa 59 Robert 59 Silly 94
SHEARS, Elizabeth E 9 Lay 9
SHELDON, Daniel 8 Laura 38 Wealthy 8
SHEPARD, Eliza 123 George S 123 Georgie 123 J K 125 Lydia 95 Marcia M 125 Margaret 111 Orlando 111 Ruth 111
SHEPHERD, Helen E 128 J K 128 Lydia Ann 86 Otis 86
SHERER, Francis 113 Helen A 113
SHERMAN, George 110 Huldah 116
SHERWOOD, Ann H 94 Catherine 120 Elder 11 14 Eleanora 92 Henry 92 120

SHINABARGER, George 58 Harriet 58 Phebe 58 Wm 58
SHIPMAN, D M 28 Daniel M 5 Sarah C 5 28
SHOCKEY, John 27
SHOEMAKER, Mary 76 Phillip K 76 Sarah 94
SHORT, Nancy 109 Robert 109
SHOVE, Sarah H 125
SHULTS, Bertha 134 J A 135 Margaret 82
SHUMWAY, Charles N 8 Daniel 18 Margaret A 8 9 Olive 18
SHURBIN, J B 127 M A 127 Sarah E 127
SIBLEY, Abijah 101 J C 101
SILLICK, Julia Ann 18 Saml D 18
SILSBE, A H 69 James 84 Sarah Jane 69
SILSE, James 74
SIMMONS, Calvin 69 Elizabeth 134 Maria E 26 Orson 26 Sarah 61 Susan 71 William 61
SIMONS, Seaman 122
SIMPSON, D 16
SINCLAIR, Celinda 77 John A 77
SINGLETON, Richard 12 Sarah Angelica 12
SITAMAN, John 13 Maria 13
SKELLER, M 86
SKINKLE, Catharine V 71 Isaac 71
SKINNER, D G 50 Eliza 50 Henry G 40 Mary Ann 41 Mary Jane 40
SKUTT, Catherine E 48
SLADE, Judson D 113 Mary E 113
SLIGHTER, Mrs 119
SMALL, Catherine 65 Clarissa 18 Hiram 18 46 Joseph 46
SMEAD, Henry D 119 Julius C 15 Manda C 15
SMITH, A C 83 A L Jr 16 Abbey 95 Albert 133 Amanda 136 Ancel C 52 Angie 119 Anna 73 Anna E 130 Annis S 70 Augustus D 66 B C 33 53 61-65 83 85 86 88 90 91 94 95 101 103 Caroline 100 Cathia 63 Charles 58 Charles C 88 Chauncey 95 Cordelia M 52 D 82 Darius 131

SMITH (continued)
David 55 79 129 Edward 20
Elizabeth 67 87 Elizabeth C 92
Elsa A 41 Elvira 83 Emma 63
126 Eunice 21 Fannie M 134
Frances 53 Frederick Ward 67
Freelove 109 George 100 H
Mariah 90 Hannah 28 Harlow
20 83 Harriet 22 69 Henry 73
Henry D Jr 92 Howell 53
James 33 James P 117 James
S 33 Jane 58 Jared 66 John 17
22 33 38 52 John J 87 103 John
L 38 Justin M 131 Laura M 38
Lois M 38 Louisa E 68
Lucinda H 67 Lucy Jane 52
Lydia 63 Margaret J 103 Maria
43 Martha 116 Martha H 133
Mary 9 Mary Jane 95 Matilda
55 Miss 52 N Margaret 88 Orrin 70 Phidelia 20 Polly 45
Rebecca M 83 Rebecca P 57
Rev 16 35 Rhoda Jane 85
Richard H 116 Rollin B 133
Rufus 45 Sally Ann 33 Sarah 16
Sarah Ann 78 Sarah H 125
Sarah J 117 Sereno 63 Sylvester 63 T J 69 Thankful 52
William 57 67 William B 125
Wm H (Mrs) 94 Wm N 52
SNOOK, Cynthia 77 Tunis 77
SNOW, David 82 Margaret 82
SNYDER, Betsey Ann 21 Daniel
21 Elsa A 41 Fanny M 79
Henry M 79 Hiram 41
SOMERS, Chas G 58
SOUTHARD, Betsey Ann 21
Emeline 82
SOUTHERLAND, Amelia 47
SOUTHWELL, Jane E 40 John B
40
SPALDING, Eliza 16 Erastus 16
SPAULDING, H G 130 Jennie E
130 Rev 30
SPENCER, H 38-40 51 53 58 60
62 66
SPICER, A J 86 D A 86 Harriet
118 Huldah 118 Mary 118
Michael 118
SPORE, John 56
SPRAGUE, John S 63 Stephen 63
SPRAKER, Maggie 135

SPRING, George 108 James 86
Lavina 86 Martha 108
SQUIRE, Sarah J 91
STAINER, Adelaide E 136
STANIFORD, A Eugene 105
STANLEY, Jane F G 9
STANTON, Myron 76
STAR, Anne 19 William 19
STARK, Almira 65 Henry L 65
STARKWEATHER, A 90 A H 90
Sarah 65
STARR, Ann D 57 D 57
STEARNS, John 113 Rev 80
STEBBINS, Elder 23 Fannie Bell
118 H 27 J E 118 M M 118
STEPHENS, Albert S 95
Alexander H 49 Annie J 120
Elias 49 Eliza 36 Elizabeth 55
Ellen 36 Franklin D 55 John 48
49 Margaret 92 Mary 87 Nathan
36 61 Olive 48 49 Rachel 61
Rachel Celestia 55 Sarah E 95
Sarah Elizabeth 19 Sophronia
55 Sylvanus 19 Uriah 55 William 97
STEPHENSON, Ann 8 D 8 Daniel
78 Mary E 78
STETEER, Hetser Ann 20
STETSON, Elsie 100 Reuben 100
STEVENS, Melissa 127 Moses
127
STEVENSON, James M 66
STEWART, Andrew 50 Ann H 94
Anthony 94 Calcina E 70
Charles D 96 Charlotte 6
Elizabeth 60 91 131 G D 80 87
103 George D 87 91 92 102 103
Henry 3 James 3 42 Jane 77 79
Margaret 3 Rachel 83 Rev 102
Richard B 6 9 Ro-Ella 96
Sam'l 3rd 60 Sarah 9 Sophia 14
Susan 50 Wellington 91 Wm H
83
STILLSON, Polly 93
STILTS, Jacob H 77 Rhoda 74
Sarah Ann 77
STINSEN, Catharine 54 George 54
STINSER, Catherine 75 Michael
75
STOCKBRIDGE, Levi 23 Syrena
23
STOCKING, John A 9 Selah 22

STODDARD, Esther A 83 Harriet 119 Peter 61 Phillip K 65 Sarah Jane 65 Thankful 61
STONE, Amos 13 Anna M 122 Charles V 24 Jane 13 Joel 112 Martha Ann 112 Samuel 122
STOUT, Byron G 125 Margaret W 13 Pamelia W 125
STRADELLA, Pamela 99 William 99
STRAIGHT, Elijah 42
STRAIT, Alvira 55
STRANG, King 101
STRATTAN, David 11 Eliza 11
STRATTON, Charles 100 Sophia 100
STRAWN, Amanda E 55 H T 55
STRICKLAND, Lucia Ann 37
STRONG, Abigail 8 Stephen 8
STROUD, J F 130 J P 117 129 Mary 125 Samuel 119
STROUGH, J 36 38 77 Rev 72
STRUBLE, Mary D 90
STRYKER, Benjamin F 11 Jane 11 Mahala G 6 Mary Ann 56
STUART, Mary 12
STURGES, S S 125
STURTEVANT, Edward B 117
SUTHERLAND, A 90 Rev 135
SWART, Ann Eliza 57 Ellen T 118 P 57 Ten Eyck G 118
SWARTHOUT, Amanda 23 Ann Eliza 84 Isabelle 42 James 18 Julia 18 Minor 84 William D 23
SWARTWOOD, E D 18 Harriet 131 Isabell 94 Llewellyn A 131 Mr 104
SWEET, Edward A 51 Jonathan 25 Meribah 51
SWETMAN, N Margaret 88
SWEZEY, Nancy Maria 19 Walter F 19
SWICK, B B 56 B R 59-62 65-71 78 Elder 58 Hily Ann 62 Rev 48
SWIFT, Harriet 18
SYTEZ, George 1
TAGGART, George L 123
TALBERT, Mary Ann 22
TALBOT, Esther Ann 14 Fidelia Jane 11 Jarvis 11 Warren 14

TALERDAY, John 111 Mary 111
TALLES, John M 111 Susan 111
TAYLOR, Augusta F 108 Christina 28 Clarisaa 17 Daniel L 77 Dugald C 17 Elizabeth 65 Esther 77 G W 28 65 Helen A 27 J B 56
TEED, Colby 109
TEMPLER, Elizabeth 131 Wm H 131
TENEYCK, M O 115
THAYER, Caroline Matilda 34
THIBOU, L 27
THOMAS, Alvira 104 Charles D 82 Emeline 82 Maria 77 William 77
THOMPSON, Bertha J 113 C H 91 Catherine 94 Cordelia 20 Giles B 94 Hester Ann 20 James 5 John W 20 Joseph (Mrs) 99 Lydia 72 Martha C 22 Rev Dr 78 Samuel 22 72 Smith 32 T C 59 Wm 20
THOMSON, Helen C 117
THORP, Joseph 43 Mary 43
THORPE, Julia 110
THURBER, Jane O 113
THURSTON, C 66 Samuel B 73
TIFFANY, Elmira 33
TIFT, C B 116 H C 116
TILLOTSON, D L 103 Helen 103
TILTON, David 84 James 84
TOBIAS, Jonathan 68
TODD, Rev 7
TOLIVER, D T 49 Elizabeth 49
TOLLIVER, Wm 28
TOMES, Amanda 40
TOMPKINS, Mary 80 Rice 80
TOOKER, Ann 65
TOPPING, Elizabeth 87 Perry 87
TOTTEN, Caroline 92
TOWERS, E A 95
TOWLE, Cecelia B 9 Elizabeth 18 Elizabeth B 68 John D 18 Lucinda 13 Mary 43 Richard 81 100 Richard (Mrs) 100
TOWNER, Hannah 34 Mary 38 Oliver R 91 Sarah J 91
TOWNSEND, Abraham 11 Diantha 130 E G 76 77 79 82 George A 116 Henry A 4 Josiah 130 Louisa V 116 Rev 82

TOWNSEND (continued)
  Sarah 18 Sarah C 5
TRACY, John 131 Lucilla 131
TRAVACE, Esther Ann 14
TRENCHARD, Patricia 32
TRENCHER, Sally Ann 17
TRIMBLE, Elizabeth 34 John 34
TRUE, Anna 134
TUBBS, Hugh 117 Jane 117
  Lebeus 1
TUCKER, Daniel 68 Harriet E 35
  Susannah C 68
TURK, David 135
TURNER, C A 66 Samuel 82
TUTHILL, Harriet Melvina 64
  Mandeville 43 Mrs 64
TUTLE, J K 64
TUTTLE, J K 39 65 127 J R 62
  Mary J 12 William H 12
TUTTON, James 126
TWITCHEL, Rev 37
TWOGOOD, R C 112 Richard C
  114
TYLER, Nancy 60 Sally 34
UNDERHILL, Charles 70 Porcia
  Maria 70 Punderson B 26
UPTHEGROVE, Kathline M 93
VANALLEN, Nancy M 69 Wm H
  69
VANAMBURG, Sarah F 70
VANATTEN, Mary D 90 Thomas
  90
VANBUREN, Abraham 12 Mr 78
  Sarah Angelica 12
VANBUSKIRK, Richard 69
VANCAMPEN, Eliza Ann 116
  Hamilton 116 Harriet A 37
  Maryette 116 Moses 59 Wm R
  37
VANCE, Elizabeth M 35
VANDEMARK, Jane A 91 Joseph
  H 91
VANDERBILT, Commodore 136
  Maggie Louise 136
VANDERHOOVEN, Annis 57
  Elizabeth 57 Jesse 57
VANDERWARKIN, Jacob 51
  Temma 51
VANDERWARNER, Hannah L 109
  Washington 109
VANDUSEN, Nancy 68 Wm H 68

VANDUSER, Polly Ann 79 Susan
  55 Wm 55
VANESS, Angeline 18 Ira 18
VANGELDER, Catherine 43 E
  Clinton 135 Henry 69 Julia A
  135 Polly 69
VANGELLER, Levi 122
VANHOUSEN, Amanda 111
  Catharine 68 Edward 111 Henry
  61 Joseph H 68
VANHOUTON, James 34 Nancy K
  34
VANLOON, James H 101
VANNESS, Abbie 79 Caroline 79
  Elizabeth 72 Lucy 49 Peter 49
  79
VANORSDALE, Charles A 128
  Emma A 113 122 Helen C 128
  J C 122 James C 113 Mellie J
  122
VANOZZLEDOZZLE, Adrianna
  Augustina 107
VANRENSSELAER, Rensselaer
  60 Solomon 81
VANRENSSELEAR, Solomon 60
VANSCHAICK, J B 12
VANSICKLE, Andrew 49
VANVALKENBURGH, Catherine
  F 119 George Rudd 19 Gertrude
  C 63 J 19 63 R B 71 119 Wm
  M 27 29 30
VANWIE, Catharine 68
VANZANDT, Cornelia 76 W 76
VANZINE, Jennie 135
VEAZIE, Eva A 133 Jason R 114
  Phoebe A 114 Stephen 133
VEDDER, Jemima 30 William 30
VEILE, Clarissa A 5
VELEY, Polly 69
VENPELT, Hiram 40
VIELE, Maria E E 29
VINTON, Rev Dr 84
VOORHEIS, Mary 16 Sarah 16
  Sebring 16
VUNK, Maggie 135 Wm H 135
WADDELL, Mary Jane 40
WADSWORTH, William 35
WAGGONER, A C 131 C C 131
  Inglehart 90 Mary E 90
WAGNER, C C 131 F R 133 Mrs
  Dr 122

WAGONER, F R 108
WAIT, Emily E 60 W W 78
WAITE, Rev 79
WAKEMAN, Joel 129 Rev Dr 132
WALBRIDGE, Philo 48
WALDO, Gertrude C 63 Gertrude L 129 James A 91 M Amelia 91 Milton 116 Otis H 63 Rev 136 Wm A 129
WALES, E V 124
WALKER, E H 41 Eliza 16 Elizabeth L 92 Gideon 69 Helen M 78 James 7 John 62 92 Mary 62 Sarah Maria 7
WALLACE, Jas 58 Joseph 89 M C 58 Marinda 89 Nancy 52
WALLEN, Mary L 78
WALLING, Amanda M 67 Eliza 36 Lucy Sane 60
WALRATH, Abraham I 10 Sally 10
WALTERS, Lisetta 135 Willis J 135
WALTON, Mrs 64
WALTY, Rachel 126 William 126
WARD, Elizabeth 67 Hamilton 95 Mary 125 Rachel 126 Sarah Jane 134 Thomas 125
WARNER, Alpheus 6 Hiram 39 Mercy 6 Susan 39
WARREN, Angeline 87 Danford 3 Dwight 87 Eliza Ann 116 Elizabeth 62 Emily 8 Gen 34 Jonathan 67 Joseph Butler 62 Mary 46 Phineas 3 46 67 Rachel 15 Rachel Amelia 30 Rev 90 Robert Harper 116 Sarah B 67 Sarah H 67 Stewart K 30 Wm G W 15
WARRINER, Bertha J 113 L C 120 W A 113
WASHINGTON, Geo 121
WASS, David 13 Elizabeth 13
WATERMAN, Eliza 56 Joshua W 56
WATERS, Lewis M 99
WATKINS, Eliza 5 Harriet 60 Joseph 5 Samuel 73 Simon 60 66 Sophira 58
WATROUS, Eleanor 71 John 71 Phebe 94 Riggs 94

WATSON, Ann 75 E 82 Lawrence 75 Lydia 66 Seneca 66
WAUGH, Margaret 91 William 91
WEATHERBY, George H 111
WEAVER, Daniel 109 Emma 109
WEBB, George W 126 Lewis 100 Z L 96 Z Lewis 97
WEBSTER, Caroline 33 39 Emma 134 Fanny Delphene 39 Harriet 57 Ithamer 65 James 33 39 76 Jane 41 Phoebe 13 Sally 25
WEED, Adelaide 114 James B 74 Mason N 114 Thurlow 74
WEEKS, Ann Eliza 71 C O 91 Catharine 91
WEIDMAN, Tharessa 75
WELCH, Adolphus 56 Ann 75 Hellen Marr 56 Louisa 100 Thankful 61
WELLES, C Adell 132 S H 132
WELLS, Henry 130 Jesse W 31 Julia 18 Maria 5 Orren 125
WELTON, Amanda 136 James P 136
WEMPLE, E J 82
WENSTER, Ithamar 57
WENTWORTH, Eunice 37 George 37
WEST, X 14
WESTCOT, Samuel 28
WESTCOTT, Elizabeth C 92
WETMORE, Elijah 79 Louisa 79
WHEADON, D A 92
WHEAT, Benjamin P 116 Josiah 6 11 Lyman C 21 Mary B 21
WHEATON, Betsy Ann 96 John M 91 M Amelia 91 Samuel W 96
WHEELER, Barbara 36 C 5 7 36 Chandler 5 Edward Ransom 135 Eliza 29 Emily E 60 Emma 48 G H 29 Geo 22 Grattan B 80 Harriet 83 Henrietta 26 Jane T 88 Jeremiah 70 John 88 John G 60 Lucy 63 M 111 Mary 70 Mary Isabel 135 Mr 48 N Sanger 36 Phidelia 29 Rev 8 Seth 32 Silas 29 Wm 26
WHIPPLE, Ellen P L 82 J Eustace 29 Maria E E 29 P L 28 Rev 33
WHITAKER, Amanda 72 James

WHITAKER (continued) L 96 Nancy M 96
WHITE, A E 75 Amanda 40 Angeline 38 David 47 Elisa 47 Emily 12 George 27 Helen A 27 Isaac S 75 Isacher 47 Issachar 12 Lugher 69 Nancy M 69 P 47 Rev 79 S 5 40 Samuel B 40 Wm 38
WHITENACK, Marilla A 132
WHITEHALL, Jas 108
WHITFORD, James 129 L D 129
WHITING, Abram 71 J W 20 21 John 3 John W 12 71 L C 40 Levi C 41 M J 64 Mariana 40 Mary 3 Nancy 70 75 Pamelia 41 T W 64
WHITNEY, Abraham Jr 6 Joshua 4 Mary 86 Mercy 6 William Wallace 4
WHITTEMORE, Moses F 25 Permelia 39 Sally 25
WHITTENHALL, Adelaide 100 D S 128 Elihu 128 Eliza A 128 Henry 134 J 107 108 James 104 James U 112 Jas 109 Louisa L 134 Sarah 94 Thomas A 94
WICKHAM, Jane R 72
WIDGER, Samantha 133
WILBER, Abigail 53 Mary E 125
WILBUR, Alice N 115 F 130 Gilbert L 87 Martin 115 Parmelia 87 Rev 62
WILCOX, George 3 Jane 41 Joseph 41 M C 118 Martha 3
WILHELM, Emeline 56 Hannah 67 John 56 Joseph 77 Sarah 77
WILKES, B 5 James 5 Mary Ann 109
WILLARD, Enos G 133
WILLIAMS, Amanda 111 Anna M 131 Elizabeth 7 Francis 131 Henry V D 36 Ira C 131 Jane 27 Maria E 48 Nathaniel P 7 Zopher 27
WILLIAMSON, Mary Ann 11 Rose 134
WILLIOUR, Sarah 54
WILLIS, Dorcas M 62 Eunice 77 Israel 94 Nancy 75 Rhoda 69 Sarah Ann 94 William H 75

WILLISTON, Clara 66 Horace 66
WILLOUR, Adeline 51 Alonzo 51 64 Jacob 62 Nancy Adaline 64 Rachel 62
WILLSON, Sarah C 109
WILMER, Charles K 83 Harriet 83
WILSON, Betsey 1 Electa 63 Emma E 130 John 1 130 Maria 82 Mary E 113 Rev 68 Robert E 89 Susan Jane 94
WILTSE, Emilie W 3 James 3
WINCHELL, Don T 112
WING, Elnathan H 37 Julia T 81 Rev 18 22 Sally 37
WINNE, Ann 8
WINSLOW, G 23
WINTON, David B 110 Frances J 110
WISNER, H 113 Rev 5 8 9
WIXOM, Alfred 81 Ann 86 Sarah Jane 96 Thankful 81
WIXSON, James M 13 Margaret W 13
WOLCOT, Margaret 90
WOLCOTT, Charles 74 Charles 3rd 89 Elizabeth 74 Hulda Jane 89 John 92 Phebe 92
WOLEVER, Mary 111
WOLLAGE, Elijah 8 10 109 Sally 109
WOMBOUGH, Albert H 108 Caroline E 94 George W 94 Henry 99 108 117 Pamela 99 Pamelia 125 Rachel 108 Wm 125
WOOD, A 129 132 Albert 119 120 122 126 132 134 135 Benjamin H 16 Elizabeth M 16 Mr 103 Ruth E 120
WOODARD, David 80 Joseph 42
WOODRUFF, Alfred S 73 Hannah 1 James 1 L J 67 Mary 67 Serepta 73
WOODS, David 75 Elizabeth L 6 James S 55 Mary B 19 Olive 75 Pamelia 41 Susan 55 William 6 41
WOODWARD, David Francis 13 Elizabeth 91 F W 91 Helen 117 Phoebe 13 Sarah S 10 Thomas 65

WORDEN, Ellen 99
WRAIGHT, Alice 101 Caroline 85
WRIGHT, A 63 100 Ann E 89 Eliza Ann 132 James 131 Mary 131 Mary A 69 Rev 68 William 96
WYLLYS, Harry 45
YALE, Catherine 116
YORTAN, James 38 Laura M 38
YOST, A C 113 Jacob S 50 Mary 113 Mercy 69
YOUMANS, Jonas 62 Mary Jane Elizabeth 66

YOUNG, Almira 109 Charles C 109 Charles H 111 Julia 21 Lucilla 131 Maria 73 Marion 111 Rev 71 Samuel 69 Sarah 16 Sebastian 73
ZEILLEY, Thomas H 65
ZEILLY, Ann 65 Nancy C 36
ZIELLEY, Nancy 105
ZIMMERMAN, Catherine 32 John 32

www.ingramcontent.com/pod-product-compliance
Lightning Source LLC
Chambersburg PA
CBHW050818160426
43192CB00010B/1809